ALSO BY EDWARD DE BONO

New Think (1967)

The Five Day Course in Thinking (1968)

The Mechanism of Mind (1969)

Lateral Thinking: A Textbook of Creativity (1970)

Lateral Thinking for Management (1971)

Technology Today (editor) (1971)

Practical Thinking (1971)

The Dog Exercising Machine (1971)

Children Solve Problems (1972)

Po: Beyond Yes and No (1972)

Think Tank (1973)

Eureka: A History of Inventions (editor) (1974)

Teaching Thinking (1976)

The Greatest Thinkers (editor) (1976)

Wordpower (1977)

The Happiness Purpose (1977)

The Case of the Disappearing Elephant (1977)

Opportunities: A Handbook of Business Opportunity Search (1978)

Future Positive (1979)

Atlas of Management Thinking (1981)

De Bono's Course in Thinking (1982)

TACTICS

TACTICS

The Art and Science of Success

EDWARD de BONO

LITTLE, BROWN AND COMPANY
Boston   Toronto

Library of Congress Cataloging in Publication Data

De Bono, Edward, 1933–
    Tactics : the art and science of success.
    Includes index.
    1. Success.   2. Success — Biography.   I. Title.
    BF637.S8D365   1984   158′.1   84-16384
    ISBN 0-316-17790-3

Conceived and produced by Pilot Productions Limited,
59 Charlotte Street, London W1P 1LA

MV
Designed by Patricia Girvin Dunbar

Published simultaneously in Canada
by Little, Brown & Company (Canada) Limited

PRINTED IN THE UNITED STATES OF AMERICA

Acknowledgment and Thanks

I wish to thank all those successful people who provided time for the interviews that provide the real value of this book. I know that successful people are extremely busy and constantly badgered by requests for interviews and comments. I am therefore most grateful both for their time and for the very focused comments. I hope I have done justice to them. I would have wished to use all the interviews in their entirety but this is not practical. So I apologize to those who feel that their views are underrepresented in the book. I would point out to the reader, however, that a single sentence can hold as much wisdom as a long passage.

There may seem to be few women in the book. We did ask several successful women (Barbara Walters, Billie Jean King, Jeane Kirkpatrick among others) for their views. They declined — probably out of modesty and a feeling that that success was too personal a matter to talk about. In some cases they felt that a recent biography had said it all.

I particularly want to thank Valerie Jennings and Piers Dudgeon, who did very much of the work for this book. It is largely due to their personality and determination that the huge amount of work required for this sort of book was completed. My role has been the easier one.

My appreciation and thanks are also due to Tony Van den Bergh for his energy, persistence and journalistic skill;

Bill Kay of the *Sunday Times Business News* for his contributions and research in the field of business;

John Graham, author and journalist, for his specialist research and contributions in the areas of sport and games;

Major S. R. Elliot of the International Institute for Strategic Studies for his research and advice;

ACKNOWLEDGMENT AND THANKS

Michael Cross of the Technical Change Centre, Dr. John Cobb of St. George's Hospital, and Robert Sheehan for their advice in the areas of management, psychiatry, and probability theory, respectively;

Paddy Hills for tirelessly laying down lines of communication between different points on the globe.

Contents

CONTENTS

CONTENTS

Introduction

At no point in this book am I going to define "success." We all have an idea of what the term means but a precise definition is impossible. (There is exactly the same trouble with the word "creativity".) Is it success in the eyes of the world: winning an Olympic gold medal or at Wimbledon; making a great deal of money; running a large organization; making things happen; being awarded the Nobel Prize? Or, is it personal success: the person who toward the end of his or her life feels that theirs has been a happy, fulfilled, and enjoyed life? Which is the more successful, a man who has made millions but is unhappy and unsatisfied or an unnoticed person who has led a happy life? I do not intend to get into that argument because there are clearly many different ways of looking at success and it is only the poverty of the English language which provides us with but a single word for them. Perhaps the simplest definition is "to set out to do something and to succeed in doing it."

In this book we shall be looking at the lessons that might be learned from a number of people who would generally be regarded as "successful." This is not a personal selection in the sense that I believe these people to be the most successful, for there are many others who are just as successful but are not in this book. Nor does the selection mean that I would choose the same route for myself or recommend it to others. For example, my own training approach is very different from that used by Werner Erhard. Nevertheless, Erhard has been extraordinarily successful with his training and is clearly a success.

To be successful you have to be lucky, or a little mad, or very talented, or to find yourself in a rapid-growth field. Each of these positions can be defended, and I shall attempt to do so below.

1

LUCKY

A hundred people set out to do the same thing. They have the same personality characteristics and they behave in the same way. Even the sequence of their actions is the same. Yet two of those hundred succeed and the rest fail. The difference between these people is that although they all acted in the same way the "timing" of their actions was different. For example, a cluster of property millionaires acted at the very moment when war-bombed London needed them most. You may argue that that is no luck but perception (and I would be on your side), but there are times when unexpected events like the assassination of a president, a change in the law, a Middle East war, or a sudden scientific discovery make success (or disaster) out of an action which otherwise would have been pretty ordinary.

Sometimes there is a series of "ifs" before something can be done. You have to find the right property; the owner has to be willing to sell; the bank has to be willing to finance you; the property market has suddenly to rise; you have to find a buyer, etc. If all the "ifs" come right — many of which may be outside your control — you are a success.

The main point is that if you only look at the two out of a hundred that succeeded you might attribute success to their personality, style, or course of action. It may actually be no more than a lucky fall of the cards.

I have no doubt that some people have been very successful through sheer good luck. There will be times when readers of this book will spot instances of such luck. This often happens when one person meets another who provides him with an opportunity. If you play tennis with a girl and then marry her and then join her father in a booming television business, then that must count as some sort of luck. In other cases luck is meeting just the right partner at an early stage. It is remarkable how many successful people have come across a backup partner who provides the solidity and financial soundness to complement their entrepreneurial flair.

It can, of course, happen the other way around. Sometimes a very gifted person has a run of very bad luck. For example, he designs a fuel-saving car just when the price of oil drops. Or, an important write-up on him (which might have changed his career) is not published because the newspaper happens to be on strike that week.

Others argue that luck may give the first opportunity, but then such characteristics as perception, determination, dealing with people, etc., turn that first opportunity into success. They also argue that if that opportunity had not come along, then another one would have. A successful person would be successful whatever the initial opportunity. The noted psychologist Professor Hans Eysenck says that he only went into psychology because he could not afford the year's waiting that would be required for entry into another science area.

For myself, I do not feel that it is necessary to take a fierce position on this matter of luck. Some people have been extremely lucky, some people have been extremely unlucky. Some people have had a certain amount of luck and have built on it. Some people have had virtually no luck and have still been successful. There is a spectrum ranging from a great deal of luck to no luck at all.

As in so many other areas, I see no great virtue in taking a strongly polarized position. With regard to the role of luck in success, there is, however, a practical point which must be considered. If success is largely due to luck (a factor outside our control), then there is not too much point in reading about successful people except to admire the luck they have had.

For some people it is a comfortable thought that success may all be due to luck. It means that they do not have to do anything different but just to carry on and hope that luck — like winning a lottery ticket — might make them successful. They may also feel that there is no point in striving because without luck nothing will happen. It is always comforting to feel that you are just as talented and just as worthwhile as the successful person but not quite as lucky.

There is a parallel attitude, prevalent in England, where success is more often a cause for jealousy than, as in America, for admiration. The attitude attributes all success to a small talent plus a great deal of salesmanship. This enables the less successful person to feel just as good as the successful person except that the latter has used salesmanship (often much despised in England) to market the talent.

The positive attitude toward luck is very different. The positive attitude is that you put yourself in a position to take the maximum advantage of any luck that comes your way. The positive attitude means that you are able to carry to success whatever turns up by luck. The positive attitude means that you are very ready to spot opportunities, and it also means that you may generate such opportunities deliberately. This attitude acknowledges luck as a possible ingredient in some cases of success and then places the operational emphasis on the other ingredients, such as determination, strategy and style.

A LITTLE MAD

As the reader will discover in this book, successful people are often very single-minded and determined. Indeed, it would be possible to pick this out as the single characteristic common to almost all successful people. It can take the form of drive: if you want something hard enough, you will get it. It can take the form of ruthlessness: let nothing stand between you and your goal. It can take the form of a strong sense of purpose: know exactly where you want to go and get there. It can take the form of determination and persistence: accepting failure only as a step on the path to success.

This type of determination comes close to fanaticism and what might be called "a little madness." It implies a rather unnatural view of life, because one single goal becomes more important than any others. A person may be willing to sacrifice his wife, his children, his friends, his health, and even his life for his goal. At times the goal may seem very much like an obsession. At its extreme, obsession is a form of madness.

There are many advantages to powerful determination and a strong sense of direction. The sense of direction urges action. The sense of direction shapes the action. The sense of direction allows the value of the action to be assessed: has it got me nearer to my goal? The sense of direction allows all judgments and decisions to be made more easily: does this help me toward my goal or does it hinder me? Most people in their ordinary lives lack such a strong sense of value when taking a decision. Most people may have to take into account a soup of different factors such as family, health, enjoyment, career, etc., when making a decision. The strongly success-oriented person only takes into account one thing: the path to success.

As with luck there is, of course, a spectrum. At one end is the ruthless obsessed tyrant who could properly be called mad. At the other end of the spectrum is the person who enjoys what he or she is doing, enjoys his life and friends, and just seems to stumble into success (as with Nolan Bushnell, Norman Lear, or Sir Clive Sinclair). Readers may be surprised to find that most of the people in this book seem to fall into this second grouping.

Determination and ruthlessness always seem to suggest a person who wants success and power for their own sake and as an extension of his or her personality. There is, however, another sort of obsession. This is when a person is enslaved by an idea. The person wants to see the idea work, wants to make it happen. Power, riches, and fame have virtually nothing to do with it. Determination can spring from this sort of obsession.

There is even a further sort of determination. This is where someone sets out to do something and takes the first few steps. There is then a determination to see things through, to finish that job. Once one block has been placed on top of another, there is a compulsion to finish the building. This characteristic also becomes clear in some of the people mentioned in this book.

All these characteristics are somewhat abnormal insofar as normal people tend to be rather passive and multidirectional (less focused). That is why I have said that successful people may seem to be a "little mad."

From a practical point of view it does matter whether we attribute success to a particular type of personality. Some people may feel that since their own personality is not "driven" in this way, then there is little they can learn by reading about people who are so driven. Like the "luck" explanation of success, this is defeatist and passive.

I would not want to get into an argument as to whether people can or cannot change their personalities (through awareness, training, counseling, or environmental change). It is not easy for someone to become ruthless by just willing himself or herself to be ruthless. Later in the book the reader will see how some very successful executives still find it difficult to be ruthless (Lord Forte says that he hates to fire people). A reader can, however, try to become more single-minded and more focused. Once a reader perceives that a strong sense of direction may be an ingredient for success, it is possible to do something about it (for instance, by dropping other projects). A person who will not take "no" for an answer and writes ten letters runs the danger of being a nuisance and a pest but may be more successful than the person who is turned off by the first refusal. Such things may arise naturally from a personality or they may be adopted as a strategy. You cannot will yourself to have a foul temper (even if this often seems to be most useful for success), but you can become much better at saying what you do not like. It may well be that having success-oriented characteristics by virtue of your personality is much more effective — nevertheless adopting some of them as deliberate strategies can also be valuable.

VERY TALENTED

Chess geniuses, athletes, tennis players, pianists, architects, dress designers, advertising creative directors may all seem to owe their success to a great deal of talent. Obviously the talent is there at the time of their success. Has it always been there — at least potentially? Whether it is always true or not, we can accept a "yes" answer at this point. But that is the beginning, not the end of the story.

There can be talent but there may have to be hard work and training before that talent can succeed against others. There can be talent but there may also have to be strategy — for example, Bjorn Borg's "low-error" strategy was important. There can be talent but there may also have to be the right mental attitude: for example, the "killer instinct" which Virginia Wade seems to lack.

It may be a matter of unlocking the talent, or maximizing it or building upon it. Maria Callas put a great deal of effort into making the best of her talent. There are times when a phenomenal natural talent soars above all others — and so it should be. Most of the time, however, it is a competition between talents which are not so phenomenal, and in that competition the difference is often made by the effort put in to make the most of the natural talent.

5

In practical terms, what is the most useful attitude toward natural talents? For people with high natural talents, the practical step is to make the most of them. For people with moderate natural talents, the most practical step is to make the most of them. For people with no talent at all, the most practical step is to focus on a field where success does not depend so heavily on a natural talent ingredient. In both the first two instances it is rarely sufficient to sit back and leave it all to "natural talent." So in reading this book it is useful to see how those with talent have made the best use of that talent.

Where there seems to be no natural talent, then it makes sense as far as possible to substitute for talent (preferably in a field where talent is not essential) by hard work, training, experience, and strategy. If you can do complicated mathematics in your head, that is very talented. If you cannot, then use a pencil and paper. Even better, delegate the math to a computer. There are said to be detectives who work through a Sherlock Holmes–type flair. There are others who use hard work and detail work.

The key question is whether hard work and training are really a waste of time where there is little talent. The only useful answer is to try it and to see what happens. If hard work is really getting you nowhere (as in a talent area) then it may well be a waste of time. More usually, hard work will make a great improvement but will not take you to the very topmost ranks.

This brings us to another question: are there levels of success or is the topmost success the only one worth having? Does every player who goes to Wimbledon really think he or she is going to win the championship — or is it success enough to play there?

In conclusion, as with luck and "a little madness," there is a difference between the passive and negative attitude and the positive one. The passive attitude says that there is nothing that can be done: either there is talent or there is not. The positive attitude says that natural talent can be maximized and also that without further effort natural talent will be wasted.

RAPID GROWTH FIELD

The computer industry is a growth industry, and within that industry software is a growth field. The steel industry is not a growth industry. Clearly it is easier for a company to be successful in the computer industry than in the steel industry. There are fields where it is easier for an individual to make a fortune than it is in other fields. Real estate (property development) has always been such a field. So is insurance. The oil industry has its ups and downs but it has also been an area in which individuals could make fortunes. It is both the growth of the field that matters and also the nature of the transaction within that field. It is

6

easier for a person to make his name in investment banking than in retail banking. It is easier to make a name as a journalist than as a schoolteacher.

Clearly there are some fields in which it is just easier to be a success than in others. It is easy for a general to become a success in war but rather more difficult in times of peace. Possibly the most likely way to make a living out of creative imagination is to go into advertising. With the term "rapid growth field" I intended to indicate also another point.

If the field is really growing rapidly, then any person in that field may simply be carried along with the growth and not have to contribute very much to his or her own success. Riding the bandwagon has always been one road to success. There is usually room for several people on the bandwagon. The pioneer in the field may or may not be successful, but those who come in very soon after the field is established can be carried along by its explosive growth.

Getting into a rapid growth field may be a matter of luck or choice. You may simply happen to be in a field that starts to grow rapidly. You may choose to get into a field that you think may start to grow. You may choose to move smartly into a field as soon as you spot that the field is on the move. In show-jumping you can be a brilliant rider who gets the very best out of a difficult horse. Or you can make sure that you choose for yourself the very best horse around and then just hang on and let the horse do it for you. There is a certain heroism in the first approach and more sense in the second.

What if your temperament and talents are suited to a field that is not growing? What if the growing field demands talents you do not have? If you are no good at writing software, should you get into that field? You could always market the software or finance software companies or hire people to write the software for your company. It is well worth looking around to see the many ways you can be in a field. The real estate world has deal makers, developers, financiers, lawyers, contractors, etc.

Sometimes there is a sort of "talent trap." A youngster is good at math at school so he or she gets channeled into a career that uses mathematics. But that youngster may have been almost as good at organization and might have become a chief executive of a major corporation instead of a professor of mathematics. Talent in one direction does not always mean that there are no talents in other directions. If you are suited to a slow-moving field, it is only too easy to feel that you will not be able to shift to another field that is growing more rapidly. Far too many youngsters who showed some aptitude for art at school have had their lives ruined by that small talent which has lead them into a field so difficult even for the most talented.

I do not really believe that to be successful you have to be lucky, or a little mad, or very talented, or to find yourself in a rapid growth field.

I have put forward this view simply because it is one that many people hold. I believe, as I have tried to show, that these things may all be ingredients in success. In the case of any individual, one or other ingredients may have played an important role. In other cases it would be hard to ascribe an important role to any of these ingredients. The explanation provided for the success of a person may be simple or it may be complex. Determination in a rapidly growing field may be enough. Talent and some luck may be enough. In other cases, it is a complex composite not only of the ingredients mentioned but also of many others. For example, a sense of humor may be an ingredient that protects an individual from the depression that may accompany failure. An ability to assess people may be a hugely important ingredient to someone whose success has depended on choosing the right people and then letting them get on with the job. That is why this book is worth reading.

In this book there are things that are obvious and clear. There are things that I shall comment upon and spell out — sometimes even when they are so obvious that they hardly need spelling out. There are things which are hidden and subtle and can only be noticed by reading between the lines. There are also complex constellations of factors and characteristics which the reader is entitled to assemble in any way as he or she wants. There is always the reader's privilege of noticing what I have noticed and then going further. Agreeing or disagreeing with me is not particularly relevant because the book is offered as an exploration rather than a thesis. Read and explore and use my conclusions to help you reach your own. If you do not agree with my conclusion then make yourself a better one.

T A C T I C S

1. **You do not have to want to be successful. You do not have to value success. But if you do want to be successful, then there are two attitudes. The first is the passive attitude, which tells you that there is nothing you can do except wait for luck or pray for the right talent and temperament. The second is the positive attitude, which tells you that there are things that you can do that will make a difference. For example, reading this book and taking note of what seems important to you.**

2. **The positive attitude toward luck is to be ready for it, to spot it, to make the maximum use of it — but not to sit around waiting for it.**

3. **Knowing what you want to do, determination, and persistence are important. You may have these qualities by temperament or as a strategy.**

8

4. Make the most of your talent and do not expect it to be enough by itself. Do not be trapped into one field by some talent for that field.

5. In some fields it is just much easier to be successful than in others. The me-too and bandwagon effect has always been powerful, so try to choose not only an opportunity field but preferably a growing one.

6. Read this book in an exploratory sense. Note what I have noticed and then go farther.

List of Interviewees

WILLIAM AGEE   Agee was chairman and CEO of the Bendix Corp., the $4 billion automative and aerospace supplier. Because he felt that in a recession shareholders' interests are best served by investment in new and wider businesses, rather than relying upon internal profit increases, Agee set about taking over the mighty Martin Marietta Corporation. Marietta defended their position aggressively, bringing in some of the big guns from Wall Street, on whose advice Marietta in turn moved to take over Bendix. The two giants started to eat each other up in what became known as the Pac-Man riposte. Agee lost the company and his position, but left with his shares up in value by some 60 percent and a "golden parachute provision" of $850,000 a year for six years.

SIR OVE ARUP   Sir Ove is the founder chairman of Ove Arup Associates, one of the U.K.'s biggest architect builders. Among his many projects is the Sydney Opera House.

JARVIS ASTAIRE   Astaire's fortune is solidly built on opportunities seized at critical points in the areas of boxing and real estate. However, it was in recognizing the moment to strike with his then novel idea of intercity and then intercontinental closed-circuit televised boxing championships that demonstrated best his entrepreneurial spirit.

DAVID BAILEY   Bailey is widely known as an art, fashion and advertisement photographer. In the 1960s with Jean Shrimpton and *Vogue* magazine, he helped shape a whole generation's fashion, and, in particular, gave us the miniskirt. What his close friend Mick Jagger was doing for rock music at that time, Bailey was doing for photography. And the Bailey style? "A kind of existential thing . . . if I could, I would put it in bottles and call it 'Focus' and get a company to manufacture it for me."

CHRIS BONINGTON, CBE mountaineer, adventurer, journalist and photographer, Bonington's many accomplishments include Annapurna II, the Eiger North Wall, Kangur, Ogre, Annapurna South Face, Southwest Face of Everest — none of which would have been possible, despite his supreme climbing ability, without a talent for team choice, management and logistical planning. He believes that successful management "is where people at the end of the day say, 'Yes, that was a good thing.' "

MIKE BREARLEY In the 1978/9 series, Brearley led the England cricket team against the Australians with the best-ever result achieved by an English side in Australia. At Cambridge University, Brearley read Classics and Philosophy in addition to setting a batting record of 4,068 runs. In 1964 he became Young Cricketer of the Year. In 1967 he captained the Under-25 side to Pakistan and achieved his highest-ever first-class score of 312 not out. In 1976/7/80 he led Middlesex to the County Championships. This sometime England captain had a unique grasp of strategy and how to get the best out of a team. In 1982 he retired from cricket and became a psychoanalyst, a decision which may be unusual but suggests the nature of his skills as captain: "Captains have got to be able to stand back and not just be one of the boys — that's for sure."

NOLAN BUSHNELL Bushnell is worth an estimated $70 million just over a decade after starting a company with a $500 investment. This entrepreneur/inventor created the billion-dollar video game industry from an idea that came to him when watching people throwing baseballs at milk bottles in an amusement park. Atari was his company; "Pong" the first video game. Having sold Atari to Warners for $28 million just four years later, he has since launched the first personal robot, Androbot, having signed a contract not to compete in the video game area for an agreed period. Bushnell puts his personal success down to "a 'can-do' attitude. I mean, I always feel there is a solution.' "

ROY COHN Described by *Esquire* magazine as "a legal executioner . . . the toughest, meanest, vilest and one of the most brilliant lawyers in America," Cohn has clients which range from Benson Ford and Warren Avis to Carmine Galante (the reputed boss of bosses), from Bianca Jagger to the Cullen oil heir and statesman, Baron Enrico diPortanova, and from Studio 54 to the Catholic Church in New York. At fifteen, he made $10,000 as a broker in the sale of a radio station, which he divided to pay for stock in the New York Giants and for his education (which led to his appointment as an Assistant United States Attorney, aged twenty-one). A survivor of more crises than Richard Nixon, Cohn has been indicted four times and acquitted. He combines an impressive natural intelligence and strong personality with an awareness of the value of the complementary skills of his partner, Tom Bolan. It's a combination which has allowed Cohn to turn his apparently outrageous reputation to his company's advantage.

SIR TERENCE CONRAN   In the 1960s, Sir Terence, designer business-man, was as important to home furnishing as Mary Quant was to cos-metics. Conrans and Habitat provided the style that Conran knew would appeal to the new high-spending middle class of the '60s. His unusual combination of skills and ability to motivate his employees ("enthusiasm rubs off on people like pollen on bees") have enabled his success to spread through varied businesses. One of his maxims is: "People are much hap-pier if they feel that their talents and qualities are being exploited to the best." Today, following his takeover of Mothercare, his companies are worth about £350 million.

MICKEY DUFF   Still the youngest world-class boxing promoter (it being, in his words, "an old man's business"), but the most successful international boxing promoter and matchmaker from Britain. An appar-ently instinctual, and certainly well proven, judgment for what he refers to as "star quality . . . macho . . . box-office appeal" is combined with a great respect for timing in opportunity-seeking.

WERNER ERHARD   A sometime used-car and encyclopedia salesman, Erhard was born Jack Rosenberg and changed his name after reading an *Esquire* magazine article about great Germans, including Werner Hei-senberg and Ludwig Erhard. Eleven years later he founded est — an enormously rich and powerful movement (not totally unlike Zen) de-signed to help people transform the spiritual and material quality of their lives. ("What I think determines whether you really accomplish some-thing is where you are coming from.") To some he is a disconcerting mixture of super salesman and philosopher; to others he embodies the meeting point of American "Will" and oriental "Intellect."

HAROLD EVANS   Evans became editor of *The Sunday Times* in 1967 and developed an editorial style which gave the paper a new and wider readership, and earned him the accolade of Editor of the Year in 1975. He created controversy with timely and incisive investigations, notably the highly successful Thalidomide campaign ("A bleeding heart I try to ally to technical strength"). In 1981 he became editor of *The Times*, tried unsuccessfully to impose his style on Britain's most conventional paper and was sacked by Rupert Murdoch the following year. In 1983 he pub-lished his view of the Murdoch wrangle, *Good Times, Bad Times*, which became a best-seller.

HANS EYSENCK   Controversial and successful psychologist, Professor Eysenck was educated in Germany, France and England. He has held professorships in London, Pennsylvania and California, and since 1946 has been Director of Psychology at the Maudsley Hospital, London. His theories about IQ being genetically determined have led to suggestions that blacks have lower IQs than whites and that a proportion of men occupy a higher IQ level than women. In a field used to theory and speculation, Eysenck has brought an individual style which tends to demand strict measurement and statistically based results.

ALAN FINE   Fine believes, like the Inner Game Organisation for which he works as an instructor, that success in sport and business is a question of removing our own unconscious barriers to achievement. The aim of the Organisation is to open our eyes to these barriers and allow the individual to determine his/her program for development. "It's not our assessment of the obstacles," Fine explains. "It's that person's assessment. The important thing is that they devise most of the program. My role is a facility."

MALCOLM FORBES   In 1947 Malcolm Forbes became associate publisher of *Forbes Magazine*, founded by his father. The following year he launched unsuccessfully a magazine called *Nation's Heritage*. In 1954, on his father's death, he was elected editor and publisher of *Forbes Magazine*, an event which marked an extraordinary growth cycle which has continued unabated, and made Forbes a multimillionaire. So-called "the most happy millionaire," Forbes is the owner of a palace in Morocco, a copra plantation in Fiji and a private, gold-colored DC-9. He is an internationally famous balloonist who, in 1973, became the first person to so fly across the United States of America. Other interests include motorcycling (he is a world-touring motorcyclist) and collecting (he has a fine collection of Victorian art and a collection of Fabergé eggs equaled only by the Kremlin's). His love of adventure, which he sees as quite separate from a desire to take risks (a desire he does not share with some other sportsmen), characterizes his entrepreneurial spirit. At the same time he recognizes that "you can't beat parent-picking for success."

LORD FORTE   Born in 1908 of a middle-class Scottish-Italian family, Lord Charles Forte of Ripley is seldom before the public eye, preferring to keep a low public profile. In fact this chairman of the mighty hotel and catering group — Trusthouse Forte — has managed to create an organization valued at approximately £1000 million. Sound business principles rather than detailed strategy are the hallmarks of his style. Asked what he would have advised his son Rocco, were he much younger now, Forte replied: "You must be able to go into any room anywhere in the world and know there'll be no one there who can point a finger at you and say: 'That man did me down.'"

DIANE VON FURSTENBERG   Started as a designer entrepreneur in 1972 with a $30,000 loan. By the end of the 1970s her business was worth $30 million and she appeared on the cover of *Newsweek* as the "Princess of Fashion." Today she has total financial and operational control of a fashion/beauty/home furnishing empire worth $250 million. Asked why she does it, von Furstenberg replied: "It's the warmth that you get, you know, in the fruit of your work, in the fruit of your efforts."

HARRY HELMSLEY   Helmsley, who has been in the real estate business for over half a century, attaches a $5 billion market value to his property. Helmsley Enterprises bill through their subsidiaries more than $445 million a year in rent alone. Besides owning the cream of New York real estate (including the Empire State Building), Helmsley owns 30 hotels (including the Park Lane and Carlton House), numerous out-of-state properties and estate brokerage and management firms. "It's the deal that's fun," says Helmsley. "It's the shaking of the jigsaw and putting it together."

ANTONIO HERRARA   Herrara is considered one of the world's best polo players (9-goal). Among this Mexican's wins are the Coronation Cup in England, and the U.S. Silver Cup. He plays nine months a year for the Rolex-Abercrombie and Kent team.

ROBERT HOLMES À COURT   Brilliantly unconventional millionaire businessman Holmes à Court shuns fame and media visibility, preferring to channel his energies into carefully laid takeover strategies: he is the chess player, a businessman for whom the moves are what count. "My goal is business — it is not important to me which business, or which customer it is." A lawyer by training (a South African by birth), he has built his business empire from Australia to include TV stations, newspapers, tire, transport, quarry and onshore oil companies. His experience has made him aware of the difference between the romantic image and reality of big business: "Big business is only small business with an extra nought on the end . . . just more dried ink on paper."

MARGERY HURST, OBE   Following the breakup of her first marriage (when she was in the army), Margery Hurst began typing from home for a living. The one-woman business expanded as she began to use freelance helpers. A friend of her father's found her a small office in London and Margery Hurst made the subtle change into what became the first employment agency — the Brook Street Bureau, now an international, multimillion-pound company.

TONY JACKLIN   Britain's leading international golf player in modern times, Jacklin assured himself a place in golfing history by winning the Open Championship and the U.S. Open within the space of twelve months. From that moment, the pressure was on Jacklin to stay on top: "I felt that after winning the U.S. and British Open in a year the public expected me to win everything else." The fact that he did not win everything else posed a personal challenge which served to demonstrate how mental resources and stamina can be as essential as technical skill to success in any field.

HEATHER JENNER Ms. Jenner started the first marriage bureau and has since arranged over 15,000 marriages. In India in her late teens (where she was living with her family) she observed the plight of young tea planters with little chance of marriage, and who planned to travel to the U.K. in search of suitable ladies. At the outset, her idea was derided as an "outrageous concept" and provoked stern opposition.

RAFER JOHNSON In 1955 Johnson became the world decathlon record holder, an achievement which seemed impossible seven years earlier when he critically injured a foot in a conveyor belt accident. Talking about how we can discover what makes a winner, Johnson said: "The great champions are the ones who react to defeat in a positive way. . . . I'd much rather climb into the head of someone who's lost and see what made that person come back and be a victor, than climb into the head of a winner and see what made that person sure to win." In 1960, in Rome, Rafer Johnson won the Olympic decathlon gold medal; today he is a coach for the Special Olympics.

HERMAN KAHN Erstwhile chairman and director of the Hudson Institute, advisor to presidents and leading pioneer in modern future studies, Herman Kahn (who died in 1983 shortly after being interviewed) was strongly criticized for "thinking the unthinkable" in his book published in 1960 *On Thermonuclear War*, and right up to his death, he challenged conventional opinion — in 1982 with *The Coming Boom*, published during the worst recession since the '30s. He described the fount of his own success as "two thirds inspiration, one third persistence; without persistence, nothing works."

DR. NATHAN KLINE Kline introduced the first of the modern tranquilizers to the United States of America in 1953 and 1954. Two years later he first used antidepressant drugs for the treatment of psychiatric patients. The winner of two Albert Lasker awards, he was director of the Rockland Institute of Research until his death in 1983. He also held professorships at Columbia University and the University of California, San Diego. A self-described "natural" lateral thinker, Kline claimed (not wholly in jest) that ignorance, laziness and poor memory were major factors in his success. Among his many organizational affiliations, Dr. Kline held a Founding Fellowship of the Royal College of Psychiatrists in England.

ALEX KROLL Runs Young and Rubicam, which claims to be the world's largest advertising agency. Ex-pro football star (the New York Titans, later renamed the Jets), Kroll is six foot two inches tall and weighs 222 pounds. Personally highly motivated — "I'm in the habit of setting goals that are uncomfortable. I used to say to myself, 'What is really a stretch?' " — he has the ability to act as a creative catalyst, eliciting original ideas from employees by game playing in order to shift the way a complex problem is viewed. Between mid-1977 and the end of 1982 he was personally responsible for bringing $400 million worth of new business to Young and Rubicam.

VERITY LAMBERT   Ms. Lambert belongs to that small band of British film makers dedicated to commercial success based on fresh and original products. She has worked her way up through television, having started as a secretary and then being fired. As head of drama at Thames Television and chief executive of Euston Films, she achieved a blend of contemporary relevance, entertainment and production quality in her work hitherto unequaled in her sphere. In 1982 she was appointed head of production at Thorn EMI Films.

NORMAN LEAR   One of America's most successful television writers (*All in the Family*, etc.), essentially a collaborative individual who needs the stimulus of working with others and has also developed an ability to be a catalyst in collaboration. To this successful writer power means "the ability to persuade people, to communicate . . . and to reach; there can be no greater power."

PAUL MACCREADY   President and chairman of AeroVironment Inc., dedicated to providing products and services in the fields of energy and the atmospheric environment. As a child he was a serious model plane enthusiast. At sixteen he soloed in powered planes. At twenty-one he took second place in a glider at the National Soaring Championships. At twenty-three, twenty-four, and twenty-five he won, and then pioneered high-altitude wave soaring in the U.S. In 1956 he became international gliding champion. In 1977 he won the $95,000 Henry Kremer Prize when his Gossamer Condor made the first sustained, controlled flight by a heavier-than-air craft powered solely by a pilot's muscles. In 1979 he won the new Kremer Prize for $215,000 when his man-powered Gossamer Albatross crossed the English Channel. In 1980 his Gossamer Penguin made the first climbing flight in a plane powered solely by sunbeams, and in 1981 his Solar Challenger flew 162 miles from Paris to England at an altitude of 11,000 ft.

DAVID MAHONEY   Named in *Fortune Magazine* as one of the "ten toughest bosses" in America, Mahoney was until recently chairman and CEO of Norton Simon, a major international consumer marketing company. Mahoney ceased to be associated with Norton Simon in 1983 when he sought to privatize the company by bidding a ludicrously low price for the company. The move at once encouraged others to bid and the result was that Mahoney's own shares rose phenomenally in value. He became a multimillionaire. Before helping form Norton Simon he was

executive V.P. at Colgate-Palmolive and before that president of Good
Humor Corporation, a client of Mahoney's when from 1951 he ran his
own advertising agency.

A. MORGAN MAREE Morgan Maree's management company special-
izes in taxation, corporate formation, security analysis, real estate and
insurance, mainly for TV and film people. Among his clients, past and
present, are Stewart Granger, Cary Grant, Clark Gable, William Wyler,
Tyrone Power, Robert Wagner, David O. Selznick, Hanna-Barbera,
Robert Taylor, Humphrey Bogart, Rock Hudson, Lauren Bacall, Carol
Baker, Tony Curtis, Elliott Gould.

ROBERT MAXWELL Chairman of one of the world's biggest educational and scientific publishing groups, Pergamon Press, and the British
Printing and Communication Corporation, Maxwell was born in Eastern
Europe and came to Britain at the age of sixteen. During the war he was
commissioned for gallantry and awarded the Military Cross for refusing
to obey an order to retreat. One year before Maxwell took over BPCC,
the company made a loss of £11.3 million. In 1983, just two years later,
its profit line was £22.1 million. On Friday, July 13, 1984, Maxwell bought
the Mirror group of magazines from Reed International for £113 million.

MARK McCORMACK Founder chief of the International Management
Group handling most of the world's top sports stars and many personalities. His company is worth around £100 million. At a time when the
media was hungry for heroes he offered the world's best his services as
manager, agent, accountant, promoter — all in one unique package. In
one year he increased Arnold Palmer's earnings from $60,000 to $500,000.
Besides sportsmen, he has handled the Pope, marketed the Nobel Prize
and Miss World. His advice to others is "not to accept, just because a
certain thing's been done a certain way, that it will always have to be
that way."

LIONEL (LEN) MURRAY, OBE General Secretary of the (British) Trades
Union Congress from 1973 to 1984, Murray has held office since 1954.
He was awarded the OBE in 1966, became Visiting Fellow of Nuffield
College, Oxford, in 1974, a Privy Counsellor in 1976, and Honorary Fellow of Sheffield City Polytechnic in 1979. It took a heart attack to convince Murray that "being a workaholic is a very inefficient way of using time."

JERALD NEWMAN Newman has been president and chief administrative officer and trustee of the Bowery Savings Bank in New York since
1982. Bowery has $5 billion in assets and hired Newman for his experi-
ence in commercial banking to improve its weak net-worth-to-assets ratio. Newman had been executive V.P. of the Bank Leumi Trust Company of New York since 1976 and helped build the Leumi from a three-
branch bank to its current twenty-five branches and $2 billion in assets.

SIR PETER PARKER   Sir Peter "came into industry almost with a sense of reforming zeal," and recently retired as chairman of British Rail. Since joining Booker McConnell in 1954 he has held numerous directorships in diverse fields and has been on the British Airways board. Between 1943 and 1947 he served as a major in the Intelligence Corps, has played rugby for Bedford and the East Midlands, and once played Hamlet on Broadway. He is now chairman of Rockware, the glass and plastics group.

LORD PENNOCK   A past president of the Confederation of British Industry and former deputy chairman of ICI, Lord Pennock believes in the importance of seizing opportunity: "If you get too far ahead of change you'll make a mess of it and get your head chopped off. But if you don't respond to change you'll also get your head chopped off." He emerged at the forefront of the development of cable television in the U.K. as chairman of BICC until his retirement on December 31, 1984. BICC, which stands for British Insulated Callendars Cables, but is now the company's official name, is the largest cable manufacturers in Britain and stands to benefit from the new technology.

RON PICKERING   Pickering is the well-known athletic coach and broadcaster whose world renown is grounded in his success with long jumper Lynn Davies, who won the first Olympic gold medal by a Welsh athlete (the long jump in 1964) and went on to win the first gold medal triple by capturing both Commonwealth and European titles. In 1968 Davis improved the U.K. record to 27 ft. Pickering also coached Mary Rand, long jumper, hurdler, sprinter and pentathlon competitor for Britain and indisputably the best woman athlete up to her retirement in 1968. She became the first British woman athlete to win an Olympic gold medal (again in the '64 games with a jump of 22 ft. 2¼ in). Despite a long history of encouraging others to come first, Pickering's view of American society is that "their great dropout rate and a lot of their great losses of talent are due to the fact that American society sees no role or place for the guy who comes second. This is utter nonsense!"

SIR MARK PRESCOTT   Businessman, race-horse trainer, Sir Mark's management strategy is based upon shrewd analysis of the competition. His advice to others is "find what you like doing best and then find someone to pay you for doing it." He plans his horses' careers for profit, matching them carefully with events rather than running them for the Society pages in magazines. A strong, ruthless man-manager, he breeds fighting cocks as a hobby.

LORD ROBENS   Sometime Labour Party Member of Parliament, Robens rose to become Parliamentary Secretary to the Minister of Transport and was tipped as a future PM. Between 1945 and 1947 he became Parliamentary Private Secretary to the Minister of Fuel and Power, and later Minister of Labour and National Service. In 1961 he became chairman of the National Coal Board and managed to reduce the work force by a quarter of a million in an ailing industry without causing a rash of strikes.

JIM ROGERS   James B. Rogers, Jr., self-described "poor boy of Alabama," turned his personal wealth of $600 into $14 million in just twelve years. In 1973, he and George Soros formed an offshore hedge fund money management company. Rogers' idiosyncratic personality converted the company's original investment of $12 million into $250 million by 1980. Like Len Murray, he was a workaholic ("the most important thing in my life was my work; I did not do anything else until my work was done"), but unlike him, Rogers did not suffer a heart attack, perhaps because he restricted his work time to twelve years! Like Forbes he is an enthusiastic adventurer and motorcyclist. But unlike anyone else, his judgment was best, yet "everyone had the same facts as I did; it wasn't as though I had some pipeline into heaven!" To Jim Rogers, instinctual judgment is not God-given, it "has been honed by twelve years, twenty hours a day."

BARONESS SEEAR   Baroness Seear of Paddington helped pioneer modern-day management techniques with responsibility for labor force motivation firmly in the lap of experts, rather than foremen in their spare time. For 32 years, she lectured at the London School of Economics.

SIR CLIVE SINCLAIR   A self-made multimillionaire inventor/businessman, Sir Clive's first business foundered in 1979 despite such an incredibly successful invention as the pocket calculator. Now the head of Sinclair Research and in his mid-forties, his more recent products include the flat screen television, a highly profitable range of personal computers, and as yet still promised, the electric car. Sinclair was knighted in 1983.

JACKIE STEWART   Stewart began racing in 1961. In the 1969 season he gained so many points that two-thirds through it, his world title was unassailable. In Formula One racing he has been world champion on three occasions. Despite winning twenty-seven Grand Prix races out of the ninety-nine he has raced, risk is anathema to Stewart: "I hate fear; I hate it; I really hate it. . . . I've seen a lot of free-fall artists stagger their way in and out of situations — you can call it a couple of times, but you get found out." Now he earns vast off-the-track rewards promoting and making personal appearances. Recalling how he learned to manipulate other drivers on-track, Stewart reflects: "It worked tremendously well until some of the young, uninhibited drivers arrived and I had to exercise my authority on them, before they got the idea."

STING With Police, Sting has sold over 10 million records, and during the 1983 tour of the United States performed before more than one million fans — "to see 20,000 people react exactly the same way to this musical code is quite astounding!" Police became the biggest rock act in the world partly due to the voice and composing talent of Sting and partly to their carefully orchestrated strategy. "I spent five years polishing and honing an image. . . . To a certain extent you taper your creativity to a particular model." Before being a rock star, Sting, alias Gordon Sumner, was a teacher. Before that, he was county champion at the 100-yard and 200-yard sprints, but gave up athletics when he came third in the national championships.

VIRGINIA WADE Born in England, raised in South Africa, she makes her home in New York. She won the first U.S. Open in 1968 and won Wimbledon in 1977 (the year of its centenary). She was ranked Number One in England for ten consecutive years and was among the world's top ten tennis players continuously between the years 1967 and 1979. As of January 1, 1981, Virginia Wade earned over $1 million in tournament competitions. In 1982 she became the first woman ever elected to the Wimbledon Committee. The secret of her success? "The trick is being able to get outside yourself and work from outside and watch yourself as an observer."

MARK WEINBERG Millionaire entrepreneur Weinberg started an insurance company from scratch called Abbey Life. It became a success, but he left to start another called Hambro Life, backed by Hambros bank. It is now valued on the stock exchange at around £500 million. Also a financier of inventive products, Weinberg has launched the microwriter, an ingenious six-key "pocket" typewriter. Despite his total involvement in company strategy and ideas for the future Weinberg confesses, "I don't like playing poker in business."

SIR HUW WHELDON Broadcaster and chairman, Court of Governors of the London School of Economics, since 1975. Joined the BBC in 1952 at the outset of the television revolution. There he worked as producer, director, commentator and author, becoming controller of programmes in 1965, managing director in 1968 and special advisor in 1975.

CHARLES WILLIAMS, CBE Managing director of Henry Ansbacher & Co., the London-based merchant bank, since 1980. In 1955 he was captain of Oxford University Cricket Club. Between '53 and '59 he played for Essex County. His career in banking runs parallel to his political activities; he became chairman of the Price Commission in the Harold Wilson government, Labour Party candidate for Colchester in 1964, and vice chairman and founder member of the Labour Economic Finance and Taxation Association in 1975. For Williams, and thus his merchant bank, company strategy is inextricably linked to the personality of its architect, and as such is instinctual: "I am psychologically unhappy with unstructured situations."

PART ONE

SUCCESS

1

Styles of Success

United States: **Alex Kroll · John Nieman**

United Kingdom and International: **Sir Terence Conran · Sir Clive Sinclair · Robert Holmes à Court · Jack Gallagher**

Superficially, the most noticeable feature of successful people is that each has a discernible style that is unmistakably theirs. Imagine a huge hall filled with every breed, shape, and noise of dog. Imagine the famous Cruft's dog show in London. The Great Danes, the elegant borzois, the perky Yorkies, the imperial Pekingese, the friendly beagles, and the sinister Dobermans. Each in its own style. Each with its admirers. Each to be judged according to its own style.

What is style? It is a coming together of elements and actions which form a distinct pattern which is thereafter consistent with itself. There are philosophers who have declared that man is no more than his style. There are women, painters, decorators, and politicians who exist only to nourish their styles.

Is there one particular style of behavior that leads to success? There does not seem to be. There is a very wide variety of styles among the people who were interviewed for this book. Does that mean than any style will do? Probably not. There can be many successful styles and also many unsuccessful ones. A successful person may like taking risks or may

23

like avoiding risks. But cautious is not the same as timid. A timid person is unlikely to be successful.

Even if successful people show a variety of styles, is there one style which — if adopted — would be likely to lead to success? The traditional image is that of a person who is strong-minded, ruthless, and hardworking. It is surprising how few of the people in this book fit that image.

Tennis is a good game for observing different styles of play, because it is a game in which styles are made continuously visible. Bjorn Borg has a style of play that allows a wide margin of error. His ground strokes are hit with a considerable amount of top spin, which means that the ball can travel well above the net and still dip sharply to fall before the baseline. Another player, Jimmy Connors, hits the ball much closer to the top of the net and is therefore more likely to make mistakes.

MACRO-STYLES IN BUSINESS

By macro-style is meant the overall style of behavior that deals with broad strategies and decisions. Although in battle or on the tennis court or at the negotiating table, unpredictability may be an important factor, it may be seen that many legendary tycoons have remained true to the overall style that is supposed to have been the basis of their fortunes.

Paul Getty ran his business upon the principle of not spending a penny more than absolutely necessary. It is a style hard to fault purely in business terms: if you can keep costs to a minimum, you can concentrate on making profits that much more easily. When Lord Thomson came to London to buy the *Sunday Times,* he stayed at the Savoy Hotel for the sake of impressing his business contacts, but had breakfast at a workmen's café nearby. Conversely, Jack Gallagher, chairman of Dome Petroleum, one of Canada's ten largest companies, recalls, "I started out with $250,000 equity and over $7 million debt, and have tried to keep that ratio ever since."

MICRO-STYLES

There are times when the macro has to come down to the micro. How does a person deal with his team? How does a person deal with his opponents in a negotiating situation? There are people who succeed well in macro-strategies and fair poorly in micro-strategies. There might be a powerful film-maker unable to frame a simple family shot. Napoleon said that he had much more difficulty getting rid of the cook's mastiff (which used to terrorize Josephine's lapdogs) than in beating the Austrians at Austerlitz.

The Catalyst

Let's look at the way Alex Kroll, president of the world's largest advertising agency, gets the best out of his creative team. In *New York* magazine John Nieman described how the team solved a problematic selling line during a special project for Ford. The problem was solved not by Alex Kroll's providing the final answer but through his acting as a catalyst. He provided a framework around which the answer could form itself.

"Our car people in New York had thumbed their thesauruses for weeks. They'd come up with more than one hundred entries, and no winners. Y & R Detroit had also come up with a hundred different entries. The art directors had their lists. Still no winners. Everyone knew it. Everyone also knew there was a meeting in Alex's office at 3 P.M. . . . with the 'line.' Before the meeting the supervisors narrowed the list and focused on three recommendations.

"Alex looked at them. Obviously no winners. Then he told us what he thought the line should say. Not the exact words, just the attitude or stance of the line. Someone seconded the thought. Someone volunteered a first word for the line. Someone completed the sentence. Someone improved the set of words. Alex said, 'That's it!' After three weeks and reams of paper, the line had been written in five minutes. And everyone felt it was theirs."

Kroll's style is to infuse his staff with enthusiasm, exciting their imagination by involving them in a problem: "Remember Raymond Rubicam's edict!" he exclaims, " 'Resist the usual.' The only way to achieve this is to pour a strategy through an individual so that it comes out personal.

"There are a couple of things that I can do well. One is that . . . I can make up games better than anybody else. . . . It could be a new game. It could be a variation of some other game. But I could invent a game which had goals and enough handicaps. The one place that this ability is useful is in creative direction. What I've found is that you can reduce a complex, commercial situation — an advertising strategy for 'X' product — to a game, and produce a shift in attitude. To say, 'OK, here's the goal': this is what we want to accomplish. Now by making it a game, a little bit of a game — here's the object; here are the people we're talking to; here's what they believe now; here's what we want them to believe about this product; and here's the reality — you begin to catch their enthusiasm for it as play.

"It's never quite play because there's too much money involved, but if you can reduce the level of tension (the level or thread of danger that's inherent in a commercial situation) by talking around it, analogizing, and

25

throwing in everything from Henry Miller to Pope John, you begin to create a sense of enthusiasm in the team to get to the goal — a good tension comes into it, the tension of winning or accomplishing a goal rather than the dread tension of failure down the line. If you do that, they (art directors, writers, producers, etc.) will come up with a solution that will be far more original, idiosyncratic, and interesting than I would.

"In the process of getting there I'm going to become involved and I'm going to make mistakes. That's not a problem. In the process I'll become exposed as fallible, get my hands dirty, make risky propositions. Now, put that behind us, step away from being the guy mucking around in the mud puddles, and I can do the other part: 'OK, we've all screwed around long enough, now we're going to do this.' Somebody has to say A, B, or C."

MANAGEMENT STYLE

Another businessman's ability to get the best out of people became crucial to his success: in 1982, Sir Terence Conran, designer/businessman, chairman of Habitat and Mothercare, bought through Hepworths (of which he is a director) a chain of 70 women's fashion shops called Next. He expanded it to one hundred or so shops and transformed the business into a great success. He claims now that the idea was very simple, that the market was there already: 25-to-40-year-olds wanting reasonably fashionable clothes at a competitive price. But clearly if that was the whole answer then other people would have made the apparently simple equation work. "They didn't," says Conran, "because they didn't do it with conviction; that is the difference.

"People like the Manchester Business School looked at it and said, 'This is a terrible risk.' It was like talking to a lawyer! But the very conviction of everybody who worked on the project — from the designers to the shop staff to the people who did the advertising and the people who manufactured the clothes — produced a totally convinced team effort. That total conviction, where every detail was in place, was almost compulsive to the general public. Everything added up together and gave the public a feeling of confidence. . . . I think enthusiasm rubs off onto people like pollen on bees."

Here we may notice some interesting points. There are times when the conviction and enthusiasm of a leader rubs off on everyone else — as seems to be the case here. (It would also seem to be the case with Lee Iacocca's amazing rescue of Chrysler.) There are other times when a team spirit and confidence are built up less through a process of charismatic "rubbing off" than by careful nurturing and a sensitive use of people. In English politics the contrasting styles would be those of Churchill and Attlee.

The Inventor

The uniquely innovative Sir Clive Sinclair acknowledges that he lacks such management style. His success is in thinking up new ideas — the pocket calculator, the digital watch, his own home computer (which has sold more than any other), his flat-screen TV, and (hopefully) his new electric car — a totally different concept: "Both the success and the failings of the company are due to my personality. We do a good job in thinking up new ideas and marketing them effectively (there's often as much creativity needed in the marketing of a new concept as a new product itself; often you cannot sell a new idea in the same way you can sell a conventional one). But then the failings of the company are again related to my personality in that I'm not a manager either by inclination or by training. I'm a fairly reserved person in some ways, so I find it very difficult to cope with hundreds of people." The demise of his first company, Sinclair Radionics, in 1979 was probably due to a number of different factors, but Clive Sinclair recognizes the limitations of his personal style: "I try to avoid general management as far as possible."

There is no doubt that Sir Clive Sinclair is a brilliant electronics genius. He is also an entrepreneur who has to work alone and could not be happy in a large organization. His boldness in concept and in business is the surprising boldness that is often to be found in someone who is rather shy. His success depends on his willingness to have bold concepts and to market them at astonishing prices (astonishingly low, that is). Almost all his ideas would have been rejected at once by any product development team sitting down in a large corporate company to examine proposals. All his pricing levels would have been rejected even faster.

The Predator

Robert Holmes à Court's style is almost totally different to Sir Clive Sinclair's, but no less successful. Born in South Africa, he moved to Australia and set up a practice in law. Pretty soon he became involved in business.

"I had a client interested in purchasing a public company, but he didn't go through with it . . . probably wise. It was the smallest, worst company on the Stock Exchange. I hadn't seen it, but I bought control for $75,000. After six months it had got considerably worse than it was — without hope — so I took a month off from my legal practice to see what I had bought and what I could do about it. I haven't gone back!"

Today his interests range from TV and newspapers to transport and oil. He has built his empire with deliberate, clinical strategy and not a trace of showmanship. In conversation he makes the process seem self-evident, a logical product of that first deal. In fact, it is the logic of the chessboard. Robert Holmes à Court is a keen chess player and business strategist; he believes in making every move count.

In 1982, he took over Lord Grade's ACC (Associated Communications Corporation), a film and television company with worldwide interests that had been energized by the Hollywood-style razzmatazz of its executive chairman. Holmes à Court, recognizing this as its essential weakness, moved in — the low-key negotiator and stealthy predator seeming to have a hypnotic effect upon its quarry.

As we watch some of the moves in the power dance which Holmes à Court himself describes, note the difference between someone who has an idea and pursues it through to success (like Sir Clive Sinclair) and someone whose success lies in the way he moves and reacts to the moves of others. It is the difference in style between a scientist, who deals with ideas, and a general, who deals with the moves of others. It is the difference in style between an artist, who does his own thing, and a politician, who needs to work with and on others.

The Takeover of ACC

"I actually came over to London on other business at that time; I was on my way to America to look at cable investments. But there was a strong Australian dollar and weak sterling, so I was looking to move into that currency. I put a tender in for *The Times* newspaper, but then ACC announced its disastrous results — it was the first thing that caught my eye, this complete management disaster — chaos."

ACC was not at the time looking to be rescued by an outside purchaser, and there were more fundamental problems connected with Holmes à Court's takeover:

"The first fascinating thing is that it was agreed by everybody that ACC was takeover-proof. There was a small number of voting shares held by the Board, and the IBA (the Independent Broadcasting Authority) wouldn't allow anybody (let alone a foreigner) to take over a UK television station. So ACC appeared to be safe. But the share price collapsed and I bought 50 percent of the nonvoting shares over nine months. 'Lex' in *The Financial Times* explained the situation fairly well; perhaps because I was an Australian I didn't understand that it couldn't be done — I'd obviously made an awful mistake."

Holmes à Court's first major public acquisition had been to take over Bell. On that occasion he had moved in, in stages. With ACC, he essentially repeated this two-stage strategy, the first stage providing him with a seat on the board.

Not only did the undoubted charm of the man persuade Lord Grade to sell his shares, Grade even made a number of public statements that he was delighted to sell to him.

It was then that Gerald Ronson's Heron Corporation asked the Takeover Panel to censure publicly Robert Holmes à Court for alleged breaches of the Takeover Code. Holmes à Court continues the story:

"Ronson paid a lot of money to public relations people to try and promote the thought. I can't remember the name of the firm, but he paid a very big fee, and they set up a cry and had their Australian agents do the same. I sued the Australian agents for defamation and was paid as much money as they were able to pay without going insolvent."

In the United Kingdom, newspapers were following every move in the tortuous struggle. This is a very important factor. There are negotiations and actions which work well when no parties other than the negotiators are involved. A totally different style and strategy may be required when every move is exposed to the scrutiny, interpretation, and extrapolation of the press. For example, "red herrings" do not work too well in private but they work very well in the public type of fight. The moves may not be made through the press (though that is always an option), but the fact that the press is watching makes the difference. When you are expected to say something and do not, that can be a powerful move in a public negotiation. Holmes à Court continues:

"Ronson made a very good play in the press and I decided to meet it with silence. I didn't want to give him credibility or argue. I got on with the job." To the British public Holmes à Court still remained a shadow. "In reality I was chairman — the situation never changed except publicly. I owned it and I ran it."

And the critical step of share negotiation with Lord Grade himself? "I follow a policy (in negotiation) and it's very simple; it's open and clear; it's as it shows. There's no great tactic. There's no more to it than shows on the surface. I don't enjoy any complicated mating dance or any subterfuge, which I don't think ever works.

"I was absolutely tough with him. I gave him nothing. Nothing other than a price for his shares that I offered to all the others. In fact, I got him to rescind his contract — he had a contract to continue working here for two years at £200,000 per year and I said that was exorbitant and I wouldn't make an offer."

There is a commanding logic to his approach, to his ability to spot an opportunity and then with strategy and cool determination sort out the fundamental realities of the deal. In his opinion it was Lord Grade's style — which epitomized the weaknesses of Holmes à Court's strengths — that was an important reason for the chaos at ACC:

"He [Lord Grade] had an image of himself as a 1950s movie mogul and he had to play up to that image. He had to tip the headwaiter in America $100 and he had to live it, he had to say, 'Yes, you're on, we'll do it, and we'll spend more.' So he had to do what he perceived was the obligation to that image and he was, or he thought he was, happy with that image.

"What was really happening was that Grade only had that facade for the public — not privately. He was a sad, frightened, worried man privately. Behind the facade people were tearing their hair out because they were facing failure.

"The ideas you want are real ideas; they're not fantasies. There is a difference. The real ideas can be put into action. They are not dreams; they're something real. And what gets the team confident is that the entire team, the whole company, is successful.

"The bankers of ACC were very concerned a year ago, were withdrawing their support. I have their total support. They get the real answers from my accountants. They get disclosure — that's one of the things I believe in. I would eliminate seven-eighths of the company legislation that controls company behavior and would replace it with total disclosure requirements.

"You see the general public is led by the financial journals to believe that big business is a romantic exercise and they look for romanticism. It's not there. Big business is only small business with an extra zero on the end. . . . In reality it's just more dried ink on paper. I'm just motivated by doing what I'm doing as well as I can. . . . I could play chess with you and be motivated in the same way. It's making every move count."

There is a tinge of sadness in the strong contrast of styles. The gazelle has its style, but in the end the lion will prevail. Lord Grade had the style of an entrepreneur who took risks and enjoyed the building up of his entertainment empire. Holmes à Court had the style of the negotiator and deal maker. There is a sort of inevitability about the triumph of the latter style. Without the former, nothing would ever get built up. Yet within the entrepreneurial style are the seeds of its own destruction because it thrives on change and expansion. Sooner or later there comes the point of relative failure and with that a vulnerability to the "realism style." The stag may be magnificent, but the stalker usually wins in the end — through patience and making the right moves.

2

Characteristics of Typically Successful Styles

THE PLAYERS:

United States: **William Agee** · **Nolan Bushnell** · **Roy Cohn** · **Werner Erhard** · **Bobby Fischer** · **Malcolm Forbes** · **Rafer Johnson** · **Dr. Nathan Kline** · **Alex Kroll** · **David Mahoney** · **Paul MacCready** · **Morgan Maree** · **Mark McCormack** · **James B. Rogers, Jr.**

United Kingdom and International: **Christian Bonington** · **Robert Holmes à Court** · **Tony Jacklin** · **Miyomoto Musashi** · **Sting** · **Virginia Wade**

ENERGY, DRIVE AND DIRECTION

As a teenager, Alex Kroll developed obsessions: "They could be anything . . . it was a period of time where I was totally devoted to baseball, Russian novelists, weight-lifting, taking high-protein pills obsessively (I was very thin, very skinny, and very clumsy . . . but the more I worked out, the better, because the faster I'd get stronger). I became obsessed with certain goals. And the thing I guess I learned was how really hard it was to win, for me to win. And how terrific it felt to win. And I got into the habit of setting goals which were uncomfortable. (I've always been very confident that I'm very lazy at heart, and in order to suck me out of my lethargy, in order for me not to allow that natural compulsion to be a slug, I had to set uncomfortable goals)."

31

David Mahoney was nominated by *Fortune* magazine as one of the "top ten toughest bosses in America."

"I just keep moving every day as hard and fast as I can. High-intensity and high-voltage. Light comes from that, not from passivity. I insist we all do our best every day. I'm intense in everything I do and I expect others will be, too. There may be timing factors in it, good luck and fortune factors, but the question is, do you utilize it? Some of it you can't control — some of it goes against you — it works both ways. You run to daylight — where you see the break you go. Most people aren't even aware of what's happening around them. Two-thirds of the people don't know what's going on to them, personally.

"I don't forget what my role is. My role is to run this company as well as I can financially, substantively, pick the right people, get the goals correct, see that they're implemented. . . . Has it worked out well? Damned right. Company's tripled (since 1968). It ain't bad . . . I really don't care so much as I used to about what other people think . . . I think that's true of many chief executives after they've been banged around and kicked."

Sometimes "direction" goes awry only to offer another avenue for drive and persistence. "We had a crisis in the acquisition of Max Factor. We bought it and we had a lot of problems. We thought we could run it better than they did. There was that wonderful synergistic time in the sixties when everybody thought you could just fix anything, 'Synergy' — the worst word that ever happened in American industry. . . . The world believed you could transfer every skill to the other. We bought a company and the market really wasn't there. But we thought we could fix it. We're still digging our way out of it. But I think we've finally got it worked out.

"The other night some lady came in and said, 'That's your Vietnam,' and I said, 'Wait a minute; Vietnam they got out of, we're still in here, baby, and we're going to win it.' That's the difference."

At first sight it may seem that Mahoney's style is one of intense drive, energy, and positivism. All that is true, but it can give a misleading impression. There is a powerful element of realism. In assessing styles it is easy to be carried away by the most obvious attributes and to ignore those other factors on which success also depends. Boundless energy is useful but rarely a complete style in itself.

EGO

Is ego just a strong sense of personality or an aim in itself? Do people do things in order to satisfy their ego or in order to create that ego?

Chris Bonington: "The successful climber usually has a strong ego and he wants to be the first person to either stand on a summit or find a new way up a mountain, but in actual fact this is then combined with an intellectual curiosity. So this drive to be the first there is not just to be the first there to say 'Hoorah, I'm great!' It's also the great drive to find something in yourself, or a curiosity of finding whether this can be done. So you have these two things. You have an ego, in that I think most climbers enjoy being able to say, 'I did this,' which is ego, but that is not the sole reason why they did it."

"CAN DO"

Sometimes we may mistake for an ego drive what is really the challenge, and subsequently the obsession, of an idea: "This is impossible, but I can do it."

Working with a few friends but without the support of a large design laboratory, Paul MacCready made the first plane to fly using man's muscle power on its own. Many mathematicians had claimed to show that the muscles of a man would never be sufficient to enable him to fly without some outside source of energy. Various teams had tried to build airplanes that would be powered only by the energy of man. All had failed. The task was to build a plane that would follow a figure-eight course over a mere half-mile. The task seemed impossible. But, "I went single-mindedly and with considerable assurance towards the goal. I knew I was going to get there. There was no barrier that was going to stand in the way. We just charged ahead, and everything worked out." Mac-Cready and his group suceeded in winning the Kremer Prize by flying their plane across 24 miles of the English Channel. This represents an incredible achievement. Later Paul MacCready was to build an airplane that would cross the English Channel when powered only by solar energy.

Nolan Bushnell, the man who created "Pong," the first electronic game, and who has recently launched the first "intelligent" robot, Androbot, explains: "I think it's very much a 'can-do' attitude. I mean, I always feel like there is a solution. I believe that there is a truth. It's not always obvious what that truth is and it's not always obvious how to get to it, but if you keep searching you can figure it out."

CONFIDENCE

"I think one of the biggest problems most people have is that they are too bashful. In the formative years of your life, drive should be accompanied by some need for recognition. And it's only after you are recognized that you don't need to be recognized."

— Morgan Maree

Self-confidence and a sense of mastery are important ingredients to any successful style, and we have seen examples of them in Paul MacCready's and Nolan Bushnell's belief that they could solve the problems they tackled. Confidence is extraordinarily difficult to understand. Does it arise from knowledge or from ignorance? Is it just (as I suspect) a chemical state in the brain that may follow different circumstances in different people? Some people are nervous and some are not; reverse that and put in confident. I am not at all sure there is a logic of confidence. If you know your stuff, you will be confident in an examination. If you have beaten your opponent, you may be confident of doing it again. Mastery can give rise to confidence, but confidence can also exist without it.

The twenty-one-year-old chess master Paul Morphy's outstanding characteristic was also an almost unbelievably supreme confidence. He knew, as though it were a simple fact of nature, that he was bound to win, and he quietly acted on this knowledge. This enabled him to play with outstanding audacity, sacrificing piece after piece with what appeared to be sheer recklessness; it was the result of precise calculation. The same confidence is displayed by the newest chess star, Gary Kasparov. In the 1982 Olympiad in Lucerne, Kasparov, still only nineteen years old, played an amazing game against Victor Korchnoi, the official world title challenger. He left one piece *en prise* for seven moves and advanced his queen to the enemy back rank, where she was apparently totally cut off from safety. A report in *The Times* written by David Spanier described the scene:

> He held the spectators, following the game around the board and on the television monitor, spellbound. Yet so complex were his ideas that even the experts could not analyse if or how Kasparov was winning. Instead there was an overwhelming sense of mastery. Of inevitable fate. Perhaps Korchnoi might have found his way through.
> But with his King surrounded, a rapid series of exchanges took place in which Korchnoi gave up his Queen. It was all over in 36 moves.

At the time, Kasparov was ranked number two in the world. Twenty years earlier, Bobby Fischer (then also nineteen years old) had set standards of confidence which can never be beaten. "There's no one alive I can't beat," was his constant boast. And when asked if he was the greatest player who had ever lived, he replied, "Well, I don't like to put things like that in print; it sounds so egotistical. But to answer your question, yes." The champions make these cosmic claims and then justify them. They are able to justify them because they are very, very good indeed at their game.

It is in the nature of some people not only to underestimate their own qualities but, in millionaire publisher Malcom Forbes's own words, "To admire the people who have qualities the opposite of your own. I wish I had the patience of Job. I see other people who are less kinetic, and I think I'd like to be that calm, cool, collected all the time." Nothing erodes self-confidence or the ability to turn ambition into success more than a feeling that others higher up the ladder have all the answers. David Mahoney, late of Norton Simon: "When I was young I thought that people at the top really understood what the hell was happening . . . whether they were cardinals or bishops or generals or politicians or business leaders. They knew. Well, I'm up there, and now I know they don't know!" Nolan Bushnell, the inventor, makes the same point: "I consistently believed that there are experts and there aren't. Whenever I've wanted to surrender good judgment to a Santa Claus, I get disappointed."

STAMINA, HARD WORK

Stamina and hard work are not the same thing. There may be hard work in training or in putting together a deal. Stamina is the ability to maintain a high level of importance throughout the "confrontation" or "operation" time. Some hardworking people do not have stamina, and some people with stamina hate hard work. How important is hard work for success?

"I don't know if I have the distance, judgment, and balance to be correct," says James B. Rogers, Jr., a low-profile money manager who turned $600 into £14 million in the space of twelve years. "But what I ascribe my success to most of all is enormous hard work. You see, the most important thing in my life was my work. I didn't do anything else until my work was done. That was it. That was the be-all and end-all. That's what I focused on, what drove me; that's what I had to do.

"I also know that I could have been successful, as normal people justify success, not working as hard, but my definition of success is not normal people's and that's the problem. At the time I worked most intensely, I really knew an enormous amount of what was going on in the world, I really knew just about everything to the extent a single human being could. That was how I was able to make judgments. I was doing the work of eight or ten people. I was so narrow-minded; I was driven; I was dedicated."

"Efficiency is a function of effort and result," states Robert Holmes à Court with customary clarity when told of Lord Grade's public reputation for starting work every morning at 7 A.M. and working a twenty-four-hour day. "He used to sleep all day on the couch! I try to make light work of something. I put in all my time, but on each particular time I prefer to make light work of it so that I can move to the next thing, or take it to the next stage. But my total waking hours are working hours."

Len Murray, until recently general secretary of the TUC (Trades Union Congress), did suffer a heart attack from overwork. "I had to stop — that's the thing that came out of that [the heart attack]. I found that being a workaholic was a very inefficient way of using time. It was a very valuable lesson. I'd been in a descending spiral of ineffectiveness. If you want anything badly enough, you can go and get it. But time you can't. And, therefore, you've got to use time. It's a God-given gift. You've got to extract the most out of it. There's an obligation on you to use time."

So what is the verdict? Is hard work essential? Successful people so often enjoy their work that it does not seem like work. Then they retire and quickly deteriorate through lack of the stimulus of work. It does happen that some aspects of the work are enjoyable (like setting up a deal), but other aspects are just hard and tiring work (like travel and working out the paperwork for a deal). Certainly there are people who seem to think that hard work must have its rewards and that hard work is a substitute for strategy, but filling time is not the same as time management. Being busy is not the same as working. Dealing with the urgent is not the same as dealing with the important.

There is also what we might call the urgency of laziness. This is an apparent paradox, for laziness and urgency would seem to be exact opposites. In practice, however, laziness can be a powerful spur to thought. This point is neatly made by Dr. Nathan Kline: "I always try to do things the simplest way. And I think laziness is a virtue. If you have to get your work done and you're lazy, you'll find a better way to do it and one that requires less effort and time, so laziness is a virtue when you combine it with enough compulsiveness to be sure you get there."

EFFICIENCY

It might be said of Mark McCormack that he owes his success to a single good idea, the timing of which was perfect. He had the idea of marketing sports personalities at a time when the media was hungry for heroes.

"Having secured Arnold Palmer, Gary Player, and Jack Nicklaus, and launched them as the first in a new firmament of sports stars [Palmer's earnings went from $60,000 to $500,000 in the space of a year], a strategy emerged. We then flew vertically down the sport after that, and IMG spread from that. We took that approach in more sports. Jackie Stewart was our first race driver and he was the world champion. Killy was our first skier. . . . That was the method that we used to get into sport. We took what we had done in another sport (which was good, was unique), and we went up to another person in another sport and said, 'Look what we've done in that sport, we can do that in your sport.' "

But perhaps the secret of McCormack's success lies as much in his controlled, computerlike efficiency, which has earned him the nickname "Mark the Machine." His liking for punctuality is, he claims, part natural: "A little of it was me before I started; a lot of it was me not wanting to be totally involved in business all the time. The punctuality really related to the fact that I want to finish on time just as much as I want to start on time. 'To finish on time' means 'at the end of the day' as much as it does 'finish this interview about nine A.M.' More importantly, if my last appointment on a given day is six, I want to finish at seven (if that's when I'm scheduled to finish), and when I've finished I want to be able to relax and get it all out of my mind. That works better for me. I can be more efficient as a person in business, and it makes me more relaxed as a person out of it."

McCormack is a stickler for detail. He logs the amount of hours he sleeps every night (aiming to ensure an average of about seven), how many days of the month he gets out and jogs, how many miles he flies in a year, and what percent of the time he has managed to spend with his family in Cleveland, Ohio. "Also, I wallow in these yellow pads. The real purpose of those things is that I can make notes during the day and usually will deal with those notes very early on in the following morning — it maybe takes me a half-hour to take little notes and decide what I'm going to do about them. The key to me is that when I go through them I don't think about business at all. When I wake up in the morning I have this sheet which starts on both sides of the line — starts in the morning and goes to the evening. There are things to do and there are calls to make, and so I look at it and know that between nine and nine-thirty I have four phone calls and I know which order I'm going to make them in, and then at nine-thirty I'm going to the golf course and I'm going to do a television commentary for the BBC. I don't worry about a thing anymore, and then tomorrow morning I'll turn over and here's the next sheet and that's what I'll do tomorrow. That goes up usually a month or two in advance."

His cool, methodical efficiency enabled him to suggest to skier Jean-Claude Killy, without flinching, that marriage might harm his marketing potential. He was being promoted by everybody as the bachelor, jet-setting ski superstar. "He came and asked me what would happen if he got married," McCormack remarked in an interview with the *Sunday Times* magazine. "I told him I thought his image would maybe be better if he didn't get married. He waited a couple more years."

RUTHLESSNESS

Where single-mindedness and efficiency meet, ruthlessness is the charge. "In single combat," the Samurai warrior Miyamoto Musashi advises in *A Book of Five Rings* (Overlook Press), "if your opponent's rhythm is disorganized or if he has fallen into evasive or retreating attitudes, you must crush him straightaway with no concern for his presence and without allowing him space for breath. It is essential to crush him all at once. The primary thing is not to let him recover his position even a little." In an arena which shares some remarkable similarities with single combat in seventeenth-century Japan, tennis player Virginia Wade isolates a lack of "ruthlessness" as her particular Achilles' heel.

"I think one of my problems was that I was afraid to win. I never really won as much as I should have won. I think I'm afraid of winning because the moment you win you have much more pressure on you and you have to sustain it, and that is always the thing that starts to bear down on you. It's always harder to be the holder of the tournament and play it the next year than be the challenger. I would find myself in winning positions and then I would chicken out. To have the guts to go through with that final little bit is an enormous step to make. You have to think how bloody-minded you're going to be when you lose. You have to think those things. It's so easy to think, all right, I've had a play in this tournament, and in the final I know exactly what I'm going to do, and I'm going to be so happy when I win it. You play it because you want to win, and then suddenly the day comes, and when that moment comes it's much harder to tackle. That is when you think, God I feel tired today; I feel awful; I don't even feel like playing. And that's when your desire goes when all these things — when the pressure of the moment — finally comes. Wanting to win, it's being totally childish not to go through with that final little bit, because if you lose you have this huge drama and all these tears and misery about losing, and it really is masochistic. This is why I take my hat off to the Borgs and Chris Everts of the world who win consistently. They do it very much through mental ability. I don't have half as much respect for someone like Martina Navratilova, because she's got so much ability and so it's easy for her to win. It's just a natural consequence to win with that strength she has, and that ability."

Here we see a high degree of self-knowledge (see page 77ff.) and the realization that there may be a certain lack in a style. Clearly all successful people do not have perfect styles. Often they find ways of compensating for these deficiencies or try to overcome them. Sometimes the weakness is unsuspected and only comes to light when it is tested directly. There are generals who are brilliant at retreats and others who are better at advancing. It is rare to find a style that will be successful in all circumstances. This is, however, different from an acknowledged weakness in the main area of activity.

Combat on the sports field, in the courtroom, and in war demands a style that is different from that of the idea-follower and the deal-maker. There is the element of ruthlessness which Virginia Wade sometimes seems to lack. Ruthlessness has a bad odor simply because it is almost impossible to determine how much is necessary and how much is excessive.

It attracts criticism when it prevents fair play and becomes overkill.

In the late summer of 1938, England and Australia met at the Oval, London, to decide the cricket Test Match series. The first four matches had been drawn, and for this fifth Test the time limit had been waived; the match would go on until there was a decision.

England won the toss (an initial advantage) and went about setting up a big score. On and on they batted, far past the score at which the innings would normally have been declared closed. At last, late on the third day, they declared at the unprecedented total of 903 for 7 wickets. No such total had ever been amassed in Test cricket and, what is more, no such total had ever been necessary.

Eventually, Australia were defeated by the highest margin on record, a classic case of overkill on behalf of the English captain. Nevertheless, there is no doubt at all as to the effectiveness of his tactics. A writer in *The Times* stated that Walter Hammond (the England captain) would not even have declared at 903 unless fate had intervened and removed the only human being capable of prolonging the match, Australia's Don Bradman. Bradman had been injured and was unable to bat for his side.

This ruthless power play left a nasty taste. Because of World War II, it was ten years before the Australians were able to return and avenge their humiliation, but in 1948 revenge it they did, with Bradman himself as the chief avenger. He was just as ruthless as Hammond.

Roy Cohn is in his early fifties and has his own law firm, Saxe, Bacon and Bolan. An article in *Esquire* magazine pulled no punches in its assessment of the man Cohn. "He's the toughest, meanest, vilest, and one of the most brilliant lawyers in America." Clients range from Carmine "Lilo" Galante ("the reputed boss of bosses") to the Catholic Archdiocese of New York, from Bianca Jagger to the biggest names in New York real estate, from Warren Avis (of Avis Rent-a-Car) to Thomas and Joseph Gambino (sons of the late Carlo Gambino). His client list expands in proportion to the publicity Roy Cohn generates. "The more you say he's a ruthless bastard," says his partner, "the more it helps."

In fact, Cohn's style is an amalgam of contradictions. For every accusation of evil, there is another voice attributing to him friendship and loyalty. "To accept a client I either have to like the client or feel they are getting a rough deal. The same kind of rough deal I got [there had been unsuccessful indictments of Cohn for obstruction of justice, bribery, conspiracy, extortion, blackmail, in violating banking laws]. I have to develop an equation, a community of interest with the client." He would do anything but hurt a friend's interests. "I can think of no circumstances under which I would testify against a friend. . . . I'd do everything within the bounds of legal propriety not to hurt someone whose friendship I had accepted."

Ruthlessness, ferocious loyalty, and the desire to win even if that requires a sometimes cynical approach to the ground rules ("I don't consider myself a one-man ombudsman") overlay a technique that annihilates, intimidates, and impresses courtroom witnesses, prosecutors, and juries respectively.

"I have packaged a strategy in dealing with cases, in dealing with legal situations. Very simply, it's a bottom-line strategy. I'm not a time waster. For example, if a client in a matrimonial suit wants to start her story in 1935, I say forget it. Just shut up. I'll ask the questions. Don't tell me your life story. And after I'm through, if there's something you feel I still should know, tell me.

"After five to ten minutes asking 'Is there any chance of getting back together again?' 'What are you looking for — a divorce, a separation?' 'Is there a custody question?' 'How many children?' 'How much money do you have?' 'How much does he have?' 'What do you need?' — by then I have the story, usually, and I'm able to get to the bottom line and see where I want to go."

For Cohn there is no letup between the early stages of confrontation with his client and the coup de grace in the courtroom itself — once he tastes victory, his is a single, crushing movement that, in Musashi's words, "leaves no space for breath."

"Life is so quick for me, that I operate almost instinctually and I don't think out where I'm going to go. I'm just propelled . . . I make up my mind and do it."

In cross-examination he may provoke terror in a witness, using his ability to absorb and develop the key factors of his case extemporaneously — never using notes or reading a speech. "It's just not my style. I have found a couple of cases where I am so well prepared that I lose spontaneity. I particularly love working with juries because it's eyeball-to-eyeball communication. Not using notes or reading to a jury, I find I can have eyeball contact with every one of the jurors when I'm summing up."

Cohn thrives on crises, loves the challenge and courtroom drama. His success, he believes, is due to his "makeup" as well as his training, to the way he has been molded by his friends and other strong, people influences. Training, drive, energy, ruthless ambition are not, however, the only factors which he sees at the core of success: "You also have to have a certain amount of conceit, which leads you to believe that you and you alone can get things moving."

FAILURE STYLE

Any style of success must also include a style of failure. How does a successful person cope with failure? Failures there will be. Failure takes different people different ways. It can utterly destroy or build a personality's confidence; it can activate a spiral of depression or be a stimulus.

Golfer Tony Jacklin has, along with most other successful people, experienced troughs in his career. "I hated it, but I got shoved into a situation a lot of the time that I didn't want to be shoved into. I couldn't even go into how I felt a lot of the time. As time went on, I slowly realized the reasons why I was getting the way I was. I was pushing myself so far, so hard to win everything. I felt that after winning the U.S. and British Open in a year the public expected me to win everything else. If I had a bad day, the Press wrote about it; if I had a good day, they wrote about it. They wrote about me whatever the hell I did. If I picked my nose, they wrote about it, and I just got to the point where I was pushed and pushed and pushed — and I couldn't go any further; it began to affect my game. I got mentally very, very down. Three years ago, maybe it sounds an exaggeration, but I was damn close to having a mental . . . you know something blowing. And then I backed off and I said, 'Hey, what the hell is this all about? Golf's a game and it's a life, and to let it beat you up like this is not sensible. Start to try and look at things more rationally.' I've done that to a point, but not as well as I should have, I don't suppose." As this was written, Tony Jacklin was named captain of the European Ryder Cup team to play in America.

LEARNING FROM FAILURE

If you win an argument you end up with a feeling of glory but little else. Success is an affirmation but not a learning process. There are times when failure has a value as a teacher.

Olympic Decathlon champion Rafer Johnson develops the point farther: "The most enjoyment I had was not always winning (although I dislike losing very much). But what gave me the biggest thrill was the way I reacted when I was beaten — what I thought about when I was beaten, and how I came back from defeat. To my mind, the great champions are the ones that react to defeat in a positive way. I'd much rather climb into the head of someone who's lost, and see what made that person come back to be a victor, than to climb into the head of a winner. You can probably learn more from failures. That somebody wins all the time does not necessarily mean they are successful."

It could be argued that, rather than teaching military history by emphasizing victory, a nation would gain more from studying its defeats. By doing so, it would identify its weaknesses and, by analysis, produce a catalogue of precepts to enable it to avoid — or to counter — such weakness in the future.

Remember, however, that generals are always more inclined to fight the last battle over again (trying to avoid losing it) and economists to solve the last crisis than to prepare for the future. We can survive mistakes and we can learn from them, but learning from the past is no more than part of our adventure into the future. If we treat the past as an experiment, then we devise a better experiment for the future.

"I always went back," says Johnson; "I really took a close look at how I performed and how I approached what I did. I'd just go back to work, get more physically tough, get more mentally tough. I might try approaching it a little different way. Let's say, for instance, I ran 1500 meters in 60-second quarters, well, I might push that down to 58-second quarters, just to see how I might react physically and mentally to that. I might lay back a little more and use a sprint at the end. I would use, maybe, a little different tactics."

"When I first started on Wall Street," recalls hedge-fund manager Jim Rogers, "I went to visit a man. I was twenty-six and he was probably forty-two or forty-three. I'm not quite sure why I went to see him; I believe somebody said we should meet each other because I was a bright young man and wet behind the ears and he was a very rich, powerful guy who backed bright young men. I remember he said to me: 'You know, the best thing that can happen to you or any young person starting in this kind of business, or any kind of business, is that you go bankrupt.' And I said, 'What! Bankrupt!' That was my greatest fear. That was the worst embarrassment. How could you tell a man to go bankrupt? How could I pay the rent? How would I eat? And I said, 'I can't conceive of what you're saying; how could you possibly want somebody to go bankrupt?' And he replied, 'Not only is it best to go bankrupt, but it would really be better if you go bankrupt twice!' A year or two later I actually did lose everything I had. It really was a very, very good thing to happen to me. Years later I understood that you learn a lot about yourself, you learn a lot about making mistakes. One of the best things you learn is that you can make mistakes. When I lost everything, I did so because a few months earlier I had taken everything I had and invested it in such a way that I would gain provided that the stock market collapsed. (I shorted the market.) And lo and behold, the stock market did collapse (a fact that nobody in his right mind would have banked on). I tripled my net worth when everyone else was losing their shirts. It was 1970 and the worst bear market America had seen for thirty-two years, and there I was tripling my money and people were furious at me. I thought, this is so easy. On the very day that the stock market hit the bottom, I reversed my position (covered my shorts is what you call it), and I said, 'Now wait for the market to go up for a while and then I will sell short again.' I waited about two months (the market did in fact go up dramatically) and said to myself, 'Boy, this is really easy; now I'm going to short the market again and I'm really going to be rich.' So I shorted the market again and two months later I was wiped out. The market didn't see it the way I did and I was wrong. I was totally wiped out, I lost it all.

"First of all, I had learnt I wasn't as smart as I thought I was, and second, that the market could do strange things no matter what I thought. In stock market parlance, I didn't know the market could discount the immediate future (or see far into the future), and even though things were terrible at the time, the stock market could still go up knowing things would get much better in the future. Of course I'd read that in books, but books are a lot different from the real world!"

Werner Erhard believes that the all-important thing about failure is that you accept it: "For me what determines whether failure stops a person or not is how the failure is held — not whether people have failures or not. Success includes failure. There is only one other thing I have to say about failure that I think is valuable, and that is that I am responsible for my failures. By that I do not mean that I am to blame or that I am guilty, simply that I recognize I am the cause. When I explain failure, when I justify it, even when I feel badly about it, I've lost my responsibility for it. When I can hold my failures, it makes me bigger than the failure."

Sting follows a similar line: "I face the prospect of failure as a social being, as the reverse side of success. I don't like it. I accept it. I do foresee it, both intuitively and logically. It's obvious that eventually people will stop being interested in the way my voice sounds and stop buying my records. Which is why I'm extending the parameters of my expression and trying to become an actor." At the time of writing, Sting is starring in the film of Frank Herbert's *Dune*.

REINTERPRETING FAILURE

For two years or so William Agee, then the boss of Bendix, one of America's largest business corporations, has been divesting the company of some of its businesses in order to build up cash for a future major acquisition. Agee justified the strategy on the basis that in times of recession, expansion from within is impractical. It was, he felt, in the shareholders' interest at the time to mount a strategy of acquisition in order to seek the highest possible return on stockholder investment. In 1982, all set to make his play — he had more than half a billion dollars to spend — he launched the strategy that he and his protégée Mary Cunningham had devised. His quarry, the huge Martin Marietta Corporation, resisted the incursion — Agee had seriously underestimated that company's financial muscle. Whoever was to blame, the reconnaissance of the situation left much to be desired, and once the brawl got going, some of the biggest Wall Street heavyweights, including Harry Gray, the shrewdest dealer of all, the uncrowned master of mergers, became involved. Agee was out of his depth. Gray, chairman of United Technologies Corporation, who is reputed to keep a current list of 50 potential takeover targets in his desk at all times, teamed up with Marietta. The deal? UT would retaliate by buying Bendix stock, and so would Marietta. It was an aggressive riposte, particularly as the two agreed that whoever ended up with Bendix, UT and Marietta would divide the spoils. Whatever happened, Marietta would retain its independence, and Gray could only gain. It became known as the Pac-Man defense.

Afterward, Marietta's board claimed that their counterstrategy was designed to make Agee go home and that they gave him three opportunities to do so. But, for whatever reasons, Agee continued Bendix's purchase of Marietta's stock, with the result that the two companies were just eating each other up in an orgy of corporate madness. Finally, and too late for his own good, Agee enlisted the aid of Allied Corporation, which negotiated with Marietta for its Bendix stock. Result: Allied Corporation owns Bendix. Agee had not only failed in his takeover bid, but in the process had himself been swallowed up.

This was William Agee's assessment of his predicament at the time: "It isn't that terrible. People who are engaged in acquisitions consider it to be 'a loss' if your company's taken over by somebody else — if you don't continue to come out on top. But they fail to realize something I believe that I have felt strongly from the moment I entered the business world, and that is that my job as chief executive officer is not necessarily to preserve my role or to perpetuate all of the things that only make sense to me as an individual. That's what shareholder value is all about. Many managements confuse shareholder value with their own personal interest. You know, what makes them tick. So, they feel unless they can control it all, shareholder value isn't being enhanced. Given the alternatives that we had in the light of the way the thing played out, there was no choice. . . . It's the American way to come out on top. It's the macho way to come out on top. Well, time will only judge who came out on top; you can't judge that at the moment."

In re-tracing the tactical background of what became known as the Bendix War, one cannot help feeling sympathy for the criticism Agee levels at "the American way, the macho way to come out on top." It is an aspect of American culture which some see as a source of dynamism and others as, in coach Ron Pickering's words, "the most eroding factor in American sport, in their society. There, success is paramount; winning is the sole object, and there's no room for failure, and I think a lot of their psychological problems, their great dropout rate and a lot of their great losses of talent, are due to the fact that their society sees no role or place for the guy who comes second. This is utter nonsense. It has to be paradoxical. There's absolutely no way that you can survive on that. I think they have the greatest reservoir of talent in the world and they use it so badly that other countries can come along and beat them. We, as teachers and coaches and philosophers, must convince kids that being second out of a whole mass of participants has still got something magnificent about it. What I'm saying is that if Daley Thompson at seventeen had been told that he's got to take on the Olympic Decathlon champion on his eighteenth birthday, if he's told that the only judgment of success is whether he wins it (when he has no chance of winning it), then you will destory the athlete. Whereas, if he can get four personal bests out of ten, that surely would be something that would be a terrific step up the ladder. If he gets 7,300 points, that will be something that no other seventeen-year-old has done. He's going to convince the other twenty-three athletes [that are competing against him] that there is a kid of seventeen, and the next time they see him at the Olympic Games he's going to be fearful. That's not about winning; that's about using your placing and your nonwinning intelligently."

T A C T I C S

1. It is comforting to know that there are many styles of success. Those who have always felt that their particular style is not the traditional style of success should be encouraged by this.

2. Try to determine your own style even to the point of verbalizing it or writing it down on paper. You might even ask your colleagues how they would describe your style. Do not always believe what they say. Do not be trapped by this assessment of your style.

3. Build up the strong points of your style rather than try to alter it to a completely different style.

4. Use your style as a way of making decisions, plans, and choices. Does this fit my style?

5. Be aware of any deficiency in your style, but don't be cowed by this or use it as an excuse.

6. Choose the circumstances that best suit your style.

7. Be bold, be confident, be egocentric, but do not expect me to tell you how.

8. Use failure as the shadow that gives dimension to the picture.

9. An inflated balloon is vulnerable, but that is the only way it is going to fly.

3

What Stimulates Success?

T H E   P L A Y E R S :

United States: **William Agee · Nolan Bushnell · Malcolm Forbes · Harry Helmsley · Hermann Kahn · Jeane Kirkpatrick · Norman Lear · Mark McCormack · Jerald Newman · James B. Rogers, Jr. · Diane von Furstenberg**

United Kingdom and International: **Christian Bonington · Sir Terence Conran · Alan Fine · Robert Holmes à Court · Robert Maxwell · Lionel Murray · John Ritblat · Sir Clive Sinclair · Jackie Stewart · Sting · Virginia Wade · Mark Weinberg · Charles Williams**

What is the dream in the mind of someone who sets out to be successful? What is the vision up ahead that draws them on? Or is it a sense of duty rather than a dream?

Champion driver Jackie Stewart: "I remember dreaming that maybe one day I would be famous (like every girl dreams she might one day be a princess). . . . There is no question that it is a wonderful feeling for 10, 20, 40, 200,000 people to stand for you when you enter a racetrack. They respect you, and you get a great warm feeling — 'My God, I've done something.' That's a wonderful feeling."

Jeane Kirkpatrick, at the time of writing United States Ambassador to the United Nations: "There is only one reason, one, that I am doing this work. It's not the status perks, the prestige perks. I think it's my duty. I have a demanding conception of citizenship. I have an obligation to

46

confront serious problems, to use whatever means are at my disposal to strengthen this democracy."

Rock star Sting: "What set me on this particular trail was to make a living solely out of being a musician. Success and fame were a side effect, if you like, not a driving force, until it became apparent what was at stake. Success in the artistic field is unique. You are put under all sorts of pressures from the media — your craft becomes secondary to the side effects, fame, money. . . ."

In this section we shall look at some of the traditional concepts of motivation to see whether they are true. Is it money? Is it power? Is it fear? These are the usual motivators attributed by analysts to the successful. Since these things often follow success, it is natural to assume that that is what is being sought. A gambler may win money, so it is assumed that he gambles to win money. That does not seem to be the case. He gambles to enjoy the tingle of anticipation as he waits to see the outcome of his risk taking. Winning money is somewhat irrelevant — except that gambling would be pointless without money to be won or lost.

First, there is motivation to get going in the beginning. What makes a successful person take the very first step or head off in a certain direction? Why does the entrepreneur set up his or her own first business? Why does the real estate developer make the first deal? This may well be the most interesting aspect of motivation.

Second, there is the motivation to keep going. Many successful people have more than enough to live on and could cease what they are doing. What keeps them going? Is there a fear of letting people down or of being regarded as a failure if they drop out? Is it the increasing enjoyment of the whole game which becomes easier and easier? Is it a search for bigger and better challenges? Is it that success has become so effortless that there is no point in stopping? Is it just a lack of anything more enjoyable to do?

Third, there is the motivation to focus on one particular area that is to become the basis of the success. Why does a person choose one area rather than another? It can be chance or a chance meeting. It can be opportunity or a family tradition.

NEGATIVE STIMULANTS

"If you're saying was there a fear of failure, then the answer is, sure there was, particularly during the early days of Abbey Life." Abbey Life was Mark Weinberg's first experience in starting up an insurance company. It was a stepping stone to his enormously successful Hambro Life. "At Hambro it was mingled with an excitement of potential. The fear was something I was prepared to live with because I did the cost-benefit balance and came to the conclusion it was worth it. I was prepared to live with the fear." Weinberg still enjoys "the excitement of the start-up" and at first refused to accept fear as a prime motivator — "It can motivate me to do something, but it's not something I'm looking for. There isn't fear of being wiped out personally, financially, if you like." But later added, "There is fear of Hambro Life flattening off and going downhill, which would be financially disagreeable but not critical. Much more important, I've got something of a public reputation, I've got my colleagues in Hambro Life, hundreds of branch managers, literally thousands of salesmen to whom one has a first-name relationship of some kind and who quite wrongly personify me as a person who gets the credit if things go well and whose fault it is if everything falls out of balance. That is a very strong fear and it is a very strong motivator and it's probably the major single reason why I don't pull up stumps and say I've been in the same job for twenty years (two companies, but the same job) and let somebody else do it, and say to myself that I'd rather concentrate on farming or some other venture (which I probably would actually prefer to do)."

Anxieties

Security is one antidote to anxiety. But at other times entrepreneurs seem to simply outgrow anxiety. It is rare to find an entrepreneur who never knew anxiety at all.

Robert Holmes à Court: "My commercial security is that I own half the company. I will not be dislodged by some young pup from Australia or anybody else. So I have that security."

Earlier in the life of a successful entrepreneur there are anxieties and there are pressures. What is interesting is that with successful people the anxieties are "propellant" rather than "retardant." The anxieties push the entrepreneur forward rather than hold him back. There does not seem to be a search for the easy way or for security as such.

"I get overworked at times, but I don't get anxious now," says Sir Terence Conran. "I sleep well; I don't think it worries me much these days. It has done in the past. I remember at one stage in my early years of building up a business that my accountant said to me, 'Look, I really do think you should put your business into liquidation because you've not got enough money to pay your debts,' which actually made me determined that that was the last thing that was going to happen. I would get through somehow or other. So I suppose in the years from about twenty to thirty I had an extremely hard time. Ten years of really tough life taught me about being a businessman, taught me just how tough it is for people. But now I've got an extremely good team around me. We're now a business that's worth £240 million, something like that. So when you get to that level, all right, you can have bad years, but unless you entirely mismanage the business, you're very unlikely to plunge into bankruptcy. This is one of the points about Mothercare — in some ways it was spreading and making the business even firmer-based than before because it gave one a bigger international spread. It gave us a lot more assets, certainly property assets, than we had before. A much wider audience. A fantastic cash flow. All sorts of things that you've been taught in business school are good for your business."

Jim Rogers, entrepreneur money manager: "My main anxiety was that I'd never get the work done. I'd never get anything done. I could never know enough. I could never work hard enough. I also had anxieties imposed by outside forces such as women. Women would say, why don't you come home, or why don't we go to the movies, or something, and most people never understood. I had anxiety imposed by outside forces. But I never felt anxiety about whether we were right or not; I always went to sleep. Other people can't sleep at night. I hit the pillow asleep."

For the experienced businessman, the anxieties that may stimulate the early years can sometimes be replaced by what property developer John Ritblat describes as a "natural nervousness." "You know, the volatility of the currency market, the volatility of world affairs, the unpredictability of happenings in further parts of the world, which can impinge upon one's best judgements overnight.

"These are, I think, a little frightening.

"One may have a large position in the gilt market, a perfectly normal and sensible thing in which to be involved and tied . . . but when you think of the banking situation with the Eastern Bloc in South America, when you think what can happen literally over a single weekend and how exposed one can be — and really it's quite beyond one's control — it's no satisfaction to me to be able to say, 'Well, we'll all be in the same boat.' "

Herman Kahn takes up the point: "I almost never had anxieties until a couple of years ago. The kind of work we're doing — we're dealing with issues of war and peace and with proper national policies and so on — you worry a lot about a briefing, for example. Maybe you only get one chance to brief a senior person to make your point. If it doesn't go, it doesn't go, and that's it; you've had your chance. We worry about these briefings a lot, but the worry there is constructive. I have found in the past that every now and then I give a briefing or give a talk that does very badly. In all cases I wasn't worried about it. I was just totally confident. So now I consciously try to make myself worry about a briefing, and if I'm not worried, I worry.

"I'm also worried about the world. *The Coming Boom* says that the economic and technological picture is quite good; it isn't at all clear that the political and intellectual future is that good. The people who ran this country at the beginning were actually unique in world history. The people at the Constitution Convention were a terribly talented group of people. It would be very difficult to find their like at any point in the last, say, 1,000 years, say 2,000 years, maybe since Ancient Greece. These were impressive people. We just don't have their like today."

POSITIVE STIMULANTS

Power and Money

Everyone knows that all politicians are motivated by "power." Power means different things to different people. Underneath all the different definitions there is "the power to make something happen." In the case of famous television producer Norman Lear it seems to be the power to communicate.

Norman Lear: "Somebody asked me — Helen Gurley Brown for *Cosmopolitan* — what I thought power was, and I said something to the effect that 'power is the ability to persuade, and if one fails at persuading, that person is not thrown out with the effort.' If I succeed, terrific; that's power. If I don't succeed, power is also not having you think, what a fool; rather, I don't like his idea, but he's still OK. It seems to me there can be no greater power than the ability to persuade people, to communicate . . . and to reach."

Merchant banking provides a platform for making big money and for exercising great power over other companies. Charles Williams of Ansbacher was also chairman of the Price Commission under the last Labour Government. "Going back to my education, I am used to power. I was the captain of everything. I do get very dissatisfied if I don't fulfill my own self-image of being somebody who's captain of things. I don't sit there and say, 'Ha ha ha — exercising power,' but I think my own image of myself would suffer if I wasn't in a position to." Many people who were interviewed put "making things happen" as their prime motivation, but, as Williams points out, "You can't disassociate the two. You can't have one without the other. If you're chairman of the Price Commission you can make things happen, but you can only do so by being chairman of the Price Commission, which gives you a certain power."

And Money? "My life-style is one which requires a certain relatively finite amount of money. Beyond that I have no interest. I do not wish to be a triple millionaire. That doesn't motivate me. If somebody said to me, 'Look, I'll offer you a lousy job, but you'll get paid £3 million a year,' I'd say, 'Thank you very much, no.' That is not a motivating factor."

Power is a complex subject. Power may mean being top dog or being first. Is this simply the end point of a race in which competition is the main element — is it outperforming people rather than getting there that matters? Power may mean being important and being noticed and having oneself taken seriously. Power may mean the ability to give orders and have other people carry them through. Power may simply be a measure of achievement: a scale on which self-worth can be measured.

Do you get pleasure out of power? Robert Maxwell: "The only thing I get pleasure out of is that I have a car and a driver and I don't have to worry about car parking problems!"

Jackie Stewart: "To get picked up at the airport and to be taken shopping and to be taken to business meetings and not have to park the car: that to me is one of the rewards of my success."

Malcom Forbes: "Leadership does involve power. You're not the leader if you don't have the power — if you don't have the decision-making authority. People who like authority for itself are never successful, but exercising authority is part of what is required from somebody in a responsible position. You've got to be able to do it, but when it's an end in itself, usually you're not successful."

William Agee: "I've always wanted to be at the head of something; I mean, when I was in the first grade, it was cleaning the erasers. We had one of those funny little machines that you'd run the erasers across — that was kind of a choice job because you got out of class. I wanted that job. And I wanted to be captain of the sports team, and have the best grades. Safety Patrol was the first office; the captain of the Safety Patrol had a blue badge and a white belt that he wears. The lieutenant had the red badge and a blue belt. The top position at my grade school was to be captain of the Safety Patrol. And I did it. And when I got into junior school, seventh grade chairman — that was the top job because it was elected by the students, and so on. Then student body president — that type of thing. I'd say to myself, 'What's the best job out there, what do I see as being a leadership position?' I really wanted people to appreciate. . . ."

Power and money are often presented as the caricature ingredients of the capitalist property magnate. Harry Helmsley, who should know, has this to say: "I don't care about the power. Forget it — there's no power in a real estate man. He has money, but he doesn't have any power. And money doesn't give you power. It's helpful, it's nice, but I don't find I use money for power play. If you're semisuccessful, you make $50,000 — you add another nought, and you make $500,000, but the principles are all the same. There's nothing different about it. You can be just as smart and never make the big money, and yet be doing a better job than some fellow who's making the big money. It's just the fellow who knows how to add the big 'o' who becomes the big success. It's the deal that's fun. It's the shaking of the jigsaw puzzle and putting it together."

Robert Maxwell: "I'm an industrialist. I make things. And if as a result of making things, I make money . . . then so be it!"

Robert Holmes à Court: "Money is a measurement, it's like a scoreboard, it's a measurement of how well you're doing. It's not an end in itself, and personal money is an illusory thing. You do not need very much, really, nobody does; it's trite to say, but it's awfully true. I think that a lot of people think that they want to make some money because they want more physical things than they've got, but I don't think making money is itself success — it's a by-product of success."

An artist paints in oil on canvas. A composer works with musical notes and notations. In the same way, an entrepreneur works with money. The entrepreneur has the advantage because money is both the medium in which he works and also a very direct measure of success. Here the man whose success can be measured in money has a reward system that is superior to almost all others (except perhaps the record-breaking athlete's). Success can be measured step-by-step in a way that is impossible in science or the arts, where the opinion of others matters so much and may be unfairly given. The money man can count his money without giving a damn as to what other people may think. As a medium, money also makes success into a game, since the outcome of the different plays can be calculated. Beyond a certain point it seems very unlikely that money as such is accumulated for its spending power.

Image Improvement

I would name self-image as a prime motivator. This is a view of oneself as being significant, of being different from others, of being someone who can stand out and someone who can make things happen. I am not suggesting that a person sets out to become important (though that may happen with politicians), but a person's self-image motivates that person to start things and to take risks.

Charles Williams: "Self-image is all-important. It is for everybody, and anybody who says anything different is telling lies. If they haven't thought of it like that, either they're telling lies or they're being disingenuous or they're being psychologically unsophisticated."

Mountaineer Chris Bonington: "Yes, it's the satisfaction of having done it, a feeling of self-worth, but I think it is more than that. It is the fascinating, intriguing quality of wondering whether you *can*, whether something is possible. When you look at a new route, whether it's a lump of rock in this country or whether it's something like the southwest face of Everest, there's a fascinating intellectual question in whether this can be climbed. It's the fascination of problem-solving and you look at it, you work out the way in your own mind of how it can be done — you plan it and everything else. Then you actually go there and you try and put your plans into action. That, to me, is one of the vast satisfactions. Then, when you stand on the top, there's the physical thing of actually having got your body up there."

Most successful people are motivated by the challenge, discovering whether they are equal to it. Virginia Wade: "I suppose the satisfaction is really of knowing what you have — all the technical, physical and mental things — and then going out and pitting them against somebody else. Just seeing if you can, if you've got enough strength, enough determination, to overcome obstacles."

The value of a challenge is that it wonderfully focuses energies and thinking. For some people, this sharp focusing is something to be desired. Instead of drifting about, there is something definite to be done. There is almost a therapy in being focused in this manner. There is a destination and a target and also a measure of achievement. The complex world is reduced to the specific challenge, and as that is overcome, so is the world. Accepting the challenge thus becomes part of the self-image of an individual: "I can do it."

But Alan Fine of IGO sees an inherent problem in equating sporting or business performance with self-worth: "Can you imagine in the business you've got — if you make this business representative of your self-worth and the market goes flat and your business is in trouble? Are you telling me that overnight your self-worth is going to go all the way down? It simply isn't a representation of it. Even if you got into trouble just out of bad management, it has nothing to do with your worth as a human being. It's a representation of the ability you've developed so far to manage your business. Now that's just like learning to play squash. It's entirely separate. The pitfall is if you think it's representative of your self-worth. Let's take tennis — if you don't hit that bit of fluff over the net are you worthless? Do you go home and beat the wife?"

Status

When General Electric (U.S.A.) looked to see what motivated their research staff, they found that "recognition" came out at the top of the list. A person who has done a good piece of work wanted it recognized. Status and recognition are known to be powerful motivators because they are rewards that nourish the self-image. Some self-images are weak and need nourishing. Other self-images are inflated and need even more nourishing. Status is not the same as importance. Many Japanese executives may have a high status but no importance. Importance suggests power. Status is more of an acknowledgment. The giving of honors and medals is a practical exploitation of this powerful motivator.

Making Things Happen

If I had to choose the one motivating factor that seems to me to be op-erating in most successful people it is the wish "to make things happen." This is a direct extension of the child's wish to place one block on top of another in order to make something happen. I believe it to be exactly the same urge that drives an artist to create art. For successful people, life without making things is just time-filling.

"I realized that money wasn't the be-all and end-all. I think every-body looks for money at the beginning," says Mark McCormack. "Their initial financial requirements — their concrete requirements — are those of a family, and I think after you reach a certain level that's no longer the intriguing factor. I think trying to accomplish something that's unique and, in my case, that had never ever really been done before, was very challenging and very exciting."

Diane von Furstenberg: "It's the warmth that you get in the fruit of your work or in the fruit of your efforts. It fills you up with a warmth and you wink at yourself, you smile at yourself. You don't need to share it with anybody and it's not 'ha ha'; it's just warmth."

Jerald Newman: "The most enjoyment is in seeing a plan or a program that my staff and I conceive — seeing that it happens. The most impor-tant single thing is having an idea and putting it into practice and seeing it bear fruit."

"The main excitement is when you suddenly see a way of doing some-thing that hasn't been done before. It's the moment of solution. What is also nice is the recognition that there is a solution; one has found the solution": Sir Clive Sinclair.

"I think the most important factor in my life is boredom. I just hate boredom; I hate redundancy. I hate repetition. I think that has been a heavy motivating force. I just can't let ideas be ideas. I have to sort of push them until I've found how to make them real — how do you make things happen?": Nolan Bushnell.

"Understanding something which you haven't understood before, get-ting a really good insight, an intellectual explosion of some kind — when you see something you never saw before. Once I see it I really enjoy it, even if it is a disappointment. It's an enormous pleasure": Herman Kahn.

If "making things happen" is really the key motivation, then there is a crucial question that could be asked: "Would you be content to make things happen anonymously — so that the thing would come about but you would get no credit for it?" I suspect that most successful people would accept this distortion, albeit with a certain reluctance since ego is also part of the success profile. Perhaps we should rephrase the ques-tion: "Would you prefer to see it happen moderately well with your name attached, or very well without your name attached?"

Doing Something Worthwhile

We know how important drive is for success, but "being driven" is something different. The desire for revenge or the desire to redress an injustice can drive a man to perform and to succeed. The important question is whether that person is really driven to success or whether the choice of field is determined by the event and that the success that follows arises from the success profile of that person. I always find it difficult to believe that a person can be permanently driven to success.

"The first trade unionism I saw," recalls ex-union leader Len Murray, "was the absence of trade unionism! It was a man being evicted from a tied cottage. A one-legged man who could no longer work effectively. I knew his children. And I saw them living under a tarpaulin by a hedge. But then I didn't realize this was the absence of trade unionism; nevertheless, it was my first conscious awareness of what could happen to people. When later I learnt about trade unionism — considerably later on — it clicked into place and I realized it was the absence of a collective organization which made that sort of thing possible."

. . . And In Business

"Now I'm just motivated by doing what I'm doing as well as I can, and I was equally motivated practicing law. The difference between the two is hardly noticeable. I could play chess with you and be motivated in the same way. It's making each move count. You have to believe it's worthwhile, but you can believe a game of chess is worthwhile at that time and place. It doesn't have to be worthwhile in an idealistic sense, just that it's worth doing and worth doing well. Now every man in the company can apply that criteria to his job; it may be to do the accounts well. The test is that it's got to be done well by my own criteria; I must be satisfied. People who are just in it for money — they usually fail.": Robert Holmes à Court.

This last quote seems to sum up the more general feeling among successful people. There is an enjoyment in doing what seems worth doing. All along the tantalizing thing is that "wanting to be successful" does not seem to figure as a motivation unless it is already built into the self-image of the person. Either successful people do not like admitting that success can be an end in itself or else success is only a by-product of what they find themselves doing and doing very well. That conclusion may be somewhat depressing for readers of this book.

T A C T I C S

1. There probably is no such thing as a general-purpose motivation "to be successful," so if you have such a motivation, convert it as quickly as possible into a choice of field and a direction. There can be a motivation to succeed at something in particular.

2. Motivation seems to be a natural part of the expectation and self-image of the successful person. Be positive and cultivate such an expectation. Expect to succeed.

3. Use and set challenges in order to have a specific focus.

4. Use anxieties in order to push yourself forward rather than to hold yourself back.

5. Do not use money as an end in itself but as the method of play in the game of success (at least one type of success).

6. If you do not enjoy making things happen, you should reconsider whether you want only the end-point of success (and what goes with it) or the process of getting there. If you only want the end-point, then forget it — unless you can find a way of getting there very quickly.

7. If your own motivation is insufficient, then marry someone who can push you along.

4

Talent, Training, and Expectation: How Far Is Success within Your Control?

THE PLAYERS:

United States: **Nolan Bushnell** · **Werner Erhard** · **Harry Helmsley** · **Jeane Kirkpatrick** · **Herman Kahn** · **Norman Lear** · **David Mohoney** · **Morgan Maree**

United Kingdom and International: **David Bailey** · **Professor Hans Eysenck** · **Alan Fine** · **Tony Jacklin** · **Lord Pennock** · **Ron Pickering** · **Sting**

HOW FAR IS SUCCESS WITHIN YOUR CONTROL?

How good have you been at choosing your parents? Is it still possible for you to be successful if you have been rather careless at parent choice? Is success born or is it trained?

> Give me a dozen healthy infants, well-formed, and my own special world to bring them up in and I will guarantee to take any one at random and train him to become any type of specialist I might select — doctor, lawyer, artist, merchant-chief and, yes, even beggar man and thief, regardless of his talents, penchants, dependencies, abilities, vocations and the race of his ancestors.

This well-known quote is from John B. Watson, the founder of the behaviorist school of psychology. The behaviorist school holds that all behavior is really built up from a series of stimulus-response conditionings.

57

If we follow this school, success is clearly a trained habit. In our early environment as children (and perhaps later as well), certain aspects of our behavior are rewarded: either by our parents or the surrounding world. If a baby cries a lot and is each time rewarded by its mother, then we could interpret the training in two ways: "It is enough to demand and you will receive" (contrary to the entrepreneurial spirit) or "If you want something, take action to make it happen" (which is the entrepreneurial spirit). I suspect the first explanation is more likely: a child that is much scolded becomes conscious of the known and unknown limitations of action and dares little. In reaction to that, the famous Dr. Benjamin Spock advocated the freedom from constraint that some believe to have degenerated society. But freedom from constraint may mean lack of the discipline and drive that is necessary for success. Freedom from constraint may mean lack of the discipline and drive that is necessary for success. Burton L. White would go so far as to claim that the first three years of a child's life set the temperament, emotional, and behavior patterns that dominate thereafter. Certainly for many successful people, early environment would seem to have had a marked effect upon their future, though as in the fictional examples above, behavior patterns were not governed solely by the nature of the stimulus (e.g., a poor upbringing can be interpreted advantageously).

"My folks really gave me a lot of latitude as a kid, and gave me the opportunity to expand — we had a forty-foot antenna on the roof when I was eleven or twelve": Nolan Bushnell, founder of Atari.

"I had a wonderful Oklahoma childhood. My family imbued me with the frontier spirit. What's that? Oh, it's a can-do spirit. It's the frontier ethic that you can do anything, everything. Always what I heard was: 'Jeane, you can do this!' I was always told that doing something well was just a matter of trying hard enough": Jeane Kirkpatrick, United States Ambassador to the United Nations.

Norman Lear: "I've often thought that my father's demands on me must have had something to do with the fact that I wished to do my own thing."

NO INFLUENCE

Many successful people claim that in their particular cases parents had very little to do with the subsequent success of their offspring.

"Dad was an unskilled, untutored construction man," recalls David Mahoney. "My mother was unskilled, untutored, and worked for the phone company. . . . I was the first kid in the family (in the whole organization!) that went to college. I did it on my own."

Whereas Herman Kahn, Werner Erhard, and billionaire Harry Helmsley found poor backgrounds positively stimulating.

Herman Kahn: "It forced me into what I think is a practical mode. I worked all my life from the age of ten — shoe-shine boy, selling things, and so on. . . . In general, upper-middle-class children are raised in a kind of protected way; they're raised in a way which doesn't put them in much contact with reality."

"My mother and father and the way they raised me were worthless to me," reflects Werner Erhard. "So what happened is that I shifted the context in which I help my parents and my childhood so that what was a source of problems became a source of power in my life."

"What gave me my drive?" laughs Harry Helmsley. "When you don't have any money you've got plenty of drive!"

BORN TO SUCCEED

The genetic view starts out at what seems to be the opposite pole to the behaviorist view. It holds that our behavior patterns are just as much inherited as the color of eyes or the shape of our nose. In the end, these inherited behavior patterns will determine our behavior.

In the matter of performance on IQ tests, for example, studies claim to show how much of the performance is due to genetic factors and how much to other factors. The conclusion put forward is that most is due to genetic factors.

It is not difficult to imagine that the chemical profile of the brain is determined genetically. We are now coming to believe that chemical effects among the nerve endings, determined by the relative strengths of different enzymes, are even more important than the neural wiring of the brain: so a child may inherit a chemical profile which, for example, allows patterns of neural activity to change more frequently. Such a profile would give a better scan and consequently a better performance in an IQ test, while in another case the chemical profile in the hypothalamus may lead to anxiety and neuroticism.

It is not difficult to suppose that factors such as these alter attitude and behavior, and in turn the chances of success.

But are they the whole story? I used to correct papers for part of the Cambridge University medicine finals. A small percentage of the students were brilliant. A small percentage were so bad that you wondered how they had got that far. The rest formed a large middle group, among which it was very difficult to distinguish.

At the extremes of genetic endowment there are the exceptionally gifted and the exceptionally deprived. In the middle is the usual mass. The question is whether success among the mass is still a question of genetics or of what can be added to that genetic base by environment or conscious effort.

Approaching the subject of success in this way leads us to think in terms of key factors. All else might be pretty ordinary, but one key factor is different. For example, the key factor may be the ability to work extremely hard or the determination to find and develop opportunities.

There would seem to be certain activities which demand a high degree of innate talent and others which depend more on the development of such abilities. This is the case within athletics, observes coach Ron Pickering:

"Seventy-five percent of athletes will have come up because they are talented to a very high degree . . . if you can't produce results with a Lynn Davies or a Mary Rand, you're not much of a coach, because they have exceptional talent. Why I leave out Sebastian Coe and Steve Ovett is that, with the greatest respect, athleticism is not so well reflected in middle-distance running as it is in other events. What is reflected in middle-distance running (which is our Number One event and the pride of Great Britain) is a cardiovascular efficiency, which is much more trained than natural. You can make a World Class 10,000-meter runner like David Bedford out of a totally untalented athlete."

Sting, who elsewhere talks of "tapering his creativity to a particular model," recognizes that his success as athlete and singer have a similar base: "Running was a gift. Because of the shape of the muscles in my legs and body generally, I was able to run fast. [He was the county 100- and 200-meters champion.] Whereas a distance runner, well, you have to work on the tactics, you have to work on stamina, things like that. You're not born a distance runner. I could draw a parallel with my singing. My voice is not something that I have ever developed or had trained. Yet some people would regard me as one of the best exponents of a particular style in the country."

EXPECT TO BE A SUCCESS

Success in business would seem to depend much less on native talent and a lot more on thinking and personality factors. Certainly success in business often seems to arise simply from a desire to make things happen. Have you noticed how there are times when a successful person seems to have a set of concepts that are different? In a way they are expectations that affect the behavior of that person. Most people are content to receive a weekly wage and to fit into a slot provided by an organization. It is not so much that they like the security of such a slot but that they do not really have any ambition to set out on their own.

Nolan Bushnell, born to Mormon parents in Utah, describes how his "expectations" were swiftly formed shortly after his father, a cement contractor, died: "He died in August and at fifteen years old I ran the construction crew, finishing off the construction projects that he had. It forced a growing up, but at the same time I got to see some aspects of the business and how it worked and how to price out all the unit labor, and how much all the materials cost, and I saw what he was selling it for, and I thought, 'This is a good deal. You don't have to work for somebody else to make a lot of money. You just organize it and hire the people and do it.' "

At this point we seem to have three choices. Ambition (drive, etc.) could be a genetic factor. It could also be the result of the training brought about by an early environment. Finally it could be a "concept." We have a concept of "a chair" because we have experienced a chair often enough. "The ability to make things happen" might become a concept and an expectation in the same way. Thereafter, making things happen would seem as natural to those minds that had acquired the concept as it would be to sit on a chair.

It is said that in poor countries much of the poverty is psychological: the expectation that nothing can be done. Self-help schemes (with relatively little money) have shown that if this expectation can be changed, then a great deal is done.

This is one of the reasons behind my Venezuelan project in which I have been working with the government to teach thinking to every child in school. The object is to change the self-image of that child to that of a person who can think things out and put them into action. Children are very quick to pick up the "rules of the game."

Such expectations are fostered by cultures, both local and national. How companies can do this is examined in Part Three, Chapter Ten. In another environment altogether, Ron Pickering describes how expectations are set by what he describes as "the overwhelming power of the peer group. It is such an overwhelming force. We've got 85 percent black kids in our club (Haringay Athletic), and we've remained free and clear of any racial tension or aggression — but if suddenly one peer group were to say, 'Hey, lads, tonight we're going to Brixton and we're going to burn,' — that group could determine what those kids do. You can have a kid come in whom they all idolize (because he plays the guitar well, say), and he might say, 'Shit, man, forget all this, let's go and smoke some grass. . . .' "

National cultural attitudes toward success are the local attitudes writ large. There is, for example, a marked contrast between the cultural attitude toward success in the United Kingdom and the United States. In the United States there is admiration and a remarkable lack of envy. Successful people are treasured almost as national monuments. They are the aristocracy of society, certainly the media aristocracy.

In the United Kingdom the historical class structure has produced an opposite effect. A class is a club which survives if its members derive their place in society not from personal effort but from membership of the club. If you stand out — as a tall poppy — you destroy the uniformity of the club. Excellence is permitted in certain spheres such as athletics and entertainment, but not in serious matters. The phrase "too clever by half" could never have originated in the U.S. In the U.K., the only acceptable cloak for intellectual success, for example, is eccentricity. The success of wealth is vulgar and in bad taste. In the U.S., people respond to success with a wish to emulate it. In the U.K., admiration is replaced by envy, which then attributes success to some sort of unacceptable behavior (the boy does well at exams because he is "a bookworm" and studies too hard).

The purpose of this book is to provide an environment in which successful people share some of their experience. The concept of success is attainable through contact with success cultures; remember that the word "culture" is quite different from "training" because cultures encourage you to absorb concepts and set expectations, whereas training merely sets reaction patterns.

CAN YOU COPY A STYLE AND BECOME A SUCCESS?

"I have spent five years polishing and honing an image. I am image-conscious," admits Sting. "First of all, looking the right way was terribly important. Then saying the right things, giving coherent answers to intelligent questions, though it did strike me as odd that one of the first serious interviews I did involved my opinion on nuclear fusion."

I am going to make a controversial statement that many readers will instinctively object to:
"If you role-play being a thinker then you will become a thinker."

This statement is not really controversial because those who object to it will base their objections on semantics and emotions and prejudices about the nature of thinking. For my part, the statement is based on thousands of hours of the direct teaching of thinking as a skill to both adults and youngsters, across a wide range of countries, cultures, ages, and abilities. I run what is probably the most widely used program in the world for the direct teaching of thinking as a subject in schools.

"Thinking" is taught as a specific subject just like geography or history or mathematics. The very first lesson is called the P.M.I. This is a simple scanning structure which the student uses quite formally and quite deliberately. He or she looks first at the Plus points in the situation, then at the Minus points, and finally at the Interesting points. After this structure scan, the person makes a decision which may be emotional. The formula can be carried out quite consciously and deliberately. Although the tool is simple, there are many complex reasons behind its design. Some of these arise from consideration of the mind as a self-organizing information system (as described in *The Mechanism of Mind*, which was published in 1969 and is one of the first examples of the concept of "self-organization"). Many highly intelligent people are caught in the "intelligence trap." They take a position on a subject and then use their thinking skill solely to support that position.

The more able they are to support the position, the less do they see any need actually to explore the subject: so they become trapped into one point of view. The P.M.I. formula forces a scan. Once perception has been broadened in this way, then the thinker cannot unthink what is now in front of him. We have adults and children using the P.M.I. to affect major decisions in their own lives. We have children sitting their parents down around the kitchen table to put the parents through this and similar thinking tools.

Now, the P.M.I. is a very simple tool, and it is easy to use. When using it, the student *plays the role* of a thinker, he *plays the game* of thinking as written in the rules that are put before him. Carrying out this role (even if the student does not believe in it at all) will produce a broader view of the world. In turn, that broader view will affect the student's behavior.

The relationship of this example to success is important. What can we copy from others?

LEARNING BY COPYING

Imitation and copying are powerful learning methods. We sometimes tend to feel that people have to work out everything for themselves. Copying can be very effective, as suggested by Tony Jacklin. Tony Jacklin: "When I was a youngster, how I learnt more than anything else was by copying — it is the greatest facility any young individual has. It's a facility that we do have all our life, but when we're younger we tend to use it more; when we get older we tend to get more analytical. We push that copying device to the back of our minds. But I think it is probably the single thing that we do that helps our progress most — especially in golf. You see a good player and it rubs off. But that's not enough for a lot of people. They go off, get to seventeen or eighteen years of age and want to know for themselves why. They delve into the mind, and really sometimes certain things are best left alone. That you do A and B is enough, but unfortunately it's not for most people, especially if they've got an analytical mind."

Youngsters may be influenced by a teacher, parent, or mentor, and may, consciously or unconsciously, copy their style. But it is all too easy to confuse "learning from others" with "copying others." When Bjorn Borg was at his peak, it seems that many young Swedish tennis players copied his style in the hope that their game would be as successful as Borg's. They failed because they were trying to copy someone else's style instead of developing their own. For example, Borg's top-spin strokes require a tremendous sense of timing, whereas flat strokes are less critical. If a player lacks this fine timing, then copying Borg is bound to fail. With copying we try to *become* that other person, yet style is built on a person's own special qualities and cannot be transferred without transferring those qualities as well.

"Even if I try to copy somebody else," says David Bailey, "and sometimes I do copy dead photographers (their atmosphere), it doesn't work. I did Bellocq once. He photographed prostitutes in New Orleans at the turn of the century, and I did some fashion pictures where I tried to make the girls look like his. But the pictures came out looking nothing like Bellocq; they remained my pictures. Sometimes I try very hard to change the look of my girls, but I can't. No matter what I do to their makeup, the pictures come out like Bailey's (or like somebody doing a Bailey picture). I hate that. All my life I've tried not to have a style because I never wanted to get trapped into one style. I try to vary my photographs as much as possible, but in the end the girls all begin to look like mine."

But, of course, we can learn from others. We can learn lessons; we can gain new perspectives; we can learn what works for them and what does and does not work for us; we can learn what to focus upon; we can learn broad strategies that do not rely for their efficiency upon our teacher's personal style (like playing on another person's weaknesses in a negotiating position). The purpose of this book is to provide an environment for such learning.

ROLE-PLAYING TO SUCCESS

Unlike copying, with role-playing we *temporarily act out* being the other person. It is exactly the same as an actor on stage acting Hamlet or Charlie's Aunt.

"Let's say you were playing McEnroe and you were the kind of player who always gives in if there is an argument," supposes Alan Fine. "In order to withstand McEnroe himself, you could, for instance, begin acting like his double. If, as a businessman, you perceive yourself as the quiet one (someone else is always the first to speak; you're never the dynamic Mr. Go-Get), then whenever there is an opportunity for you to be dynamic, you'll say, 'No, that's not my way.' But, if you role-play and act 'as if,' then you might say: 'O.K., I know I'm not like this, but for once I'll go out and act like it,' you could do that and find you get results that normally accrue to somebody who acts dynamically.

"I've actually used the McEnroe tactic and it's paid off, in that I get far fewer people messing me around — I go into my McEnroe act and get a bit berserk. But I might find myself disqualified because of the bad behavior, and I would certainly find myself disliked, so that might be detrimental to me.

"The point is that you *can* mold your approach to a different type of player. You can do it tactically by going to the net. Borg tried this against McEnroe; he tried to get to the net more often. But you have to get so much into it that you almost believe you are that way for a while.

"It's a game of 'let's pretend.' Some people are very good at it and others aren't. Initially, on our beginners' course, we do show them a couple of tricks just to illustrate this kind of thing. It gives us a chance to see how they can use their imagination. Some people can get right into it and others find it difficult.

"The trouble is that we don't really put ourselves into the part. And if you don't put yourself into the part, it doesn't work.

"You probably know that if you watch sport on television and you go out and play immediately afterwards, for five minutes or so your play is great and then it peters out. Images, if they're used in the right way, are fairly powerful tools. We probably learn movements by images, and by feel, and we shouldn't neglect the importance of images."

WHAT CAN WE LEARN FROM IMAGES?

David Bailey: "I remember the first time I was aware of women. It was when my mother tried on a new-look coat; was it 1948 or '49? I was very young. It was in C&A's [a store in London's West End]. And I still hold this vision of my mother swinging around against the light. That vision has stuck with me always. She looked so wonderful, so glamorous. In a way I have tried ever since to recapture that in my girls. I've never told anyone that before."

Here we see one specific image influencing performance, not in the subtle, complex fashion we expect of past experience, but in a direct and powerful way. The image has become a reference point. In the artistic world, style set by an image can determine the difference between success and failure. All the ambition and talent in the world may not produce the sort of noticeable style which is required for artistic success today. Modigliani's style was said to have been set by his love for primitive African art, which was being "rediscovered" about that time. Brute ambition may provide a driving force, but content and concept may depend on particular experience.

ROLE-LIVING AND SUCCESS

There is yet another copying tactic: Japanese culture does not have the Western concept of the ego (reinforced by religious concepts of reward and punishment). Instead there are distinct compartments within each of which a different persona develops. From 9 A.M. to 5 P.M. there is the Western-style businessman with appropriate clothes, jokes, and manners. From 5 P.M. to 9 P.M. there will be the Japanese-style businessman, who is likely to get drunk and giggle and have a fun time. From 9 P.M. to 8 A.M. there will be the traditional Japanese family man, who goes home and is obedient to his wife. These are all distinct and different roles. But the Japanese is not conscious of playing these roles as an actor plays a role.

So we can have copying, role-playing, and role-living, Japanese-style. Confusion as to exactly what is going on can lead to disaster, as Morgan Maree discovered: "I was 'the business manager,' 'the steadying influence,' 'the confidant,' 'the keeper of secrets,' 'the fellow who knew you couldn't afford the last limousine you hired.' Then I became president, suffered the midlife crisis, and said to myself, 'Well, the next level is the client himself.' So I ended up getting divorced — interestingly I actually married a client! Then I found out that the two lives are quite different. One's an artistic life and the other's a business life.

"The problem with many, many artist, business, or personal managers is that they seek the level of their clients, and instead of being the steadying business influence, they become the flighty producer. . . . He gets his wings singed who tries to metamorphose from a caterpillar into a butterfly."

NATURAL VS. ARTIFICIAL STYLE: SPOT THE PHONY

"The one thing that will guarantee you don't win is that people think you're phony," says Lord Pennock. "I'm a little bit worried about your words 'adopting tactics.' It's an instinctive thing that you absorb. If I were to sit down and say, 'Right, now, so-and-so is this sort of chap, so what I'm going to have to do is this' — and get really conscious of it — he will begin to see that, and I will have failed."

On the one hand there are tactics that are phony, artificial, overanalyzed, and too self-conscious. On the other hand, there are images, role-playing, whole-picture imitation. There is a certain emotion that encourages us to believe that things which are true and natural to us must be better than things which are cultured. There are even countries where the amateur is preferred to the professional (like the U.K.). Natural food is better than artificial food — and so on. Yet we admire art and architecture that is based on care and culture and effort.

There are many natural-born salesmen. There is also a great body of expertise in selling techniques. There is no doubt that deliberate training can improve the effectiveness of a salesman. Is the trained salesman a "phony"? The answer is that he is a phony if you can spot him as a phony. If you can see him going mechanically through his routine, then he is a phony and will probably not be effective. A bad actor is a bad actor. If, however, you cannot spot him going through his routine (because it has become part of him or is acted so very well), then he is not a phony and he will be successful. That may seem a cynical view, but it is the basis of all training and most culture. An absorbed culture is no longer an artificial culture — but until it is absorbed it is artificial.

Sometimes natural style lacks just one or two ingredients that can be picked up from someone else. Then it is not a question of role-living but adopting a "gloss" or superficial image which can be practiced.

There is nothing at all wrong with the concept of education as a means of bringing out what is there. That has been the classic aim of education. But is there really anything there?

More often there is a role model into which the person grows. The English public-schools system was designed to grow boys into the role model required for running a large empire; industrial activity was no part of that image. I think there may be "true personalities" (determined by chemical profiles in the brain), but that role models are provided by society or family.

After Freud, Western society has moved very strongly in the direction of "true self," "hidden depths," and "inner man." The prevalent notion is that underneath the false exterior resides a better person. Societies in the past, and in the East, have sometimes taken the opposite route: man is crass and primitive, and the true self is a very poor thing. Civilization consists in growing Man into civilized role models and getting him to use the manner of social interaction in a natural way. There are two sorts of "natural." The first sort is the absence of artifice. The second sort is when artifice has become so completely absorbed that it becomes natural. Impressionist paintings were highly artificial at first, until we came to see them as more natural than representational paintings (Ingres, David, etc.).

Sometimes what is lacking in an individual who desires success is just one or two ingredients which can be adopted from the style of someone else. Why should a scientist be a good communicator? The answer may be that his success depends upon it.

"You tend to adopt a certain posture and behave in certain ways. And if these are successful, they get stamped upon you," says Professor Eysenck. "You probably exaggerate them.

"Very early on, I found it was important for a scientist to be successful in lecturing and reporting his work at conferences and so on. So I began to look at what really makes the scientist successful in this sense. Most are very bad at it. They write something and then they read it in an inaudible tone of voice. They show lousy slides, which nobody understands and which are invisible anyway; and they make all sorts of mistakes which could so easily be avoided. In order to be successful you have to do a little bit extra — the little bit extra is a kind of show bizz.

"For instance, I had to address a very large audience of businessmen to explain to them what personality was — a very technical subject, in a sense. We talked about 'factor analysis' and so on, but the problem was, how could I get them interested and really staying awake? So I borrowed from my daughter (who was, I think, only five at the time) a little paper parasol and took it along. And as my time came along, I put it on the desk in front of me so that everybody could see it. It created a stir of excitement to begin with. So I left it fairly late in the lecture and then, when I was talking about factors — 'factor analysis' — I said: 'Now, factor analysis is really like this parasol. . . .'" And then I took it and opened it. 'And the ribs are the factors, the middle is . . .' and so on. You can do a lot in that way — quite consciously, introducing show bizz into it."

T A C T I C S

1. Trying to be someone else won't work, and it will ruin your own natural style, which is based on your own qualities.

2. Important lessons and strategies can be learned from the behavior of others and then be incorporated into your own style.

3. Acting out a deliberate role in certain circumstances and for a limited time can be a useful strategy. It can be especially useful to overcome some basic deficiencies.

4. There is nothing wrong with artificial training provided it is pursued to the point where it becomes natural.

5. Some aspects of man are improved by digging deeper into the inner self (emotions and temperament), but other aspects are improved by moving in the opposite direction toward role models and manners.

6. Before a role has been learned well, there is always a difficult time when it works so badly that it is usually abandoned. The problem is to decide whether to persist with it or to abandon it.

5

How Far Is Success
Due to Luck?

THE PLAYERS:

United States: **Werner Erhard** · **Dr. Nathan Kline** · **Norman Lear** · **David Mahoney** · **Morgan Maree**

United Kingdom and International: **David Bailey** · **Mickey Duff** · **Margery Hurst** · **Robert Maxwell** · **Jackie Stewart**

"Why in a family does it work for one and not for another?" asks David Mahoney. "You can get into all kinds of discussions of genes, of backgrounds, drive, intensity, intelligence, IQ — 'He was toilet trained correctly. . . . He was this.' You know, I wonder if we're trying to measure things that are immeasurable. I don't know, but I think there's timing factors in it. I think there's luck and good-fortune factors in it. I mean, when someone says, 'What is it?' I just wonder. . . . There were four profootball games this weekend, if you played the four of them tomorrow they might all come out differently. Now, what *is* the difference?"

Luck can affect things directly or it may act indirectly — for example, through its effect on confidence. Success in snooker may depend on the way you react to what in effect may be a random placing or positioning of the balls by your opponent. This is what faced Dennis Taylor during the 1983 World Snooker Championship. Taylor had a 4-3 overnight lead against Steve Davis, but then watched as Davis potted the yellow with a miscue and took the frame on the black. Taylor became somewhat awed by Davis's luck. Some time later, after Taylor had been kept waiting by the hotel elevator for what seemed to be ages, he watched dumbfounded as Davis walked up, pressed the button, and stepped into the elevator, all in one continuous motion. "See what I mean?" smiled Taylor. "If it had been just me standing there, I'd still be waiting."

Margery Hurst, chairman of Brook Street Bureau: "Everyone gets chances, but it is only if you use them that they are any good to you. A successful person makes good use of fortune. Let me give you an example. One day my father came to me and told me that he knew this man, Ivor Field, who had a little office in Brook Street in Mayfair. The rent was tiny, and it was this chance which took me to London, where I started what became the Brook Street Bureau. But if that chance hadn't come along, then some other bit of luck would have done. You make your own fate. You make your own decisions. The secret of success is to capitalize on your chances."

Dr. Nathan Kline, pioneer psychiatrist: "Luck may be something that we create ourselves; it may not be due to the exterior universe, but I think there are people who have serendipity. Now it may be that they simply pay more attention.!"

Once, after Gary Player had conjured some miraculous shot from under the face of a bunker to within an inch or two of the hole, a spectator said to him, "Gosh, that was lucky." Answered Player, "Yes, and I'll tell you this: the more I practice the luckier I get."

IS THERE SUCH A THING AS LUCK?

The role of pure chance is as rare in business as — by definition — it is anywhere else. Occasionally a spectacular good-luck story comes along. Colin Forseyth noticed a company called Hampton Gold Mining Areas in a reference book. It owned land in Australia and the shares were less than a penny each. He bought enough to get himself on the board and abortively tried to develop the land. Then the giant Western Mining found nickel nearby. Hampton shares soared to £6 at one time. It was as good as a lottery win — and just as likely, even in the minerals game, where such tales turn up more frequently than in other industries.

More common is the sort of chance which led Selim Zilkha to set up a bank branch in the Paris building where Jimmy Goldsmith's father had an office. The two, Zilkha and Goldsmith, Jr., met and eventually created the chain of British shops which became known as Mothercare. It was the stroke which made Zilkha a millionaire many times over. For Goldsmith, it was a bright idea which he could not see through to its conclusion because he did not have the money to keep a stake in the fast-expanding business on a par with his partner. As that was intolerable to Goldsmith, he sold out and looked elsewhere. What was great luck for one was for the other just another business deal which did not quite work out.

Werner Erhard: "Human beings are going to get stuck in the rat-race they're in if they don't get over this notion of luck. I'm not saying that there is no such thing as luck. I'm saying that one of the ways to interpret the way life works is luck. (Another is through alchemy!) But if you're trying to find out something about success by examining how lucky people are, when you're all done and have gathered this information, you're not going to know anything worth a damn. If you look at a person through the matrix of luck, you may get an answer (you're going to say, 'Oh, yes, they were lucky,' or 'No, they weren't lucky at all') but the answer is nonsense, because the question is nonsense."

TIMING IT RIGHT

Good Luck or Good Judgment?

By definition all successful people have been in the right place at the right time. Whatever they have done has worked out. That means that the timing and place must have been right. This is a useless argument, but nevertheless true. As in the Biblical story, the conditions for the germination of a seed have to be just right.

Norman Lear: "No, I feel very blessed, very lucky. Time and place and circumstance, beyond one's control, is all good or bad luck. I mean, I was born at a time when the communication industry was reborn with television, and coincidentally and interestingly now, it's with cable and the new technology; it's in its second or third birth. It was radio, TV, and now this . . . satellite communications. So I was present at two of those births."

Jackie Stewart: "I believe that you have to have good luck to be in the right place at the right time. Timing is everything in life. I came along at a time when things were ready for me. My brother came along before his time as a racing driver and has never enjoyed life because of that. The Beatles came at the right time for the world, but they did it properly. Nobody came along and has made a giant success because of luck. They've come at the right time. But they have created it. The Beatles created music in the modern idiom, and they are still here today."

David Bailey, photographer: "I guess I was in the right place at the right time; I think everybody who's successful (whatever success is) has to be at the right place at the right moment. Had I been born thirty years earlier, I might have been something else. But I think that applies to many others. I always say, if Jesus Christ was alive today, he'd be in trouble because they've done away with capital punishment!"

71

Looking for Opportunity in Time and Place

Morgan Maree: "Being in the right place at the right time is part of what we mean by drive. The drive must be to examine every place at every time to determine which is the right place and whether it is the right time."

Sir Alec Issigonis's brilliantly original design — the mini — has become an institution in England, as British as roast beef and Yorkshire pudding. It has sold more cars than any other British design. Its key was and is "economy," and it was the rationing of gasoline following the '56–'57 Suez Crisis that gave it so successful a birth. Its long life has been sustained by several other oil crises since. The car also arrived at a point when traffic congestion heralded a need for a model that was easy to maneuver in traffic, and park. Issigonis's master stroke, so well publicized at the time, had been to turn the engine sideways, fitting the gearbox underneath and using front-wheel drive to make a transmission tunnel redundant. It was the perfect answer to what was required at the time.

Robert Maxwell: "Timing is very important, and not just to a man like me. It's important to everybody, even to the ordinary housewife. What time you put the meal in the oven to coincide with your family's arrival to have supper or lunch, whichever it is you're serving. That's vital to her. And the same applies whether you deal at the micro or macro level of things. And to go back to your point about monopoly, when you were referring to my offer to acquire Waddingtons. That is not a sudden thing. Two years ago I had approached the chairman of Waddingtons with the suggestion that he would be better to join up with the British Printing Corporation. He said: 'No.' He preferred to remain independent. And we said: 'Right!' But then somebody came in and made an offer for them recently, and it looked as though they were going to walk off with the company . . . and Waddingtons' customers said to me: 'That is something we can't let happen. We don't want to fall into people's hands who haven't had experience of printing and packaging.' . . . We then mounted an offer for the company because it was part of 'our plan.'"

In business then, timing is not always luck. It's an important ingredient, even a vital consideration, in setting off on a trail of expansion. Boxing promoter Mickey Duff explains how it affected his business. "John Stracey, who became the Welterweight Champion of the world, was the number one challenger for just over two years. And all the newspapermen were screaming: 'Why doesn't he get his chance; he's the number one contender!' But neither Terry Lawless (his manager) nor myself (his promoter) wanted that chance until I went to Mexico to make the John Conteh World Title fight. All the heads of the World Boxing Council were there. Boxing was Jo Napoles, the World Welterweight Champion, defending his title against Mumiz Emundo. It was a return match, and they'd had a tough fight before, which Napoles had won on a controversial decision. Now they were fighting again and this time Napoles won much more easily . . . but at a price. I saw him in the dressing room. He had two bad cuts. And I saw him under the shower and he suddenly looked like an old man. I went straight out to a coin box in the stadium and called Terry Lawless in London. I said: 'Terry, this is the time. We must not, we must not, miss it.' And we went to Mexico. Nobody gave us a chance. We tried very hard to make the fight in England, but we were just outgunned with influence and everything else. In Mexico we managed to get fairly neutral officials — as well as could be expected under the circumstances. We won."

Doing something you want to do and finding that the timing happens to be exactly right is one source of luck and one source of success.

Sensing that the time is right and doing something that is required exactly at that moment in time is another source of success. As with so many of the aspects that have been considered in this section, the important question is whether an individual can do much about it. Can the individual choose parents, early environment, important images, chance events, lucky timing, and a "success" culture? In the end, there are probably three paths to success. The first depends on factors outside the control of the individual (genes, background, luck, great talent). The second path is a mixture of factors outside an individual's control and maximizing them through conscious effort (talent/training, opportunity/hard work). The third path depends almost entirely on personal effort (awareness, strategy, building an opportunity, tactics). We can, of course, never prove that this third path exists, because we can always say that anyone who sets out on this third path must already have been imbued with the ambition and desire for success by his or her genes and early environment. We can, however, turn this argument around again. In the end the only practical thing that matters is whether you feel you can do it. If free will is only the illusion of free will, the illusion is so good that it doesn't matter.

T A C T I C S

1. Whether it is true or not, assume that you have been equipped by genes and early environment for a particular style of success. That belief may make up for some of the actual deficiencies in either area.

2. Note that a key factor such as ambition, persistence, or stamina can energize all the other faculties you may have. See if there is within your makeup a "drive" of this sort. Build it up and build on it.

3. Probably the most important factor is "expectation." This can be within your environment or within your mind as your "self-image." The notion is that success should be just as much part of your expectation of life as getting married and having children. If you are a parent, such expectation is the most important thing you can provide for your children. The expectation is that an individual can work toward success — not that success will be provided as of right.

4. Move to an environment which is success-oriented.

5. Keep and polish certain key images on which to build your style.

6. Don't wait for the right place and timing to happen to you, but be sensitive to place and timing, and plant the right seed at the right time in the right spot.

PREPARATION FOR SUCCESS

6

Focus

WHAT TO DO: SELF-KNOWLEDGE

This book is about success, and in this context it does seem important that a person should have a degree of self-knowledge as to where he or she wants to go. This aspect of self-knowledge is related to the person as a success machine (nothing wrong with that).

But self-knowledge, self-awareness, self-consciousness, and self-analysis are not all the same thing. My reservations about their significance arise because we so often treat them as if they were the same.

We take it for granted that knowledge is a good thing. So the more knowledge we have the better it must be. Surely that must apply to ourselves. So many philosophers and gurus have said, "Know thyself first," that it must make sense to become eager to do just this.

I am not so sure.

Analysis is the best tool of knowledge, so self-knowledge must involve self-analysis. To find out how something works you need to take it apart. That is a strong tradition in both psychology and self-help. Why do we behave as we do? What makes us tick?

At dinner parties some guests are reluctant to sit next to a psychologist because they feel that the psychologist will analyze them. There are others who delight in being analyzed and urge further details.

The problem is that our traditions of analysis were set long before we knew very much about system behavior. Nevertheless, there have always been people who have sensed when something is analyzed into its parts, much of the original is lost. There are qualities and attributes which only exist when all the parts are together as a system. If you analyze a person and find that he is shy, then it must seem worthwhile to overcome this shyness. Yet it may be that from that very shyness and withdrawal come the sort of bold innovations that we have already noted with Paul MacCready and Clive Sinclair. Shyness plus an imaginative mind may lead to innovation. It is fairly obvious that in most cases the whole is greater than the parts. So when we analyze something into its parts, we may gain some knowledge but also risk losing a great deal.

In my thinking program I have tried to overcome this problem of the whole and the parts by proposing two types of analysis. The first type is analysis into those aspects which arise only when the whole has come together. I was on the island of Malta recently, setting up a pilot program for the teaching of thinking in schools; all the lessons had to be translated into the Maltese language. This particular lesson was translated as *gebel u bini* (stones and buildings). The concept is that there are building stones which come together to give the building. But once the building exists, then there are other aspects such as shelter, comfort, convenience, living space, which form the second part of the analysis. In technical terms, we could say that the first type of analysis is that of system components and the second type is that of system characteristics.

It always concerns me that when we talk about self-analysis we nearly always mean system components, not system characteristics.

The self-conscious centipede that lay "distracted in the ditch" because it did not know which leg followed which was suffering from a surfeit of analysis. I feel that the blanket application of self-analysis can have the same effect.

The other problem of self-analysis is that it suffers from the pseudo science pose that psychology has used to entrap itself. Science searches for analytic truths. Psychology seeks to trap as analytic truths what are really no more than plausible stories. There can be a dangerous dogmatism in explanation: "This is your problem; this is what is wrong."

If we treat such explanations as useful myths (they may or may not be true), that is one thing and as valuable as the ancient myths. If we treat

78

such explanations as having the same truth value as the relationship between current and voltage in an electric circuit, then there are dangers.
The best we can really say is that "this is one way of looking at things,
and this is another way of looking at things." This perceptual enrichment
does have a value, but it is not the value of dogmatic explanation.

Self-awareness and Self-correction

Do people know what they are about? Is self-consciousness important
for success? Should it all flow naturally or should there be a consciousness of what is going on? Alan Fine, the Inner Game Organisation, has
his own views: "At high levels what we're trying to do is to get people
closer to their goals, whatever those goals are. So our approach is to look
at what obstacles they have internally, and help them to remove those.
It is not our assessment of the obstacles; it's that person's assessment.
For instance, if you were a champion squash player and you'd been having some difficulty, you feel you could get to number one in the world
but you're not, the first step is for you to find out what the blocks are.
Even if I can see what they are, I could tell you until I'm blue in the
face, and it's not going to make any difference, because you're not aware
of what those things are yourself. The very first step must be for you to
discover what they are. Then we can look at ways around them. We try
to make people more aware of what they're doing. In order to refine
their awareness, we get them to start looking in a specific area. If you
ask somebody a question, they look closer in order to get the answer.
So that is one way. If somebody is having problems, say with anxiety
before each match, I may ask them, over a period of weeks, to start a
little score sheet of how anxious they are — 1–10 for each match. Then
we get a graph and we begin to get some idea of what is happening. Up
until then all they know is they get into a tizzy. It's useful to know how
much in a tizz you are, so that then you know how much correction
you need.

   "At the very first meeting I sit down and ask a person, 'What do you
want?' 'I want to get to number one in the world,' whatever it is; 'The
top of my club,' 'OK, so what do you think is preventing you from being
first in the world?' So they say, 'I think it's this and this.' Then if something doesn't fit or I feel like I haven't got to the bottom line on any of
these categories, I'll dig a little bit. So that is my starting point. It's much
more organic an approach than systematic. The important thing is that
they devise most of the program. My role is a facility. Any difficulties
that they've got, the solution is already there. I may know about it, they
may not know about it, but it *is* in existence. And my job is to shine a

light on it so that they can see what it is. If I know it already, then it is in existence. There is a solution. Sometimes I don't know what the solutions are (particularly if I work outside tennis). My job is to keep asking them questions which will help them look more closely at a particular point of view, out of which they'll discover a solution. So when you come to the program, they devise it; they're the experts; all I have to do is bring it into some kind of shape. When they look at it, they think, 'My God what am I going to do? It just looks too big.' So I try and direct their attention on specific areas. If they then achieve something, they're much more excited. The self-discovery thing is confidence-building. You have got to learn to take the responsibility. If you can learn to take responsibility, you're going to be even stronger than the kind of player who needs a coach all the time. My aim is to make myself redundant. In doing things yourself, you do them so much more thoroughly."

Here we see how self-examination is going to lead to three things: an awareness of blocks, an achievement-monitoring system, and self-confidence. In essence, the person starts to deal with himself or herself almost as if that self were part of the external environment. That is possible so long as the basic self is intact. If, however, self-examination pulls to pieces the basic self, then there is no one to make the improvements. Up to a certain point self-examination is helpful, beyond that point it can be destructive (and can lead to a dependence of the destroyed self on the destroyer).

Although in psychology the examination of self may be pushed to the point of destruction (in the hope that the reassembled pieces will give a better result), self-examination has usually a more modest aim. In fact, there are usually two aims. The first is to become aware of blocks of deficiencies with a view to putting things right. The second aim is to become aware of your own style and (possibly) limitations. The first aim is correction. The second aim is realism.

RECOGNIZING BLOCKS

To what extent does a successful person stand outside of himself or herself to watch what is going on? Virginia Wade, tennis player: "If I watch somebody else, I'll be able to give him good tactical advice, and the trick is being able to get outside yourself and work from outside and watch yourself as an observer. This means staying really cool, calm, and collected, and staying outside the emotional thing. That is one of the most important things of all. You have to really be able to assess yourself and work on the areas where you are not so strong. This is something I had to learn because I've always been so emotional on court. As soon as the heat was on, I would panic. So those are the areas that I've had to work really hard on. I've always had more talent than my fair share, but I was weak in the mental areas and weak in self-confidence in a way."

Sting: "I find I can write things much more readily than I can play them. I was always more of a composer than a musician. The two things seem to be separate. I tell myself it is the analytical side of the brain that can play an instrument and the other side of the brain that tells the instrument what to play. An ability to create things that are original superseded the technical ability to play in a band. Today, as my composing facility improves, it leaves behind my musical virtuosity. This is why I have recently taken up manuscript score writing."

BECOMING AWARE OF LIMITATIONS AND ESTABLISHING SUCCESS

Before Mark McCormack became the manager of Arnold Palmer, Jack Nicklaus, and Gary Player, he was a golfer himself. "I was good enough to get into the championships but certainly not good enough to win them. I tried to play better golf, and it disappointed me that I wasn't better, but then again, I would tell myself how good I was, which was pretty good. Taking millions of golfers, I was in the top small group. But I knew I could not ever make a great success of it at a professional level."

Jackie Stewart, ex-World Racing Champion: "Personal awareness of one's own capabilities (that's part of kidding other people and not kidding yourself) involves recognizing your own limitations. And that is very important. You must be honest. It comes through experience but also through self-analysis. What is the point of building a sand castle around your head? I didn't get old through that. I think being able to recognize your own limitations is terribly important. I've seen a lot of free-fall artists stagger their way in and out of situations, and you can call it a couple of times but you get found out. You're not a stayer — that's the thing. There's a whole lot of people who've been successful for four years, five years, ten years, but you're in this world for seventy — threescore years and ten — let's see people being successful over that period of time. You can take any avenue you like and you will see them. The stayers. It's very easy to achieve — achieving is easy because you're competing against mediocrity in the majority of cases. It's very easy to get up there — to achieve. It's much more difficult to establish success."

INTERPRETING STRENGTHS/WEAKNESSES

We tend to have fixed ideas about strengths and weaknesses. But in many cases it depends very much on the context and on how you look at them. This point is made very directly by Malcolm Forbes, millionaire publisher of *Forbes* magazine:

"What is a strength in one context can be a weakness in another context. I'm persevering — you are stubborn. I am flexible — you are weak. I am practical — you are opportunistic. If I'm persevering, that is the same as being stubborn. I am flexible — you cave in. It depends on the context."

This raises a very important point. Who is to say what are strengths and what are weaknesses? Ordinary language and ordinary experience make strong suggestions: decisiveness is better than vacillation; goal directing is better than drifting; knowledge is better than ignorance. Yet, as Malcom Forbes so rightly points out, much depends on the context. Being goal-directed in an established industry is one thing. Being goal-directed in a changing industry may simply lock you into a goal that has become outdated: you may need to be continually looking around and noting the emerging opportunity areas.

We are much too free with our absolutes in ordinary language and thinking. The proverb "Look before you leap" makes sense. So does the contradictory proverb "He who hesitates is lost." The proverb "Many hands make light work" is correct. So is the other one: "Too many cooks spoil the broth." It all depends on the circumstances.

So it is with the value of self-knowledge. It can be useful and it can be destructive. It can be useful when offering alternative perceptions. It can be useful when dealing with blocks and weaknesses. It can be useful when determining personal style and limitations. It can be destructive when it seeks to change the personality rather than modify it. It can be destructive when analysis looks only at the components and not at the whole system. It can be destructive when it becomes dogmatic.

T A C T I C S

1. Do not believe that more and more self-analysis is better and better.

2. The purpose of self-examination is to offer tentative perceptions, not dogmatic explanations.

3. It is useful to become aware of your personal style.

4. It is useful to become aware, in a realistic fashion, of your limitations, so long as they do not thereafter become an excuse.

5. It is useful to look for blocks and weaknesses in order to try to put them right.

6. If you take your personality apart, there is no guarantee that what comes together again will be an improvement.

7. Always leave enough of you unanalyzed so that this can carry out the analysis on the remainder.

8. Remember that analysis into component parts may destroy values that arise only from the whole.

SET YOURSELF A TARGET

The simplest form of target is the acceptance of a challenge. In sport that challenge may be specific and self-defining: to win at Wimbledon, to win an Olympic gold medal, to run a mile in less than four minutes. Sportsmen and women may, alternatively, claim a more general target: to win every race. In art there may be a general ambition to be best, but targets are more difficult to define; it is probably a matter of getting better and better and striving more fully to make actual any artistic potential (self-improvement and self-expression may be the best definition).

Clearly we must make a distinction between specific targets and general purpose targets (see also page 84).

Jackie Stewart: "It's the satisfaction of doing something really well . . . that I know I have done better than I have done or could do. Whether it is a speech or an interview or a TV commercial or a driving sequence, if I have done it better than before—boy I feel good."

This same theme of always getting better might also be the aim of many successful entrepreneurs in business. The view is compatible with there being times of "treading water" until the next opportunity and challenge emerges, when the entrepreneur is off after that.

Robert Holmes à Court: "I think the point is that it is so important to find, recognize, and see the goal you are working towards. So many people do not have a clear goal. They'll do a lot of work but cannot formulate the goal that they're going towards (they may do work for other purposes, to impress the people around them, their peers, their superiors). If you clearly define the goal you are halfway to achieving it.

"My goal is business. I don't see that as wide; it's very narrow. It is not politics; it is not scientific-research philosophy, it is not a lot of things. It is one thing: business. A retailer doesn't know which customer will walk into his shop first tomorrow, but he knows that he intends to trade at a profit: in other words, successfully. But it is not important to me which business or which customer it is."

This is an excellent definition of a general-purpose goal. The goal is to develop the skill, habits, practices, and principles of business. That includes sound management but also spotting opportunities, assessing them, and acting on the assessment. It may be similar to the general-purpose goal of an athlete or even an opera singer: to become good and get better and better.

Such a general-purpose goal is very important but not much use to someone starting out. There is a business for Holmes à Court to run. Opportunities will be brought to him. None of that will necessarily happen to someone starting out. So there may have to be targets that are much more specific.

WHAT TO DO: CHOICE OF FIELD

Sometimes the field is determined by talent which appears at an early enough age and is then nurtured. This could be the case with music or athletic prowess, for example.

Hans Eysenck: "I always had a scientific way of looking at things. I remember many years ago when I was at school, a teacher said: 'All Jews are cowards.'

" 'Well,' I thought; 'he may be right.' I didn't know. I thought: 'How would you prove it?' Now how do you recognize valor? Simply by giving the Iron Cross? So I thought to myself: 'Why not go to books and see how many Jews were given the Iron Cross in the First World War? Is it a lower percentage?' But it wasn't! In fact, I found Jews got more Iron Crosses than their proportion of the population. So I went back and told this man and he was absolutely furious! So, you know, I always had that kind of way of looking at things; statistical, mathematical, analytical, and scientific."

For others there may be a routine and fairly obvious choice of career. What is much more interesting than either of these is the haphazard way in which many successful people have chosen their field. It may be a chance happening or a chance meeting. We always forget that although a road may be long, there is just one first step which determines whether we take this road or that.

An apparently haphazard choice of field seems to support the notion — which many successful people advance themselves — that barring lack of talent in talent-intensive areas, a successful person may be successful in any field he or she chooses. If that were indeed so, then the choice of field might as well be haphazard.

I am not sure I agree with this notion. I do believe that there are general characteristics of success (self-image, independence, determination, wanting to make things happen, etc.) and that in some cases these are so powerful that they will carry the person to success in any field. At the other extreme there may be combinations of timing and luck and choice of a strategy that just happens to fit. In between these extremes I feel that choice of field is worth careful consideration — for two reasons: (1) a person's style may fit a certain field; (2) in some fields it is much more difficult to be successful (or visibly successful) than in others.

It is interesting to note that many people switch careers. For example, Sir Terence Conran started as a designer and then became a retail tycoon. This suggests that personal style and inclinations are important and that the choice of field is not entirely random. Even in business it is likely that the choice of field is determined by personality. At least, the choice of field may not always be determined by personality, but success within it depends on whether the personality and style fit. For example, there are people who enjoy the risks of property (real estate) development and those who want to build things up steadily. There are people who enjoy selling and dealing with other people and then there are people who want to work alone, juggling figures in the investment market.

In dealing with success we can never forget that we are always looking at it in hindsight: backward from a successful person. So we can only look at those instances where field, style, and strategy have resulted in success.

Because in most school systems there is no direct pathway to a business career we get (at least in the United Kingdom), people who seem to drift into business because they have no aptitude or inclination for the sort of career path (academic or professional) that *is* advocated in school. This must give a very distorted picture. Highly talented youngsters get "trapped" by their early success at school, and this determines their career paths in the academic world and in the professions. Were business or industry to be a serious option at school, then I suspect there would be a different sort of person prevalent in business. At the moment, it has to be one who is very ambitious, a high risk taker, and something of an early misfit. In short, there must be a huge waste of business talent in the present system.

Several successful people point to a variety of molding influences which gradually shaped their choice of path.

HOW THEY CHOSE WHAT TO DO

Chance Meeting

Many successful careers have had a chance meeting as their take-off point. It does not mean that the career would not have been successful without this chance meeting. Nevertheless, the meeting set off a chain of events. This happened to Jarvis Astaire, the very successful property developer: "Through an uncle of mine I had got a job in the surgical equipment business. After the war I became an export manager of a surgical instrument firm . . . and then I married.

"The family of the girl I married were very, very keen on living in America. I was twenty-three, and reluctantly decided to give the American thing a try. I fixed myself up with an important surgical equipment company in America. My wife didn't enjoy America as much as she had as a college girl. We returned to England, and I decided that I wanted to go into business on my own account. I didn't want to go back into the surgical equipment business; it was a business for large companies, needing a large investment. So I looked about for a business. At that point I was very involved with Wingate Football Club. One of the fellows involved with the club was working for a menswear chain. Talking after games, we decided to go in together, and opened a menswear shop. The shop was in Bournemouth, as we were able to get a shop there and my partner (with some knowledge of the business) felt the competition in London was strong already.

"Then we expanded, opened another shop in Poole. It went very nicely until one day during the summer in Bournemouth, I was playing tennis (my wife's sister and her husband had come down to spend some time with us) and we met a fellow I knew vaguely from my Youth Club days. While playing tennis, he revealed that he was an estate agent, and talked about a particular piece of land available in Edgware. My brother-in-law and I thought we should see what we could do with it. The office building we built on it turned out to be so successful a venture that he and I decided that the property development business had more opportunity than either of the businesses we were in (he was a clothing manufacturer).

"So, we specialized, and became one of the pioneers of supermarket development in England. I went over to America and spent six months learning all that was required by supermarket operators, and we went into partnership with one of the major supermarket operators in this country. This was in the early and mid-1950s, when there were so many more sites around than there are today. Once we got going, it was like a rocket."

Several points arise from this apparent haphazard choice of path. The first is the importance of chance meetings and contacts — and the willingness to act on these (a sharp sensitivity to opportunity). The second point is the rapid appreciation that the real estate field offered much better prospects for success than the manufacturing or retailing business. A third point is the willingness to "get stuck in," to spend time and effort learning the business. A fourth is the willingness to work with other people in a partnership. A fifth point is the recognition that the supermarket field was about to become big business (again an opportunity sensitivity). A sixth point is the willingness to give up what was a reasonably successful business in order to try for something much better — risk-taking.

Bureaucratic Error

Sometimes circumstances forced by a mistake (one's own or the mistake of others) can open up a path that would not otherwise have been chosen. We must always then wonder whether the same talents applied along another track might not have been even more successful. Contrariwise, the mistake may have selected a most suitable track that would not have been selected in any other way.

Hans Eysenck, psychologist: "When I came over to England at the age of eighteen or so, I was required to do the Matric at the University of London. So I did the subjects that were easiest for me, which were Latin and mathematics and so on . . . German and English. But when I came to register, they said: 'You've taken the wrong subjects'; which was typical of the University of London, a terribly bureaucratic institution.

"So I said: 'What can I do?'

"They said: 'Come back next year and take the right subjects.'

"And I said: 'I haven't got any money so I can't do that. Isn't there any science I can study with what I've got?'

"And they said: 'Oh yes . . . there's always psychology.'

"And I said: 'What the hell is psychology? Never heard of it.'

"So I went into psychology."

This is a truly remarkable story from someone who has made such a success of psychology and also someone who strongly believes in the genetic transmission of abilities. It may be an example of "general ability," inasmuch as Eysenck might have made an equal success of any field he had entered (or any scientific field). Or it may be a good example of *fit*. We have seen elsewhere in this book that Eysenck's natural tendency is to be exact and to measure. His career in psychology has been based on his insistence on strict measurement and statistically based results. This has enabled him to stand out in a field that is usually more interested in theory and speculation and where things may be impossible to measure (in some areas). Had he taken his measurement style to other fields (economics, physics, etc.), the fit might have been much less effective because he would have been surrounded by people who also liked measurement. We can reverse the argument again by saying that in another field Eysenck would have realized that some other quality was more important (perhaps conceptualization) and that his focus on measurement in psychology was only because the field needed this so badly. Hindsight speculation allows a lot of to- and fro-ing. What is clear is that the initial choice of field was not on the basis of careful examination of the possibilities.

Innovative Thinking

Heather Jenner, creator of the first marriage bureau: "My father was in the War Office and was sent out to Ceylon, or Sri Lanka, as it is now. I went with them when I was about nineteen. Of course it was marvelous. The end of the palmy days! There were about forty men to one woman. You couldn't help being the belle of the ball (you were probably the only one there). I returned in 1938, but whilst I'd been out there, all these spare men were saying, 'When I go home on leave I'm going to get married.' And I'd been thinking that might be interesting. I knew lots of my girlfriends were sitting about in England, and I was thinking, 'Perhaps I'll start something so they can meet.' I got on a boat to come back, and on the boat was Mary Oliver, who'd been thinking the same thing. So we were very careful about it all and didn't tell our parents. Jenner wasn't my real name and Oliver wasn't hers. We thought somebody might try and stop us."

Here we see a good idea, at the right time and (as we shall see later) handled with innocence and enthusiasm. So there is opportunity, sensitivity, and a willingness to get up and do something about it. As always the key question is: how willing is someone to follow the slight glimmer of an opportunity? There are opportunities to be spotted in the me-too and bandwagon areas (which are easier) as well as opportunities that are created within the mind of an individual (as with Heather Jenner's idea).

Trial, Error, and Perseverence

Mike Brearley, ex-captain England Cricket XI, now a psychoanalyst: "The whole business of tactics — talking shop about tactics, strategy, and policy has always interested me. My father, who was a good cricketer, was also interested in that side of things. So, right from the beginning, from a very early age, I was interested in field placing, bowling outswing/inswing — changing the bowling, all that sort of thing.

"The pattern of my career seems clearer afterwards. I spent a lot of time being very uncertain about what I wanted to do. I changed subjects at university from classics to philosophy. I took a Civil Service exam, but didn't go into the Civil Service. I thought of being a professional cricketer, tried it for a year, and decided not to. Did research and lectured in philosophy at Newcastle University. Decided I didn't want to be a philosopher all my life, or a teacher at university. Played a bit of part-time cricket. Let it be known at Middlesex that I was interested (in being captain). They were in a mess. So it came together in time. I decided that I wasn't that much of an intellectual. I wasn't interested in intellectual problems. I was interested in the theory of something, certainly, but I was also interested in the practice, as in cricket or as in interpersonal relationships in psychoanalysis.

"Then I became involved and helped in this clinic for disturbed adolescents, and gradually became more and more interested in the unconscious and in psychotherapy. Now, I am really committed to what I do."

This is an excellent illustration of a combination of one field with another: people behavior and cricket. There is much power in unusual combinations like this, because by definition they must be very rare. For example, in Sir Terence Conran there is the combination of design flair and entrepreneurial talent. People can train for a particular career, but it is virtually impossible to train for an unusual combination of skills. I am not quite sure of the success path of a brilliant cook who was also a computer expert, but the combination would be most unusual — and valuable. From this arises a practical point for the reader. There is always merit in fostering unusual combinations of skills. The other interesting point about the Mike Brearley story is the repeated dissatisfaction with one field after another, and the constant searching for what he really wanted. This restlessness and willingness to change is also a feature of successful people. They do not seem to be content to make the best of what has been provided for them.

A FELLOW FEELING

When all things seem equal — or equally unattractive — then the personal element can come into it. There may be someone you get on with and want to work with. This was the starting point for James Rogers, the hedge fund manager: "I was a senior in my last year at university and I had applied to business school, to law school, and to graduate school. I was a confused young man. I didn't know what I was going to be when I grew up. When I went to university, companies would come in and interview seniors about coming to work for them. I didn't know what I wanted to do, but did want to see what the experience of an interview was like, and went to talk to these people. One of the companies represented was a stockbroking company in New York. I didn't known anything about stockbrokers at the time; I didn't even know about Wall Street, although I had heard about it. The company representative and I really got along well, the reason being that he had grown up in a section of New York City called Hell's Kitchen, which basically is a slum — but he'd gone on to Harvard! Going from there to Harvard is like going from Toxteth to Oxford! He'd actually done that. Now I had been raised in the backwoods of Alabama and gone to Yale, which is a bit like going from Toxteth to Cambridge.

"To make a long story short, when later I got a scholarship to Oxford, I called him up and said, 'I'm going to Oxford next year so I can't work for you, but maybe I can work for you for the summer.' They didn't usually hire summer people, but he said, 'OK, come down and work with us for the summer.' So I went down to Wall Street and worked with them just in a menial kind of semitrainee position and I felt like — well, it was the most wonderful thing I had ever seen: people would pay me to go down to Wall Street and invest money! What I liked about it was not so much investing money (because at that time I didn't have any), but that if you were smart, used your wits, and paid attention to the world (at that time I was extremely interested in what was going on in the world, and used to read voraciously), if you just understood the world, it was all you had to do. You didn't have to wear the right ties, you didn't have to join the country club, you didn't have to join the PTA. You could do what you wanted to do, and nobody cared, and they would pay you to do this. I thought this was the most exciting thing I'd ever seen.

"I went back the next summer and worked again; by then I realized what I liked was international finance. I wanted to be a Gnome of Zurich! I'd been to Oxford and thought I was the great international intellectual and all the rest of it, and so I said, 'I want to be a Gnome of Zurich and I want to invest internationally.' And by that time I knew enough about Wall Street to know that the best way to make money in Wall Street was to start, or be involved with, what is known as a hedge fund. "Hedge fund" means you buy and sell, and also sell short. "Sell short," just to explain, is if you think a stock is going to collapse you sell it. Since you don't have it to start with, you borrow it; then before it collapses, you sell it at, say, 100; then when it collapses, you buy it back at, say, 50. You say to me, 'How can you sell it at 100 if you don't have it?' And I say to you, 'I borrow the stock from my stockbroker; I sell it at 100, and when it goes down to 50, I buy it and I pay my stockbroker. It's a way to make money on collapses.'"

Here we see the value of personal rapport. Jim Rogers followed his instincts about the company representative and, as a direct result, entered Wall Street (a field about which he knew absolutely nothing, but in which he was to make his fortune). Second, he soon developed a strong image of what he wanted to be. Finally, he quickly spotted the area — hedge fund — in which it was going to be possible to make a fortune (opportunity definition).

REFORMING ZEAL

There are times when a strong sense of "mission" comes first and is the driving force. With Sir Peter Parker, who was head of the huge British Rail network, the sense of mission affected him in an unusual way.

Sir Peter Parker: "I thought of industry originally as being where the action was. Industry was for me the 'Here be Savages' country. I'd become very left in the course of the war — it had built on my experiences as a child in China. I was very, very lucky: my parents were mobile, so I had an informal education. And my father was always going to places which 'blew up.' For Englishmen, France 'blew up' in the slump. So we went to China. China 'blew up' against Japan in the Manchurian War of 1937. So twice I remember my family fortune breaking. That made me conscious of a kind of variety in life. I was also conscious of poverty. I'm not being horrifically obvious when I say I saw something was askew in society. And as a boy I grew up with this. So came the war, and when the war ended, I was saying to myself: 'How do you stop wars? How do you deal with poverty?'

"These were the things that really hit me. The war had been damaging to my family. I'd lost both my brothers, who were older than I was. And that ripped into me. So I came out of that experience thinking: 'Well, where do you go, where political decisions are taken?' And I thought industry — it had shaped the industrial revolution; it had also shaped our affairs. So I came into industry almost with a sense of reforming zeal."

This "reforming zeal" seems a most unusual reason for a choice of an industrial career. That zeal must clearly have been accompanied by considerable managerial talents. On the face of it, the "reforming zeal" seems quite the wrong reason for someone to choose a field. Yet we know that many people who put their beliefs above other things (Quakers, Mormons, etc.) have often been very successful in business. It would seem that at first sight the interests of the business and the interests of the "zeal" might pull in opposite directions. What in fact happens is that "running the business as well as possible" becomes a manifestation of the zeal, so the energy is synergistic rather than contradictory. The practical point is that you can be a zealot and still pursue a successful career path. It is not necessary just to rail against the world.

STARGAZING

A great many people choose a career path because it brings one into contact with the more glamorous side of life. Not many make the cross over. Verity Lambert did.

Verity Lambert: "I started off as a shorthand typist. Initially, I did temping (temporary work), but let's start with my television experience. I started working for Granada as a secretary and got fired after about six months. But by that time I had become interested in television. I suppose the only conscious choice that I made was that I didn't want to work in the sort of job where I was just the receiver of information. Some of the temporary jobs I had done, like working in a solicitor's office or typing French menus for the De Vere Hotel, I found deadening and awful — they obviously were not going to extend me in any way. If I had ambition, I think that what I had was a desire to at least fill my days with something that interested me rather than sit slogging at a typewriter.

"I'd taken a secretarial course because my mother thought it would be something to fall back on. It took me eighteen months to do a three-month course, I loathed it so much. I hadn't been to university. I have five O Levels and one A Level. I'd been to Paris for a year, to the Sorbonne, where I'd learnt to speak French fairly fluently. But it seemed just a matter of filling in time until I got married.

"So I was thrown out of the job at Granada probably because I wasn't a very good secretary. But by that time I'd become interested in television — the idea of it. It seemed like it was fun. I was just starstruck and it seemed glamorous and it seemed like a fun thing to do, and better than being a suburban housewife. I decided that what I wanted to be was what is called a production assistant. That is the next stage up from being a secretary. It's not very ambitious, sort of logical. But in order to do that I had to get back in again. So I had to get back in by becoming a shorthand typist again. I got a job in the managing director's office of ABC Television, which was then a smaller company and is now half of Thames. I was a secretary to the managing director's secretary, and she actually taught me to be quite a good secretary. Now the one thing that I had been very interested in at school was English literature. I had been taught extremely well and had enjoyed reading plays and analyzing them — that kind of thing. Finally I got a job as secretary to the head of Drama — a very good place to be, as I was then exposed to plays and actors and rehearsals. And I think that was the time that I really started to be interested in a particular aspect of television. I began to assimilate a certain amount of knowledge.

"Initially, when I first became a production assistant, I didn't work in drama, I worked on quiz shows. But finally I did gravitate towards drama and fortunately worked for an extremely talented, very individualistic director, who was, in some people's opinion, a monster. But in actual fact he was simply very volatile, an interesting man who encouraged me to read and have opinions. He wasn't somebody who would take on board people's opinions unless he believed they had something to offer. He listened to me."

This quotation brings up that practical point which is so much resented (and rightly so) by the women's liberation movement. The practical point is: "Get in there as a secretary and then show how good you are." Feminists feel that it is degrading to women to have to define themselves as secretaries, and they want to enter a field on an equal footing with men. They want to be interviewed as executives, not secretaries. I agree with that. I also think that women have, in addition, an advantage over men in that they can also enter a field as a secretary, and thus have a chance to display general ability that might not have been reflected in degree qualifications or an interview. Very often it is this general-purpose ability which is most important. Of course, it is argued that if you get in as a secretary you will always remain in that category. This, unfortunately, may be true as well. Ideally, all secretaries would be regarded as potential executives. Whatever the merits of the argument, it is true that in many cases a talented person has got in through being a "secretary" or "research assistant" (in TV) and has then gone on to much greater things. Being around and having a chance to show your abilities is very important indeed.

FOCUS

DOES THE PERFECT JOB EXIST?

How much of what you do, do you really like doing? Does this proportion vary for successful people? Do they always like all of what they are
doing? They often say they like what they are doing — but there are
aggravations, as Malcolm Forbes, the publisher of *Forbes* magazine, in-
dicates: "There is no millennium where the perfect job exists, where there
are no problems. I don't think anybody can be a success who doesn't like
what they do, and an equal thought is, you don't have a job if you don't
have aggravations. It is no job if it has no challenge; there is nothing to
it if there are no problems. If your job is repetitious, a mechanical one
. . . boring, you've got to fight. There is always a drawback, or it isn't
a job. There is no millennium, but the essential ingredient is liking what
you're doing."

Sir Mark Prescott: "Success is a very personal thing. I tend to follow
Henry Longhurst's (the golfing commentator) advice — find what you like
doing best and then find someone to pay you for doing it. I think I've
found that."

EXPLOITING OPPORTUNITY

The real estate (property development) field has always been a classic
one for making fortunes. The risk, the market swings, the gearing (money
invested to money borrowed), the opportunity for deal and package
making, the value of personal contacts, the value of flair have all made
this the ideal field for anyone who wants to make a fortune (or lose it).
The large amounts of money involved mean that enough of it can rub off
as profits to make large fortunes. Values in the real estate market are in
the eyes of the buyer. There are doldrum periods and overbuilding periods and times when government intervention kills the market (as in
rent control) but the field has usually been a good one for people who
want to be successful. Above all, it is a field in which an individual with
a very small staff can make big deals and get quick profits.

John Ritblat had played the stock market a little while still at school;
he assumed that would be his career. In changing to property, timing
and listening to outside advice proved important. "Broking all seemed
very exciting in those days, in the early '50's, when companies like Great
Universal Stores and Charles Clore were making great inroads into the
takeover business. But I thought I still needed a little bit more advice.
I really was totally outside — I had no commercial background in my
family at all. So I went to see an uncle who was a very successful property investor and also an estate agent of some note. He had a great number of leading entrepreneurs through his office at one time or another.
He took me to lunch and said, 'Why do you want to be a stockbroker?'

And I said: 'Well, you know, I just thought it was appealing; seems interesting.'

"And he said, 'Now, I'll tell you what we'll do. We'll walk down Bond Street.'

"And I walked down Bond Street to Berkley Square, where his offices were. In those days it was the time when you still couldn't get building consent — you needed a government permit — and there we were in 1951 with empty sites everywhere. He said to me, 'You don't really think we're going to leave London like this? There's bound to be an enormous rise in commercial property.' At that time, rent had stood still, not risen, and it was a dormant business. But he said, 'My advice to you is that you should come into the property business.' And he said, 'It's got many advantages over the stock exchange. You become a stockbroker and you know absolutely nothing about the property business. You go into the property business, you can still hold forth and consider yourself an expert in the stock market.'

"I think, you know, that was very good advice. He introduced me to Edward Erdman, who, although he had established his office before the war, he was quite well known and he had worked for my uncle before beginning his own business. He said, 'Well, we haven't much room for office boys,' for that office wasn't that big, 'but we'll take you.' Then he added, 'But I'm only taking you on merit, because I think you look energetic — there's a spark in your eye.' That's how I started."

This is what several of London's top property men did, and even someone who launched out into hotels, pubs, dance halls, and breweries, like the late Sir Maxwell Joseph did with Grand Metropolitan, found that his early days in a Golders Green estate agency stood him in good stead when it came to pricing takeover bids. That was why Sir Maxwell was willing to go for broke with the record-breaking £594 million bid for Warney's brewery. He confessed later that the subsequent rise in interest rates very nearly did break him, but he pulled through.

One advantage in working for an estate agent is that you not only gain a grounding, you make contacts — a vital asset when someone is starting out in business. That is what set Nigel Broackes out on the road which took him to the head of Trafalgar House, the property group which runs the Ritz Hotel, Cunard Shipping, and builders, Trollop and Colls. He has this advice for the business beginner: "If you have to start from scratch, join a good agency, as I did, and get to know its bank manager. Get him to acquire respect for your judgment but don't let him know your aspirations at once. Do one thing at a time. After a year of two, go and have a talk with him. If he's formed a good impression, and you have an attractive project, he will probably take a chance. Pick a suitable site for your first venture, and make sure you build the kind of place that will sell quickly. Never get stuck with something that won't move — it affects your reputation. I can't stress this too much. Your reputation, at this stage, is all-important and you can't afford to make a mistake. Once you do well, you get plenty of offers—but you must never risk spoiling your credit rating. Don't go to small builders or unknown architects. And don't get greedy: it wasn't until I stopped concentrating on making money that I really started to make it."

All this can be summed up as follows. Get to know the business. Get to know the market. Get to know people. Build up credibility. Credibility is in many fields a huge capital asset. It is difficult to build up and easy to lose. In the end it may be the only thing which determines whether a deal comes your way or whether you can get backing when you need it. Credibility does not necessarily require the caution that never permits error. Investors are willing to take risks as long as they know that the risks are soundly managed.

BE READY TO CHANGE TARGETS

There are heroic tales of persistence in which a string of failures and rejections ultimately leads to success. I believe that Frederick Forsyth's best-selling book *The Day of the Jackal* was rejected by some 35 publishers before it was accepted. Unfortunately, we only ever see the successes that occur after a tale of persistence. There are many people (authors included) who have persisted and persisted and have never met success. Their talents and their energies have been locked up in one direction and have therefore been unavailable for other, possibly more rewarding, opportunities.

Sir Kenneth Cork is the famous liquidator of British corporations. He is called in when they fail and go bankrupt (there is no Chapter 11 equivalent in the United Kingdom). He has been involved with aircraft makers Handley Page, with John Bloom's empire, and, more recently, with the De Lorean motor company. He advises newcomers to business not to fall in love with their products. Entrepreneurs may start off with a brilliant product or a brilliant service idea. Then the market changes or competition enters the field (perhaps at a lower price). The entrepreneur hangs on. Failure follows.

At other times a company invests all its R & D effort and marketing effort in one new product. If it fails the company fails. This, known as "product push" or "technology push," is almost exactly the opposite of Robert Holmes à Court's goal of successful business in general, where management skills and principles are more important than actual content. Idea-push entrepreneurship can be brilliantly successful (as with Sir Clive Sinclair), but it can also be disastrous).

In the future there will be a shift to flexible factories. At present factories are tooled up to produce a particular product as efficiently as possible. In the future there will be far greater flexibility so that if jeans are selling well the factory can make jeans; if handbags are selling well, then the factory can switch to that product, and so on. In short, the business and the manufacturing capacity becomes a "process" through which different products can be passed. In exactly the same way the entrepreneur can build up general-purpose skills and contacts and then apply them to different situations. Clearly experience and contacts in any one field are important. The person who flits from one field to another risks the pitfalls of the "Jack of all trades, master of none," but the epithet applies more to a dabbler. Many Californian entrepreneurs have moved from field to field, depending on where the opportunities have lain.

Salt on food is good up to a point, beyond which it ruins the food. Courage is good up to a point, beyond that point it becomes foolhardiness. Persistence is good up to a point, beyond which it becomes stubbornness.

You may have to change targets because in a rapidly changing field (such as electronics) the situation itself has changed. You may have to change targets because it is clear that the initial idea will not work or the product will not sell (or not at the right price).

When should you persist? When you feel that the idea is only slightly ahead of its time. When there have been indications of the salability of the product. When the trends are going your way. When the investment climate has been bad but is improving. How long is it sensible to wait for an opportunity break in R & D or marketing a product? Reward has no automatic virtue and there is no rule that says a break must come sometime. It may never come.

The merits of persistence may trap us in a failure path. Moderate success may trap us in a path of moderate success. Few people have the chance to escape from moderate success in order to take a risky leap into another field where there are possibilities of greater success, but no guarantees. Many successful people have made such jumps (probably to the horror of their families).

The taking of such a risk depends on: your assessment of your present path and its future; your assessment of the opportunity being offered; your assessment of your personal style and talents; your ability to take risks.

That effectively passes the buck back to you. All I can do is to point out that moderate success may be a trap — at least to someone who is more ambitious.

T A C T I C S

1. The overriding factor is that you should be doing something you enjoy doing and are good at doing (but see below).

2. There are clearly certain fields (like real estate) in which it is far easier to be successful than in others. There are also fields in which a moderate talent plus hard work will succeed, whereas in others a higher degree of natural talent is required. These are facts of life.

3. Most successful people do not seem to have selected carefully their field of endeavor — that is no reason not to do this.

4. There is no stigma attached to changing fields, careers, or targets. Many successful people have done just this.

5. People contacts are extremely important (not what you know but whom you know).

6. The ability to spot an opportunity when it is only a glimmer or a casual remark is very important. So is the ability to take action on that opportunity.

7. Unusual combinations of skills and experience can be important, because there will be little competition in such areas.

8. In many fields credibility is the major asset.

9. For many successful people, the first step has been a partnership with someone else.

10. Moderate success can also be a trap if you are interested in greater success.

11. Difficult challenges are worth taking on if the elements involved are within your control. If they are not, you may be wasting your time.

12. You can always define your challenge for yourself.

7

Opportunity-Seeking

NO STANDING STILL

The next step and the one after are there to be taken. Standing still and waiting for the conveyor belt of life to deliver your luggage to you is not a strategy much favored by successful people. Christian Bonington, the mountaineer, makes this point (and, for a mountaineer, it is particularly appropriate because climbing a mountain means taking one step after another): "Looking at anyone's career, it's not any one event. There are a whole series of steps. In my case, the first step was when we climbed the north face of the Eiger — the first British ascent. The decision to go for it and the fact we succeeded in doing it (instead of some other Brit.) helped me on. My next vital decision was to get stuck into photojournalism, because I wanted to make a living and didn't want to be a climbing guide. That gave me the media experience that I needed for other expeditions. My next vital decision was in fact not Everest but Anna-purna's south face. The decision to lead, when I'd never ever led an ex-pedition before, was crucial. No one decision is a cutoff. Each step leads you to the point that you are at this instant."

There always is a next step, and it should be bigger and better than the last one, just as the next mountain to be climbed has to be higher or more difficult. Peter Habeler ran out of mountains to climb, so he and his companions set out to climb Everest without oxygen. They suc-ceeded.

Successful people enjoy challenges and taking opportunities. There is the urge to make things happen. In a previous section we considered the role that luck plays in success. In some cases it can be a major factor. In others it is only a contributory factor. The starting opportunity can turn up in a lucky manner. Someone happens to mention a particular real estate deal and that is it — the developer is on his way. But the ability to recognize the opportunity, the willingness to take the initiative and the risk, the work needed to turn the opportunity into reality are all provided by the entrepreneur.

We often forget that opportunity seeking is not a natural habit of mind either for an individual or for a corporation. "Keeping one's head down" and "getting by" is more natural. The day-to-day enjoyment of life is more natural.

When organizations have grown to a certain size, they often feel it necessary to get rid of the entrepreneur who set it up in the first place. Maintenance takes over from creation.

The role of management is maintenance, not opportunity seeking. Yet even this maintenance may imply the need to grow.

"I think you have to get bigger," says Mark McCormack. "There's no such thing as standing still; if you stand still in sales volume your profits will decrease because of inflation. Tell me a successful business in which there hasn't been expansion?"

It is often assumed that growth will happen naturally as a result of market momentum or the inevitable growth of a successful organization. Sell more and make more. Become better known and increase the mar-ket share. This sort of growth fits well with the natural inclination and training of management. Most management idioms were developed in the 1950s and 1960s, when the U.S. economy was growing steadily. In a growing economy only two things were required. The first was effi-cient management, so that you could stay with and take advantage of the growth. The second was an ability to solve problems, so that you could tackle any hiccup and get back on track. In difficult times, caused either by general recession or by increasing competition, the twin skills of ef-ficient management and problem-solving are as vital as ever. Unfortu-nately they are no longer sufficient. There is today a need for further thinking: the thinking concerned with opportunity-seeking and change of strategy.

Is it possible to find an opportunity-seeking spirit in a large corporation? I once worked on a consulting assignment with a major European company. The chief executive felt that in a changing world there should be more of an entrepreneurial spirit at all levels. Among the steps taken was the setting up of a risk fund which could be used by executives as an additional source of seed money for trying out new ideas. Many executives had claimed that they were unable to be entrepreneurial because they dare not divert their operating budgets toward new risks. I remember talking to an executive who had access to the risk fund. He told me that he did not want to "risk" using the risk fund, because if he made a mistake and failed, he felt it would threaten his career. This is a natural, and logical, expression of risk-aversion in large organizations. A mistake can halt a career which is otherwise developing its own momentum. He told me, however, that the mere presence of the risk fund had allowed him to look more closely at opportunities in his surroundings because he knew that there was funding available should he chose to pursue an opportunity. Having looked closely, he found that some opportunities were so attractive he was following them up with his own budget — still without using the risk fund.

Most people in large organizations are so preoccupied with "urgent" matters that there is very little time for the "important" matters. That is one reason why so very little time is spent on deliberate thinking or conceptual thinking. There is always a problem to be solved. Problem-solving also implies the removal of risk, whereas opportunity-seeking implies increased risk and work. It is not at all difficult to see why problem-solving is so much preferred to opportunity-seeking. Management is forced to solve problems. No one is forced to look for opportunities until it is too late. By the time an organization is forced to look for opportunities it has probably already lost its best people, its market share, its credit rating, and its morale.

In large corporations there is an unstated attitude toward change and opportunity. Keep awake and watch closely. Follow trends rather than set them. Use muscle to get into an area as it starts to develop. Let others take the initial risk and then move in and buy those outfits up or get a product of your own in there as fast as possible. There is a feeling that a large organization cannot be everywhere at the same time. Slow organic change is seen as being less risky than major strategic shifts. For some organizations this might work. For others, like the American car industry, it can be dangerous. To be fair — in that industry anything can be dangerous.

The situation is similar in tennis, as Alan Fine of the Inner Game Organisation explains: "Some people wouldn't recognize an opportunity if it got up and hit them in the face. There's such an emphasis on stroke play in tennis. And I think it's true in other sports; people are so concerned to make sure they get the mechanics right they can't see, in an attackable sense, that there's a chance to close in on their opponent. In the business sense, we get people who are so concerned with getting all the things right that they lose sight of what the ultimate goal is. The ultimate goal is to be generating revenue in business. Yet I have seen people who are so busy on this kind of training-cum-management process that they've lost touch with the point of the whole thing."

INTERESTING OPPORTUNITY

It is sometimes claimed that a whole string of opportunities are constantly passing in front of every person, who may or may not be equipped to see them or to take advantage of them.

"I don't go looking [for opportunities]. I don't hunt. I try very hard to recognize when they're there. Most of the opportunities are countercyclical ones. ACC was an opportunity," recalls Robert Holmes à Court, "because all the conventional wisdom couldn't be obtained — it wasn't worth obtaining anyway." ACC was a company that it would have taken Holmes à Court years to build — an international network that had, in his eyes, failed to fulfill its potential because it had failed to utilize its resources. "Management problems were horrific, but I felt there was a way through. . . . I am attracted to the countercyclical — to solve that problem. So I am attracted to bad companies and difficult industries."

WHEN IS IT AN OPPORTUNITY?

It is interesting that in the world of films, Verity Lambert, who when interviewed was about to take up the post of head of production at EMI Films, does not see technical opportunity as a way forward:

"There are many talented, creative people in the [TV and film] industry and, on the other hand, there are technological changes afoot which could be seen to create a practical, realistic alternative to many of the now almost defunct cinema theaters: the invention of video, the advent of satellite television, etc.

"I agree that the changes in the industry will affect everything. But the first thing I thought about on being offered EMI was the fact that in this country there are many talented, creative film people, yet we don't really have a film industry. It seemed to me that the challenge of accepting the job was to have the opportunity of encouraging British talent, encouraging films to be made here, and, therefore, trying to recreate the film industry in Britain. So my first thought was, how do you get people back into the cinemas in this country and how do you make films which somehow or other can show that the British cinema is still alive and well?"

Since the days of the Ealing Comedy, when audiences flocked into the British cinemas, everybody has been looking for ways of rejuvenating the British film industry. There have been remarkable successes like the Oscar-winning films *Chariots of Fire* and *Gandhi*. It might seem that technology offers a way of getting films to people in ways other than the traditional cinema.

"These are different kinds of experiences: going to the cinema and seeing a movie with an audience is very different from seeing it on your television at home. I think that it is a good experience, provided one can make cinemas more attractive, make 'going out to the cinema' a bit more of an event. I'm not asking people to be in there every night."

(NOTE: Besides making films, EMI own their own cinemas. They own ABC.) "If you have a successful film, all your ancillary, back-end rights (which is cable, satellite, and everything) are improved."

But what if the industry is made to work the other way round — films are made for the "ancillary" media?

"Perhaps I'm being romantic about it, but there is something special about it, there's no question about that."

Is not one thing that is special about the cinema that it costs a lot of money?

"It does cost a lot of money. At the moment it costs a lot of money because it's dismal to go there. When cinemas were built — if you look at those poor sad cinemas that are closing, made into Bingo halls, or nothing — they were built as picture palaces. They were called picture palaces, and they were made in such a way that people wanted to go inside them. And it is interesting that in certain areas of France and Belgium where cinemas are being built now — modern, attractively made cinemas — that actually the cinema audiences are going up, not down. One of the reasons I think people don't go to the cinema in this country is — you're absolutely right — that it's terribly expensive and when you come out you want to be totally fumigated. You've queued in the rain when you don't have to. It's not a good experience."

Why don't you get rid of them, then?

"Well, I am going to be able to say it. Whether anyone listens to me or not is a different matter. And I *shall* say it. I mean, it is a very simple thing. Why can't you ring up and book seats and give your American Express card number in the same way as you do in the theater?"

But maybe somebody in your position could come in and say, OK, forget all that, we're going to turn them all over to something else, or get rid of them, or sell them off. We'll make far better films and employ new ways of getting them to people?

"I'd just be talking myself out of a job! I'm prepared to admit that when

I grew up I went to the cinema three times a week, as most kids did, and I loved the cinema. To me the idea that I can make cinema films is like a dream in a way. Perhaps I'm not being very realistic in that sense. I was brought up on the *Movie Annual of 1949* and things like that, on looking and saying, "There's Clark Gable," or whatever. I suppose I do have a very romantic attitude about it. But the other thing is that I cannot resist challenge. Yes, it would be very easy to go and say, 'Why don't you close all the cinemas and put money into something else? Why don't you make films for satellite, etc.?' But I think the point about it is — if you close down all the ABC Cinemas all over the country — you wouldn't actually make that much money out of them, because who would want to buy them? That's one thing."

We can see several influences here. One is the romantic view of the cinema based on childhood experience. Another is the pragmatic view that if the corporation owns cinemas, making them obsolete may not be a good idea. Then there is the view that if you take up an appointment to run a film division you should not seek to destroy its traditional base. None of these are very strong arguments. There are, however, two expressed arguments that do make sense. The first is that the experience of going to the movies is a different experience from watching a video film. The "going out" experience is all-important and the film experience (within reason) is secondary. (It is category buying again. Just as Sinclair may be selling home computers as "toys" (page 106) so cinemas are selling "going out".) The second point is that films in cinemas provide a much stronger publicity point than video films, and the consequent publicity enhances the value of the film when it is sold for video. In exactly the same way, a book published as a hardcover edition attracts more attention and reviews than if it comes out as a paperback in the first instance. As a consequence of this attention, the paperback rights can be sold for far more.

OPPORTUNISM

There is opportunity seeking and opportunity spotting. We often refer to opportunity spotting as "opportunism." Wait until the opportunity becomes clear and then jump in. American industry is excellent at this, but not as good at opportunity building as the Japanese. This may be the result of cultural differences or the pressure of stock analysis on quarterly profit figures, and hence the need to use opportunities rather than to make them.

Harry Helmsley: "Well, I really don't have to look for opportunities because they come to me. The main thing is to analyze them and see if it fits the yardstick and then dig in to see whether they gave you the right information."

There is nothing wrong with opportunity spotting — except that by this time the opportunity may have become visible to others as well.

OPPORTUNITY BUILDING

Opportunity building involves a particular concept (rather than just spotting an opportunity). Spotting a market opportunity may still involve the design of a concept to take advantage of that opportunity. Sometimes the concept is ready but the opportunity to try it out may not occur for some time. This was the case with Jarvis Astaire and his TV concept.

Jarvis Astaire introduced the idea of closed-circuit television to promote boxing matches in the U.K. "I wasn't powerful in boxing at the time. I was young — in relation to the people who were at the top of the field. What really made the difference was that the people at the top wanted to fight TV and I was prepared to marry television on my terms. All they did was resist, resist, resist. I said, if we work with television we will be able to make good use of boxing on TV. As a result I started the idea of arranging shows which could be televised the following night without any fears. This brought about closed-circuit television, which for five years I'd been trying to get someone at the Post Office (who control the lines in this country) to talk about.

"Like many ideas, I got this particular one at six o'clock in the morning. We were wanting to put on the World Light Heavyweight Championship between Terry Downs and Willy Pastrami. There was no venue in London available at the time that Pastrami was ready to come here and defend the title. The only venue was the Belle Vue in Manchester. This, of course, was hardly ideal for Downs, who was a great London fighter. It seemed we had no alternative. We did everything we could to find one and then one morning at six o'clock I woke up and said, 'This is the opportunity I've been waiting for!'

"I went to the Post Office and said here was this London boxer going to fight for the World Championship in Manchester. People supported him in thousands for several years. In fact he had been World Middleweight Champion, and lost it and then moved up to Light Heavyweight. To give you an idea of how the minds of these civil servants work, after five years of not even being able to find a person at the Post Office to discuss it with me, they immediately agreed to an experiment.

"Now I had to get a theater. None of the cinema people would listen to me. Then one day in the Mirabelle Restaurant, by sheer chance I ran into a man called Leslie Macdonell. He asked me what I was doing. I told him. He was in the theater business — running Moss Empires in those days — and he thought it was a fabulous idea. He phoned me back at four o'clock that afternoon and offered me the Phoenix Theatre. That was the first intercity sporting event in this country."

Astaire seized the moment and one thing led to another. "As luck would have it, it was a great fight; everything went off very well; we had a marvelous commentator — David Coleman (the BBC stopped him working for me after that because they felt a bit nervous). In fact, the following day I got a phone call from the Rank Organisation and from then on closed-circuit television was born. I then got the idea — once the first satellite was up — of bringing over a fight by satellite, and that was Cassius Clay and Floyd Patterson — November 1965 — from Las Vegas. I did the first satellite intercontinental show. We took the Odeon Leicester Square. I was worried whether people would come out in the middle of the night. In fact, people smashed the doors down trying to get in. I remember there was going to be a Royal Command Performance the following day, and there was a tremendous panic about getting the glass of the doors replaced. But they managed it!"

CREATIVE OPPORTUNITY: BUCKING THE TREND

Market awareness and market research are usually reckoned to be absolutely essential when developing a business. Yet in the new technology area there seem to be startling exceptions.

For inventors like Sir Clive Sinclair there can be no certainty, except perhaps in their terms, in their own eyes, that a market will exist for what may well be a revolutionary concept. However, Sinclair claims he sees a need even when others fail to perceive one.

For example, pocket calculators. "It always seemed to me very nice if you could have a calculator to put in your pocket," says Sir Clive Sinclair. "Of course it seems as obvious to us now too. But I remember when we did bring it out people said, 'Who on earth wants a calculator in their pocket?' " Does Sinclair, like Diane von Furstenberg in her quite different world of fashion, identify himself with his buyers? "Not always, no. For example, a personal computer is not something I want. It is designed to teach people programming and I don't want to learn programming. But I can see a lot of other people want to. The point about it was that when we got into the business, personal computers did exist. We had been designers in radionics and we had one under development, but the NEB didn't want to go ahead. But I believed there was a potential. I knew there was a market amongst the hobbiests for a low-cost personal computer and I believed there would be among the general public — that had never been shown to be the case. But I believed that it would only happen at a price well below anything that existed at the time. When we got into the business a computer cost about a £1,000; you might have been able to buy one for £500. But you can't market research. I don't believe you can do that at that stage. You can't go along to the man in the street and say, 'Here's a £100 computer.' He's not going to consider it — he'll probably dash to protect his wife from this lunatic!"

One rather unexpected interpretation of this phenomenon is that Sinclair is not in the electronics business as such but the "toy business." People buy pocket calculators and personal computers not because they need them but as amusing toys. The psychology of toy buying is very different from that of typewriter buying. In assessing opportunities, the "buying category" is of immense importance. This determines the psychology of buying. It also determines the price levels that will be acceptable.

Sometimes even when market surveys have been exercised, there is no guarantee that a new product or a new opportunity will succeed. Nolan Bushnell recalls: "We did a product called Video Music, and it was a thing that hooked up to your stereo and your television system and made pretty pictures while you were listening to the music. It was micro-processor-driven: a little thing that sat on top of your set. I don't doubt that you'd never heard of it. We did market surveys and it looked like it was an OK product, and we released parts for 25,000 or something like that, and ended up building about 10,000 of them before we went to the show and starting marketing it. It was dreadful! When the retail price was supposed to be $150, we sold about 20. We marked it down to about $99 and we sold another 20. We marked it down to $49 and maybe sold 50. We ended up liquidating the damn thing at $39.95. It turned out that most people don't have their stereos in the same room with the television. That was back at Atari [which Bushnell started and later sold to Warner for $28 million], and that was a major kind of fiasco."

The idiosyncratic approach to opportunity can work in the world of finance. Jim Rogers: "Other people in the business say we were idiosyncratic or eccentric or went against the trend. It's extremely easy to follow the crowd in anything, whether it's hamburgers, cars, books, anything — easiest thing in the world to follow the trend, but it's the fastest way to bankruptcy. Nobody gets rich following the trend. It's respectable and everybody sitting round the pub says, 'I'm doing this,' and you say, 'I'm doing this too,' and the third guy says, 'I'm doing it too.' But that is no way to get rich; it's a fast way to bankruptcy no matter what the field is.

"My ideas came from my reading and from my judgment mainly. I would look at things and I would say, 'This is not the way it is in the real world.'

"The way I bought any company was usually cynical. I can remember buying oil stock in 1972, drilling stocks, to be precise (companies that have the rigs and drill for oil). This business had been deteriorating for fifteen years, and I remember this guy saying, 'We don't know how long it is going to continue to deteriorate, but we're going to try to hang in there to the very end.' And I said, 'That's the best news I've every heard.' If the business has been deteriorating for fifteen years it means either they're not going to look for oil ever again, or before too much longer things are going to get really great. For a lot of reasons I could see that the country was going to run out of natural gas.

"Everyone had the same facts as I did. It wasn't as though I had some pipeline into heaven. I could see the reason there was an energy crisis was not because of OPEC. OPEC had tried to raise prices for fifteen years, and nobody had ever listened. OPEC got together every year and said, 'This year we're going to raise prices, folks,' and everybody would say, 'OK, glad to hear it,' and the retail prices would stay exactly where they were.

"What really happened was that the American government, in the 1950s — the Supreme Court, in fact — made a decision that the U.S. government could set the price of natural gas. The government set the price of gas at such an incredibly low price that it wasn't worth selling.

"When I used to drive through Texas as a kid, I used to see these huge flares at night. When you were drilling oil wells in the '50's in America you'd pump out the oil, and gas would come out too, but since the government wouldn't let you sell the gas at an economic price, it would be burned. They would burn it to get rid of it, because it was cheaper to burn it than it was to sell it, because selling it costs you money. So they burned enormous amounts of gas in the '50's and '60's, and the result was that by the '70's or the late '60's, all these gas companies were running out of gas. At the same time, my partner and I said, 'Well, if nobody's looking for gas because gas is not economic, then the price of gas is going to have to go up, eventually (somebody someday is going to have to pay someone to get the gas the country needs).' Then I discovered (I remember the day) . . . I remember reading an *Annual Report* from one of the drilling companies that said — things will be tough, folks; here's a chart showing that the number of people looking for gas and hiring drilling rigs has gone down since 1956 (this was 1971) and they'd been going down for fifteen years. And I said to myself 'That sounds good; here we are at least fifteen years closer to the bottom of the market than we used to be. It may not be the bottom yet, but we're getting closer and probably very close.' So I went to see all these guys in the drilling business. They said, 'It's hopeless; a lot more people are going to go bankrupt.' I went back and said, 'The world is running out of gas because they're burning it off; the price is too low; people are going out of business, and that has got to change.' So, we bought an enormous amount of gas stocks and drilling stocks in '71, '72, and '73. And lo and behold, finally OPEC tried it again in '73, in the war, and it worked! And it wasn't because OPEC did it, but because the world was ready. There was no gas left."

This is a classic example of both the "climate change" type of opportunity and also the "undervalued" asset type. Sometimes an asset is valued correctly in the light of existing techology, but a technology change can greatly increase the value. When the price of gold rose, it became worthwhile to rework the old gold-mine tips with the new technology that could extract gold from what had been regarded as waste. In the 1930s C. J. Levine floated on the Adelaide stock market a company that was going to extract gold from unusable sites in New Guinea. The sites were unusable because there was no way of getting a gold dredger to them. Levine's idea was to use the new Junker aircraft. The dredgers were designed to be broken down into bits, and each bit was ferried to the site in a Junker. The scheme was a great success. Any eye for what technology makes possible is not the same as an eye for new technology itself as an opportunity. The latter can be a high risk area, but the former is more certain because the market is known.

WHY DO SOMETHING DIFFERENT?

Almost the opposite of innovation is the *Son of Lassie* trend. So we have *Airplane II*, *Superman II*, and *Superman III*. There is the story of the television program buyer who thumped the table and said: 'What we really need are some brand new platitudes.' In other words, something that is new, so long as it is exactly the same as we had before. There are two strands of logic in this attitude. The first strand is that if you have got the ingredients right, then you should repeat the formula. The second strand is that the public knows what it is getting. When David Puttnam tried to raise backing money for *Local Hero* after his success with the Oscar-winning and money-making *Chariots of Fire*, American investors said: 'Why do something different?' 'What about *Chariots of Fire II?*' " The opposite view is put by Verity Lambert, head of production at EMI: "Once you start working to a formula, you actually maximize risk." I do not believe this is always true. The most steady success in publishing is that of romantic fiction. Here the formula is worked out extremely tightly (with many different categories). The public buy the books. There are times when people want novelty and times when they want comfort. There is comfort, not novelty, in your garden and in your living room. There are times when you want to meet new people and times when you want to see old friends.

For designer or stylist, there is virtue in giving people what they expect and danger in becoming stagnant.

THE "ME-TOO" PHILOSOPHY

Lord Sainsbury revolutionized retailing by following the example of others elsewhere. "Being old and having a long perspective, I have seen revolutionary changes in the retail food trade," he admitted to the *Observer* newspaper. "Since the last war there's been a tremendous rise in the standard of living and an increase in the range of foods, which made it impossible for the old counter shop to retain a sufficiently large range of choice.

"People used to shop three times a week because there were no refrigerators, let alone freezers. Now the bulk of the shopping is done on Friday or Saturday with the pay packet. The change started in 1949 when a colleague of mine and I went to the States, basically to see the development of frozen foods, which was in its infancy. We visited a large number of supermarkets in New York, Boston, Buffalo, Philadelphia, and both came to the conclusion that this was the future pattern.

"One reason I retired at sixty was the belief that the older you get, the more reluctant you are to change, because you won't see the result."

When Rubik's cube was a big hit, all sorts of people jumped onto the bandwagon to produce the same or different cubes. When electronic games became the rage, most of the toymakers jumped in there as quickly as possible. When a pharmaceutical company has success with a drug, then all the other pharmaceutical corporations try to produce their own version of it (for example, with the beta-blockers).

NICHE STRATEGY

The opposite of the "me-too" strategy is the "niche" strategy. Find some small area and do it so well that no one will be tempted into that market (the market is too small and it would be too expensive to catch up with you). Being able to spot undervalued assets (as with the Slater Strategy) is also a classic method — especially for financiers.

Jim Slater's technique has been described in many ways, but his own version is the most vivid. He called it the Zulu principle. Not many people know much about Zulus, he would point out. But a lot of people make it their life's work to know all there is to know about, say, England or America. So it is very hard to make much impact as an expert about those countries. But if you were to find out only a fair amount about Zulus, you could probably become the world's top expert on the subject. There's that much less competition, you see. In his case, the Zulus were obscure little companies that had been ignored by the stock market but had hidden potential. His weapons were balance sheets and the statistical cards published by Extel.

Again, Pergamon Press has been built up on a deliberately created series of monopolies. Robert Maxwell, an excellent linguist, realized that the scientists he liked mixing with had few means of communicating with their colleagues and rivals around the world. Two people might claim the credit for the same piece of research, because neither could be sure who was first. So he published a chain of journals on the most abstruse scientific subjects. It was a variation of Slater's Zulu principle. Each journal became the world's forum for one narrow topic. All the academics in a certain field compete to have their articles published by Pergamon, often at no fee. Mere publication gives them kudos and respect from their peers. In turn, every university studying a subject covered by the *Pergamon Journal* has to take out a subscription from the one and only supplier: Pergamon. Maxwell charges very high prices, in some cases over £1,000 a year, for a few issues of one title. The print runs are relatively low, but even so, the profit margins are fat. And any institution entering a field of study within Pergamon's orbit must also buy back numbers from Maxwell.

Jim Slater developed a written strategy for opportunism. At its crudest, Slater was looking for undervalued companies — as most stock market investors believe they're doing. But it is a fact that companies can suddenly hit an upturn, and it can take some months for this to be reflected in its share price as the word filters through to the city. Slater tried to devise a system which enabled him to spot when that was about to take place. In the search for the alchemist's stone he refined his search into nine rules for companies whose shares were about to go up. According to Charles Raw, the author of *Slater Walker: An Investigation of a Financial Phenomenon*, these were:

1. The dividend yield must be at least 4%.
2. Equity earnings must have increased in at least four out of the last five years.
3. Equity earnings must have at least doubled over the last four years.
4. The latest chairman's statement must be optimistic.
5. The company must be in a reasonable liquid position.
6. The company must not be vulnerable to exceptional factors.
7. The shares must have a reasonable asset value.
8. The company should not be family controlled.
9. The shares should have votes.

Items 5 to 7 are obviously a matter of opinion, although Slater himself liked to see companies have an asset backing per share which was comfortably higher than the market price of the shares. This element was to come to the fore when he graduated from buying shares to buying companies, because he would often sell surplus assets of the firms he had taken over, leaving only the profitable parts of the business. It was this technique which led to the charge of asset-stripping.

PLAY OUR OWN GAME

After a while most successful people tend to look for opportunities in areas with which they are familiar. Lord Pennock, executive chairman of BICC and past deputy chairman of ICI, seeks his opportunities cautiously but deliberately in the new technological boom: "You can't stand still. Either you're going up or you're going down. The bad thing about Britain is that people have this feeling, 'Well, right now if it's been unpleasant, at least we've done it. And now we've got it right, now it's going to be OK.' Life is not like that. All the time it's changing, and all the time you've got to be a little bit ahead of the change. If you get too far ahead of the change, you'll make a mess of it; you'll get your head chopped off. But if you don't respond to the change, you'll also get you head chopped off.

"The new opportunities always have to be related to the business, and the things you know something about. When I came here (to BICC), there was a proposition to acquire a sizable electronics business from America about which we knew very little, because we are cable makers. I said, 'Look, let me tell you the story of the twelve biggest mistakes we made in ICI . . .' (which were all to do with going into things which we knew nothing about, and thinking we can do better than the people who have been running these things for years). '. . . . Now, this electronics business may be all that you say — it's expanding at 15 percent, and so on — but if it depends upon two guys who built it up from scratch, suppose they walk out?' 'Oh, well,' they said, 'we can pick some other good people; we can always get managers.' But is there in fact anybody who could take charge? Nobody. So I said, 'Forget it.'

"But immediately, we then went on to say — what we have to do is to get into things which, like the electronic business, are going to grow fast but are based on something we do know something about. So what do we do? We make cables. So then we said, 'What about the components on the end of the cable before it goes into the computer? What about connectors? What about power service units?' Transforming power — before it goes into electronics. Now that's a business we do know something about. On the one hand we'll have the advantage of growing as fast as the computer business, as every computer has to have them; on the other hand, it doesn't involve the massive research into computers, about which we know nothing anyway. So, we get into a business that grows as fast as electronics, which we know something about, and doesn't require an enormous amount of research. The same technical people can cope. And that's what we've done. We acquired two businesses last year in America in the connector and power service unit business and they're coming along quite well. But you've got to seize opportunities — you can't stand still. If we just said, 'Well, cables are doing all right now,' we would have failed. You've got to get the new opportunities, but they have to be related to things you know about. Business has to be dynamic. You have to respond to change. Generally most nations and most people don't like change, but in Britain we are particularly resistant to change. We have a great history and it makes us want to live in the past. We spend £4 million getting a sixteenth-century wreck up off the bottom of the ocean bed, and it's national news for weeks. Famous men like the Earl of Mountbatten and Winston Churchill plan their funerals five years before they die, to ensure the traditions are preserved: we are a nation which just loves to have things like they used to be."

Moving from managing sports stars and personalities through the media, Mark McCormack was offered the opportunity to take charge of the Pope's visit to England. "It was dealing in a wholly different area, dealing with different kinds of people, different levels of people, different kinds of manufacturers; some of the principles were the same, but it was a hard job. The Vatican wanted something that was commercial. They wanted to make money tastefully and professionally, have it controlled, and feel confident it was being done right. If you're doing any kind of a one-off where you bury your manpower into something that will have an end, you have to wonder whether the long-range benefits of that diversion would outweigh the disadvantages."

Here is a true story of a poker game in hand in 1977, where a player sought opportunity in an apparently related but in truth quite a different game from that in which he had expertise. John Graham: "It began as a quiet dinner party, just six of us, and then somebody suggested a friendly game of poker, small stakes, limit raises. The crucial point is that we were playing dealer's choice: that is, the dealer could nominate his favorite variation of poker, draw or stud.

"We played along for a couple of hours, with no huge deals, and no particular winners or losers. Somebody was about £40 ahead, somebody else about the same down. A few people went home, and after midnight there were just three of us left. We were playing £1 ante, £2 initial bets, and maximum raises up to half the value of the pot. The biggest pots so far had been about £30 to £40.

"The game went backwards and forwards between the three of us, and then one player at his turn announced a stud variation known as 7-27. He knew the game (obviously), and so did I; the third party did not. . . .

"Now in 7-27 you get one card down, and can then draw one-by-one as many others as you like face-up, with a round of betting between each draw. The object is to get your hand to total either 7 or 27, or as near as possible. Picture cards count 1, aces 1 or 11. There are usually two winners; the player nearest 7 and the player nearest 27. The critical difference between this stud variation and any other is that there can be an enormous number of rounds of betting. The game only ends when all the players have been offered a card to draw and have refused. A player who is initially dealt an 8 and a king (total 8½) will often go on to try to make 27, and with picture cards counting only ½, this can take ten cards or more.

"What happened was electrifying. I was dealt an ace down and a 6 up. Perfect. I can't be beaten. I'm going to win half this pot, but I'm also going to let others do the betting. The dealer was showing a 9 up, and the third party a king.

"Dealer at once began to draw, aiming at 27; third party took no cards. After nine rounds of betting, dealer showed (?) -9-K-A-Q-2-4-J-Q-8, totaling 26 plus his hidden card. Third party had been making most of the play in the betting, but now dealer bet the maximum, and we all followed. The pot was now worth about £600, and third party was in deep trouble.

"He was looking at me (6 plus a hidden card), and at his own hand (which happened to be a hidden 7 plus king), and at the dealer (26 plus hidden card). He made a terrible mistake and began to draw cards himself, abandoning the attempt to win low and setting off after 27. He reckoned that that last 8 had taken the dealer way over the top, and that a score anywhere between 25½ and 28½ would win. Maybe he hadn't registered the dealer's maximum bet; more likely he read it as a bluff to get him out quick. The dealer might easily have assumed that third party and I would simply compete for the low and that he would be unopposed for high.

"So, third party keeps drawing cards, with a round of betting in between each draw, and when the smoke finally cleared he was busted clean over the top. I obviously won the low, and the dealer had an ace in the hole for a perfect 27. We must have had at least twenty rounds of betting (compared to two rounds in draw poker, and four or five in most stud variations), and the pot stood at £6,000! Having never even bet a total of more than £10 on any single pot over the previous three hours, third party had just lost £2,000 on one deal. Why? Because he played a game both his opponents knew, but which he didn't.

"Of course I was lucky to be dealt a pat hand. But I knew the insidious nature of 7-27, and had already decided to draw precisely one card and aim only at 7. If with three cards I had been more than half a point off 7, I would have folded there and then.

"I was gratified to read the following in a marvelous book called *Play Poker to Win* by 'Amarillo Slim' Preston, the first poker World Champion: 'If you're not exactly on seven, I'd say get rid of the hand, unless you look around the board and see that everyone's face card is seven or greater. . . . A lot of people who have passed seven go on and try to make that twenty-seven, but I say that's for the suckers. . . .

"If you're sitting on a seven, don't let on about your hand: When people bet, just call, and if people raise, don't play back — just call — because this is another one of those cases where you've got a cinch. There's no reason to run anybody out who may want to draw. . .

"But my feeling is that this game is best suited for old women and little kids."

"My feeling, too, and sure enough, you don't find serious poker players playing 7-27. It's nice to know I played the hand same way Slim would have . . . if only I could say that about all the other hands in my life."

With a problem we look for a solution: with an opportunity we look for a benefit. So the assessment of payoff or benefit is crucial. The second aspect is feasibility. Feasibility implies two questions: is it possible? does it fit our resources? We can language-cheat and say that there has to be benefit and benefit (taking "bene" in the Italian sense of "good" and hence deriving "good-fit").

The pursuit of an opportunity means the commitment of time and resources. The pursuit of an opportunity carries with it the risk of failure. The pursuit of one particular opportunity means that other opportunities cannot be pursued. There are times when a person or a corporation assesses that harder and harder work in the current direction is not going to add up to much. There is therefore a need to find a new direction, a new opportunity. At other times a booming market is seen to offer opportunities all round, and there is a desire to get in there and have a piece of the action. For an individual there may be the calculating wish to plot a path to success.

For an opportunity to work out, everything has to be in place. This means that the more things that are in place already, the better it is. So established markets and established channels are a help. There should be as few "ifs" as possible. A series of "ifs" makes the opportunity very "iffy" and liable to holdups (as so often happens with technology-based opportunities). The more things that are under the control of the opportunity taker, the better. A financier playing the stock market can make his buy-and-sell decisions as he wishes. Someone planning a factory in California may have to get dozens of permits before he can even start (and each of these may take an uncertain amount of time).

So in the end it comes down to two things: feasibility and benefits. Affecting both of these factors is the matter of "risk." There will be uncertainty about the feasibility. There will be uncertainty about the benefits. It is a willingness to take the risk that determines whether someone takes the opportunity.

TACTICS

1. No corporation is forced to look for opportunities until it is too late to do so.

2. With a problem, you look for a solution: with an opportunity, you look for benefits.

3. The two key things in opportunity assessment are: benefits and feasibility.

4. There are two sorts of risk in every opportunity: uncertainty about feasibility and uncertainty about the benefits.

5. You can hang back and wait for an opportunity to emerge and then rush in to take advantage of it, but other people will be there too.

6. The safest sort of opportunity is something already successful that can be copied and made better or cheaper. The market and buying patterns are already in place.

7. Sometimes an opportunity in the market awaits the development of a concept to turn it into success.

8. The simplest form of opportunity is to buy something at less than its value and then to operate or sell it at its true value.

9. Management and problem-solving are maintenance functions. They are not sufficient in a changing or a competitive world. Conceptual thinking is needed in addition.

10. There are opportunities that are available to everyone and opportunities that particularly fit your style and resources.

8

How to Generate New Ideas

T H E   P L A Y E R S:

United States: **Nolan Bushnell · Dr. Nathan Kline · Alex Kroll · Mark McCormack · Jerald Newman · James B. Rogers, Jr.**

United Kingdom and International: **David Bailey · Lord Robens · Sir Clive Sinclair · Sting**

For Sir Clive Sinclair, ideas are never a problem. "I've consciously got a lot of things in the back of my mind that I'd like to be able to do (I'd like to be able to make a vertical-takeoff car to have in the back garden, but I don't know how to do it), and then one day, 'Oh, crikey, yes!' I can do that. The labs might have come up with something. I might have a combination of ideas, a major breakthrough. A new material might arrive that suddenly makes something possible. Or a new process. It's constantly playing it through and trying all the combinations."

How important are ideas to the successful person? Where do ideas come from? What is creativity?

There are people whose success has been based on a single brilliant idea. There are others who have had a succession of brilliant ideas (like Sir Clive Sinclair). There are others who have not had any definite new idea but have tackled their problems in a generally creative manner. There are others who do not really seem to have used creativity at all: they have used a logical approach in a field that responds to that approach and they have just got on with it.

Creativity is exciting and it is glamorous. Probably the worst possible route to being a successful person is to sit around and wait for the brilliant creative idea that is going to make your fortune. It seems an attractive route because the idea is going to be so very good that it will do all the work for you. In practice it does not happen that way. The idea may indeed be brilliant, but no one realizes its brilliance. The inventor of the game Monopoly had a very hard time selling the idea. The idea may be brilliant, but somehow it does not make money (loss of control, competition, etc.). Having a good idea is only one way to success. There will always be stories of how a simple person had a marvelous idea and made a fortune. It can happen and it does happen. It is not, however, the most reliable route. You may also never have this wonderful idea in the first place.

There are people who have a relatively simple idea which is not really new, but they apply it in so thorough a manner that it leads to success. There are people who enter a field without any new concept, but their strategy is so sound and so well executed that they succeed. There is also the sort of creativity that does not give rise to any marvelous idea but that provides at every instant a creative reaction or response.

The reasons that creativity is so often picked out as a vital ingredient in success is that it offers a way of distinguishing those who are successful from those who are not. These two people are equally able: that one is successful because he had a creative idea. The truth is that success involves very much more than having a creative idea, and it is usually the general ability that differs between the two people and not the creative idea.

A forest would not exist unless each tree had started out as a seed, but a sack of seeds does not make a forest.

Making ideas work is every bit as important as having the idea in the first place.

A creative idea is one route to success. So is having a sound strategy and carrying it out effectively. So is the ability to spot an opportunity. So is natural talent. So is luck. So is the combination of aesthetic judgment and executive ability. So is the ability to make deals. So is the creation and motivation of a powerful team. And there are many more routes.

Having put creativity into a reasonable perspective, we can now look at the origin of ideas.

In business a powerful source of ideas is copying. Many a European entrepreneur has made a fortune by going to the U.S.A. and studying what is happening in some field over there (see "Opportunity-Seeking," page 111). Sometimes it happens the other way round. Another example of copying is the powerful "me-too" idiom. Someone is having a success in a field, so you jump in there too in order to share that success. From a creativity point of view, we may despise copying — but it does work. Many more people have made fortunes out of the "time-sharing" concept for holiday homes than the person who first thought of the idea.

Many more people have made fortunes out of fast-food franchises than the person who first thought of the idea. Many more people have made fortunes out of multilevel marketing than the person who first thought of the idea. Insurance is but a concept which at one time was new. Many people continue to make fortunes out of it. You may copy an idea and do it better. You may copy an idea and add some new sparkle to it or apply it to a new market segment. You may copy the bare bones of the idea and apply it to a different business. Your design, your judgment, and your effectiveness will determine what happens next. Would you try to franchise spaghetti sandwiches?

Let us acknowledge the real value of copying, transferring, adapting, or modifying ideas, and let us move on to the creation of really new ideas.

CREATING NEW IDEAS

There are creative people who are always sparking off new ideas. As youngsters they have always tried things out; making inventions, doing harebrained things. They have the sort of frame of mind that is caricatured as the mad inventor. Please note that a creative person may actually be very rigid and only willing to look at things in one way: his (or her) way. These creative people can be the bloody-minded inventors or they can be the bubbling dabblers who hop from one idea to another.

I have put forward this caricature as an extreme. Many people have a creative nature which is much more focused and practical than the caricature. I want to imply that the motivation for creativity is in their nature.

There are also the quietly creative people. They may not be any good at generating ideas, but in any situation they are always willing to look for alternatives. Such people are willing to listen to ideas and to explore ideas. They have a constructive approach.

Moving along the spectrum, we next come to people who fully acknowledge the value of creativity and who want to be creative. They find it difficult, however, to spark a new idea or to react in a creative manner to ideas they meet. The will is there, but the nature and the habits are not.

Then there is the person for whom creativity is simply not a value at all. He (or she) sees no point in creativity. Success is a matter of doing things properly and well.

Finally, there is the person who abhors the very notion of creativity. He (or she) regards it as pretentious, messy, unreliable and an excuse for sloppiness. Such a person is intolerant of the ambiguity that may be required for creativity. Logic and precision are quite sufficient and much more controllable.

So long as we continue to regard creativity as a gift which is made up of equal mixtures of rebelliousness and inspiration, then there are going to be people who do not understand it, do not like it, and do not want to use it.

But once we come to look upon creativity as a "logical process," all that can change. That is what I have set out to do in my books on lateral thinking. Once we can understand the nature of the information universe in which creativity works, then we can start to understand the logic of the process and go on to devise tools that use that logic. The problem is that the universe of information in which creativity (an all-human perception) works is totally different from our usual information universe (math, logic, computers). The universe of perception is that of self-organizing pattern-making and pattern-using systems. There is no mystery about such systems. They can be described and their behavior predicted (as I started to do in my book *The Mechanism of Mind*, which was published as long ago as 1969). Perception works by allowing a particular sequence of experience to create patterns which then organize future experience. Too often we are satisfied with perceptions and concepts which make poor use of available experience. What we need are ways of cutting across patterns in order to find better ones (hence the term "lateral" thinking).

THE VALUE OF A NEW PERSPECTIVE

Some of the attitudes and processes of lateral thinking have been used instinctively by creative people. Most creative people realize the "escape" value of getting a different perspective or standing back in order to look at things from a distance.

Nolan Bushnell: "I oscillate between being a morning person and evening person, and when I'm an evening person I'm much more creative. When I'm a morning person I'm a doer, and accomplish fantastic amounts of stuff. A significant number of my big-money ideas have occurred to me while on vacation or on foreign travel. At work you're on automatic pilot a lot of the time. But you go to France, and although you're struggling with the language, you're struggling with the hotel, you're struggling with the transportation, you do have leisure. The telephone isn't ringing and there aren't people hounding you, so you have time to correlate. Maybe a foreign language forces you to use different parts of your mind. If language is the vessel of thought, maybe a different language structure helps you to unlock other lobes of your mind — other senses. You're not used to dealing with such-and-such in the same way, and you see (understand) and say different things. Or maybe it's just that you get away and you get a fresh perspective. You know, you see the forest from a thousand miles away."

THE CREATIVITY OF INNOCENCE

It is obvious that innocence gives courage to an entrepreneur who does not yet know the difficulties in a field. Innocence can also give rise to a special type of creativity. "Some of my earlier pictures are as good as I'm doing now. Some may even be better — more naïve, more innocent. Maybe my pictures are sometimes too considered now. It's a valid thing that I do think about sometimes": David Bailey.

Experience has many plus points, but the one minus point is the loss of innocence. There are two sorts of creativity. The first is the creativity of innocence. Because you do not know how something ought to be done, you are able to find an original way.

Coming new into a field allows the creativity of innocence, since one is not bogged down by the baggage of that field.

Lord Robens, ex-chairman of the Coal Board: "It was picks and shovels in 1960, and 98 percent was mechanized by the time I left ten years later. That was my big thing. But there had been plenty of people who understood coal. But you needed someone from outside who hadn't got coal in his veins to be able to see the thing properly."

An innovator comes into a field and sees that the way things are done is inefficient and only done in such a way because of how it evolved historically. Railways were required (by unions) to retain a stoker long after the switch from steam to electricity. Innovation in such areas, especially in the service field, is a powerful route to success. Successful innovations will, of course, be quickly imitated.

Dr. Nathan Kline: "I went to medical school with no preparation at all. That year they ran an experiment and asked for volunteers among liberal arts majors with no science background. Anybody in his right mind would not have gone. We were in competition with people who had started studying for pre-med in kindergarten. I graduated gloriously in the lowest 10 percent of the class. But in the end it paid off, because it meant that I was able to approach medical subjects in, as it turned out, an unconventional way. I didn't know it was unconventional because I didn't know what the conventional way was. So it meant that I was able to transfer concepts, frames of references, and universes of discourse from philosophy and psychology and English to produce new gestalts that others hadn't seen."

It is not that outsiders know the rules and choose to ignore them. Often the outsider, or newcomer to a field, does not even know the rules. The newcomer may not know why something cannot be done.

Most design teams and professors of aeronautics knew that man-powered flight was impossible because the horsepower produced by a man would always be inadequate to lift a plane off the ground. Paul Mac-Cready did not know it was impossible, so he set out to do it and did it.

Sir Clive Sinclair has told me that when he enters a new field he reads just enough to get a feel for that field, to get the idiom of the field. If he were to read more, he would be constrained by the concepts and directions already established in that field, and innovation (and innocence) would be impossible. So he puts down the books and does his own thinking.

This raises yet another dilemma. How much experience do you need in a field and how much will constrain you? Some experience is necessary in order to know the pieces with which one is playing, but too much may result in sterility — unless it is accompanied by a strong creative attitude. There are two basic sorts of creativity. The first is the creativity of innocence: doing something in a new way because you do not know the old way. The second is the creativity of escape: doing something in a new way because you have succeeded in escaping from the old way — perhaps through the deliberate use of lateral thinking.

The practical point is that you do not have to know all there is to know about a field before you have an idea in that field. Get to know the general idiom. Create your new idea. Then check out the new idea.

THE CREATIVITY OF ESCAPE

The second sort of creativity is that of escape. We do know how things are usually done, but we manage to escape from that. For such escape we need provocation and some of the other attitudes and tools of lateral thinking. For innocence we need only innocence. Unfortunately, innocence is a sister of stupidity, ignorance, naïveté, and other things we would rather be without. Groucho Marx summed this up by saying that his brother was an amateur brain surgeon. Some artists manage to preserve a sense of wonder, which allows them to combine the virtues of experience with the perceptions of innocence.

The creativity of escape means escaping from the usual way of doing things or the usual way of looking at things.

Sting: "I think businessmen can and should be creative. I think society should be creative. One of my maxims is that society needs to be realized and not controlled. Most of the rules in society tend to restrict creativity to a safe level, and it's only rare individuals who manage to escape that handicap."

James B. Rogers, Jr.: "I heard someone describe me recently as 'He always goes against the trend, which is a very difficult thing to do.' You see, it's easy to follow the crowd. It's extremely easy to follow the crowd in anything, whether it's hamburgers, cars, books, anything, easiest thing in the world to follow the trend, but it's the fastest way to bankruptcy. Nobody gets rich following the trend. It's respectable, and everybody sitting round the pubs says, 'I'm doing this,' and you say, 'I'm doing this too,' and the third guy says, 'I'm doing it too.' But that is no way to get rich; it is a fast way to bankruptcy no matter what the field is. If you look at a stock that everybody in the city of Wall Street is buying, and everybody has good things to say about it, you say, 'Wait a minute; maybe something is wrong there or maybe something is about to go wrong.' To me the fact that everybody loves a thing means that it's very expensive and maybe something is wrong. And if you look, not always but sometimes, you will find 'Aha! This is what they've all been missing.' Just like Sotheby's — a perfect example, because this market had been booming for years, then suddenly they started to overexpand; they were opening everywhere. Enormous sums of money were being spent. They were adding staff like there was no tomorrow. If you could see that maybe they were wrong, you would sell that company short because you knew it was going to be a disaster. Everybody in the City loved Sotheby's; they thought it was the most wonderful thing since sliced bread, until I sold them short."

Jerald Newman: "I think being creative and looking beyond the — let's say, the normal traditional views of things is most important. I think the biggest thing is when a problem is brought to me, and people feel that they've reached the end of the trail; they don't know what to do; they're usually looking within the box, they're not looking outside the box."

I would almost offer the following advice as an axiom. If you want to make a fortune, look at fields with a traditionally high profit margin: you can be almost sure that this will have protected the field from new thinking for a long time. So get in there and do some new thinking.

HOW TO MAKE THE ESCAPE

The key point about lateral thinking is that concepts, perceptions, and structures evolve over time and are a summary of history rather than a blueprint for the future. In the mind, this is due to the self-organizing nature of the brain, which is designed as a pattern-making recognition system. So we may have to cut across and break out of patterns in order to put things together in a new way. Provocation is an essential part of lateral thinking, and there are various specific techniques such as the random-word technique (which is now used by most major advertising agencies throughout the world).

The logic of provocation shows very clearly the difference between our normal information universe and the information universe of a patterning system. In our normal universe there should be a reason for saying something. There should be a reason for making a mark in a certain place on a piece of paper. With provocation, this is not so at all. I have defined provocation in the following way. *There may not be a reason for saying something until after it has been said.* The point is that the provocation allows a different entry point, and this allows us to use different patterns; the value of these patterns then justifies the provocation.

I invented the new word "po" (which can be taken to stand for provocation operation) in order to indicate that the statement being made was intended as a provocation and to be used as a provocation. In the following quotation from Sting we can see this process working. The title of the song becomes the provocation. In this case the title has "turned up." In other cases the provocation can be produced deliberately.

"Initially the essential caucus of a song comes through inspiration. I don't sit down at the piano at nine o'clock or nine-thirty in the morning to write a song. I wait until the creative side of my brain mentions an idea, suggests a line for me. I write backwards — I write from song titles. Song titles usually coincide with what is called the 'hook line' in the trade. 'Don't Stand too Close to Me' came to me as I was walking along and simply struck me as a good line; it also linked up with an idea I had had for a long time about sexuality in the classroom, which also linked with my love of a book by Nabokov called *Lolita*. What really happened in the creative process was in the relaxation of walking — three separate ideas clicked together.

"I think the brain goes through different stages. The conscious brain is very formal and ideas don't often veer off-course. They stick, stay in their own way. But when you relax, your unconscious takes over and links things up — look at dreams, for examples. Then I do start to finish and click; ideas that were formerly totally separate click together into a synthesis which is something new. So I had those three ideas in my head at the same time, and some electric charge, or whatever, put them together.

"I do go through the writer's block; everyone does. What I've learned to do is control it. I realize that to worry about it only makes it worse. So, I go through periods of intake as far as experience goes; then I go through periods of output. Right at this moment I'm going through a period of intake (which I used to call a writer's block). There's just so much going on in my outside life that my unconscious is absorbing it. I mean, your brain does have two sides: it has a left side and a right side. One is involved in analysis, logic, and strict things; the other is the creative side. It is when those things meet that you have an idea. The toil comes later. Then I sit down at the piano with the idea and begin to join things up, and that is tough work."

Dr. Nathan Kline, the American psychiatrist, explains his way of generating ideas: "If I don't get there headed straight, maybe I get there by zigzagging or jumping over the problem. The great changes in science have all been not the result of a particular discovery but the result of a shifted frame of reference, seeing things in a new gestalt, so the ability to play with things — how about if you change the rules and play the game this way — is very important. It's that ability to shift your frame of reference. The fact that in a sense it's a game doesn't mean the consequences don't have great meaning and that you don't work at it, but when you deal with the framework of the theory you have to be a little whimsical."

Shifting the frame of reference is shifting the frame of perception. It is extremely difficult to do that by an effort of will. Sometimes an experiment provides the trigger, sometimes a remark or a chance event. If we do not want to wait for such things, then we can try to do it through deliberate provocation (which may take the form of what Dr. Kline calls "being a little whimsical").

Mistakes have also been a useful source of creativity. They provide a type of provocation. *The essential point of provocation is that we create an unstable situation from which we can then move forward to a new perception or a new idea.*

Alex Kroll: "I had my own mathematical system, which makes no sense to anybody who knows. It follows no pattern for arriving at answers. When people add, I subtract. When people divide, I multiply, but I get to the same point!"

The processes of humor are the same as those of lateral thinking. The logic of humor arises from the logic of patterning systems. The "impossible point" of humor is similar to the use of a provocation. The punchline in humor is similar to the insight in lateral thinking. Computers cannot laugh because they are not yet structured as patterning systems.

The incidences of humor and creativity are totally interlocked. People that are funny are already creative because they see the improbable and the upside-down logics. It is one of the things we actually look for; these people who have a finely gauged sense of humor are likely to be most creative.

The way the brain makes sense of the outside world is to allow the incoming information to organize itself into patterns. These patterns then tend to organize future input and the way we see things. All this is immensely useful for ordinary life: the brain is designed to be brilliantly uncreative. Our normal mode of perception is based on judgment. Judging what pattern is appropriate to use in the present situation. Judging whether what we see fits the pattern we are seeking. So it should be. In lateral thinking there is a different idiom. It is the idiom of "movement." Movement has a forward effect. Judgment takes us back to existing patterns. Movement takes us forward to new patterns. We normally look at an idea and judge whether it will work or not. With "movement" we look at an idea to see how we can move forward from it — hoping eventually to arrive at a useful new idea.

If I said that motor car wheels should be square you would judge that to be a silly idea. But if I said, "po, car wheels should be square" then you ought to treat it as a provocation and ought to try to use "movement" to go forward. The following line of thinking might emerge. As the square wheel rotated, the vehicle would rise up on the corner of the square. This would make for a bumpy ride. If, however, the suspension contracted to counter this rise, there might be a smoother ride. This concept of a variable suspension leads on to another idea. Imagine a vehicle with three pairs of wheels. In front of the vehicle is a set of jockey or "feeler" wheels, which sense the bumps on the ground. This information is fed back into a microchip which also calculates in the speed of the vehicle. When a pair of wheels comes to the bump (or individual wheels) the suspension adjusts or lifts that wheel clear of the bump. We now have a vehicle which "flows" over the ground. This makes for a more stable ride (as for weapon systems) and a more economical one, since with a bump the whole vehicle has to be raised, while with flow, only the wheel is raised, etc., etc.

In considering river pollution the provocation "po, factories should be downstream of themselves" leads to the notion of legislating that the input to a factory should always be downstream of its own output so that there would be a greater incentive to clean up the effluent.

There are many formal ways of obtaining "movement" from an idea and these are part of the formal techniques of lateral thinking.

Consider a typical escape example. We expect watchdogs to bark and bite. Suppose (po) a watchdog does not bark: what use would it be? We can imagine a rather frightening notice which says: "Beware of silent watchdog." It is frightening because the dog may attack without any warning. We can go farther and suppose that the dog does not bite. In fact the dog may be so feeble that it flees from an intruder and hides in its box. What use could that be? In its box there could be a microswitch which is activated by the dog's weight and then sets off any manner of alarm system one wants. At this point attention has shifted from the "output" value of a watchdog to the "input" value (animal bearing, smell, alertness, mobility, etc.). We then provide the dog with a more powerful output system. At this point we can forget about the dog and think in terms of trained mice in cages. They are trained to respond to an intruder by pressing a bar which activates any system we like.

In the pharmaceutical industry a drug is developed for and found to be useful for the treatment of a particlar condition. That is the pattern of perception of that drug.

Dr. Nathan Kline, who discovered an antidepressant drug that was to be very useful in treating mental patients, describes how the discovery came about. 'Its use had been practically discontinued because patients who took it for tuberculosis felt so good that they overexerted themselves — they very often didn't follow the regime anymore that they were supposed to. Everybody, including me, walked right by the fact and paid no attention to it. It was only subsequently, after seeing the animal work on the first drug I'd introduced, that I went back and found this was the same drug that produced these side effects. And of course it fitted in perfectly with the idea that this might be an antidepressant. Now I do this sort of thing routinely. I look at the side effects with the idea that maybe they're not side effects. That maybe they have major effects. How can you use the side effects to treat some other condition? You see, you shift your frame of reference."

This quotation shows clearly how a deliberate habit of mind can become a creative strategy: looking at side effects as useful effects. This is a typical example of a reversal type of provocation. It illustrates how certain habits of thought, or techniques, can be learned and applied deliberately. In lateral thinking it could have been put as follows: "po the side effects are the really useful effects."

Clive Sinclair: "Right now I am developing the electric car. There have been lots of reports published in the House of Lords which show the electric car not making economic sense. And it's a very interesting thing. I believe that those reports are produced very genuinely and with great skill, and they do conclude very positively that electric cars don't make any sense. But they can be very wrong. Electric cars don't make sense if you just take the existing knowledge — of course, that's not what you do." Q.: The problem with the electric car would seem to be you can't get sufficient power to go fast unless you load them up with enormous batteries. "That's the sort of thing; that's right." How, then, is Clive Sinclair approaching it? "You will have to wait and see, because I can't tell you much about it. But the answer is, it is lateral thinking in the sense that it's other than an ordinary car — suddenly it makes sense. It was something somebody said, actually, and suddenly I realized . . . but I can't talk about it."

Things are often assumed to be impossible because of an existing perception. It was calculated that a space rocket would have to weigh a million tons in order to reach the moon. This was because the concept of a "staged rocket" had not been considered.

"Don't accept that just because a certain thing has been done a certain way, that it will always have to be that way": Mark McCormack.

Once we understand the nature of patterning systems then we come to realize two things. The first thing is that such systems are absolutely essential for ordinary life and immensely valuable. The second thing is that we are locked into those patterns which are but a summary of our sequence of experience and that already existing experience can be used to form new ideas.

I am not suggesting that all creative effort is due to conscious or unconscious use of lateral thinking (a chance provocation is similar in action to the random-word technique). In artistic creation many other elements may be required. What I am saying is that once we understand the patterning nature of perception, then the deliberate changing of concepts and perceptions is something that we can attempt. We can use lateral thinking as a formal thinking process alongside our other thinking equipment (analysis, logic, mathematics, etc.).

T A C T I C S

1. A brilliant new idea is not the only — or even the best — route to success.

2. One of the routes to success is innovation within a field. For deliberate creative effort, try using lateral thinking.

3. There is the creativity of innocence and there is the creativity of escape. You can only use the first while you are innocent.

4. Making an idea work is more difficult and more important than having the idea in the first place.

5. The "logic" of lateral thinking arises from the nature of perception as activity in a self-organizing information universe. Humor is a good parallel.

6. With provocation there may not be a reason for saying something until after it has been said. The provocation does not fit in with existing perceptions but is used to lead us to new perceptions.

7. In lateral thinking we use "movement" rather than judgment. We use movement to move on from a provocation to a new perception or concept.

8. Shifting perspective and frames of reference can lead to new ideas and insights.

9. Having to react continually to immediate pressures and problems makes creative thinking difficult (except in solving those problems).

10. Lateral thinking should be treated as a routine part of our thinking equipment.

11. Look at any area with a traditional high profit margin and apply the innovative thinking that has probably been lacking in that area.

9

Do You Have to Take
Risks to Succeed?

T H E   P L A Y E R S :

United States: **Roy Cohn · Werner Erhard · Malcolm Forbes · Harry
Helmsley · Antonio Herrara · Herman Kahn · Dr. Nathan Kline · Morgan
Maree · Diane von Furstenberg**

United Kingdom and International: **David Bailey · Christian Bonington · Lord
Pennock · Jackie Stewart · Sting · Mark Weinberg**

ARE SUCCESSFUL PEOPLE RISK-TAKERS?

Risk taking and gambling are quite, quite different. This is made very
clear by the attitudes of successful people towards risk. These attitudes
are expressed succinctly. We tend to feel that successful people must
have taken risks. They do not always see it that way.

"Gambling is not my sort of polo. If you're in that sort of position,
you're a different polo player": Antonio Herrara.

"Every deal is a calculated risk. But you have to know the percentage
of risk; you have to have a pretty good feel for the business. You don't
take decisions on the basis of 'win some; lose some.' No, not at all. In
every deal there comes a point where you have to put up the money;
that's when you have to know what you're doing. Early on in the game
we had a very big deal, buying a building. We had worked out a plan:

we had the mortgage money lined up; we had the syndicate money lined up. It looked like a piece of cake. Only one problem. We went to the fellow who was organizing the remainder of the money and he said, 'Times have changed.' That meant coming up with two or three million dollars — we sweat bullets putting that one through": Harry Helmsley.

"If you don't take risks," says Dr. Nathan Kline, "the possibility of accomplishing something sizable is reduced. For me the excitement of risk-taking is important and I feed on that kind of excitement."

"You always risk losing — it's risk/reward ratio that determines what you do. But no matter what you do, you risk losing. Let's say, 'Do you want to invest in my invention for half the profits or would you prefer to loan me the money if I guarantee to pay you back plus a small amount of interest?' The questions are 'How much are the profits likely to be?' 'Can I afford to take route A, which is more dangerous?' or 'Must I, because of my responsibilities to others, remain in the conservative route B and take the lesser return?' You determine for yourself every day of your life how much risk you can afford to take. And that is a measure of your courage": Morgan Maree.

"I don't mind taking a risk if it's necessary. It doesn't frighten me. I'll give you an example. Once a client of ours was operating a railroad at a tremendous loss in New Jersey, and he was forced to keep it open by court order.

"Well, I don't think any court constitutionally has the right to order somebody to keep on losing money. So after they had been through ten lawyers in Jersey, I said to him, 'Shut it down.' So he shut it down. He said, 'They could put me in jail.' So I said, "OK, if you're nervous about it go down the Caribbean for a couple of weeks, but I don't think you have anything to worry about.' And, of course, it worked out. We shut down the railroad cold . . . and the court changed its order and the Power and Utilities Commission ruled that we had the right to close down the railroad": Roy Cohn.

Anyone who takes an initiative or pursues an opportunity is taking some sort of risk. It is said that some of the entrepreneurial spirit of America is due to the fact that every emigrant who left Europe was sufficiently a risk-taker to leave Europe and set off for the unknown. The security-minded genes stayed at home.

At the beginning of their enterprises many successful people have given up a secure job or mortgaged their houses in order to start on their own. Clearly these are risks which many people would regard as unacceptable (if not for oneself then for one's family). Do those who take such risks actually consider them as risks or are they so sure of the value of their ideas that — to them — the risk element is slight?

Here is how photographer David Bailey became a household name overnight, and revolutionized the fashion industry by creating the miniskirt look: "I took a few risks in the early days. In fact, the first risk I ever took was using Jean Shrimpton. I'd been at *Vogue* for about a year and I saw this girl and thought she was wonderful. She was doing a Kellogg's picture with someone called Duffy, a photographer at *Vogue* at the time. And I said, 'Introduce me; I like her,' and then I said to *Vogue* I wanted to use this girl and they said I couldn't because I was sleeping with her! (In fact, I wasn't sleeping with her at the time.) Eventually they gave me a fourteen-page lead, which in those days, when *Vogue* was much smaller, was quite something. They finally agreed to let me use Shrimpton. After that session it just sort of snowballed. Jean and I just worked together for about three years." The session launched the miniskirt: "I liked Jean's legs, you see. I never really cared much about fashion; I only really took pictures of frocks because girls were in them! I used to pull the skirt up higher and higher every time I did a picture and *Vogue* used to airbrush it down. And the more they airbrushed it down, the more I put it up. Suddenly it became acceptable that you could wear a skirt up to your knickers!"

GAMBLER'S RISK

Are successful people gamblers? Have they reached their position of success by taking a big risk and winning? Those who take equally big risks and fail are not around for us to look at. Is the relationship between success and risk-taking the same as that between success and luck: we only see the good outcomes? Do all successful people see themselves as risk-takers?

Mark Weinberg, Hambro Life: "I don't like fear. I don't seek brinkmanship. If Jim Slater (see pages 109–110) had to grow to a stage where he knew there was danger in what he was doing, I wouldn't. I used to belong to a dining club which he belonged to, and one night they had the casino owner John Aspinall to talk. He was describing the excitement of being a gambler and how you put your £1,000 on the table and it doubles and it's £2,000, £4,000, £8,000. He said the difference between a gambler and a nongambler (the gambler was the person he was glorifying) is that the nongambler keeps on doubling up when he feels he's on a winner. Then we had questions, and I attacked him very strongly. I said it was totally irrational — you ought at some stage to garage; that was the right thing to do. Jim Slater supported me on it, but with a bit more of a gambler's instinct. He would enjoy the thrill and keep wanting to run on, but rationally ask the question — at what stage (sooner or later) would he run out? He's a terribly keen backgammon player, and I don't know whether some people need the fear (it gives you some adrenaline) or whether they're happy to live with it. I'm much too cautious for that. I go for the cautious solution."

Do You Have to Take Risks to Succeed?

The contrast between businessmen Mark Weinberg, Jim Slater, and John Aspinall nicely illustrates the spread of risk-taking. At one extreme is Aspinall the gambler, who enjoys the adrenaline of gambling: the anticipation, the reward, the chance to "play," the action, etc. At the other extreme is the "designer" Mark Weinberg, who wants to think things through and leave the minimum to chance. When chance has provided a bonus, then that is to be saved and invested rather than chanced further. In between is Jim Slater, who wants to think things through — his method both here and in the rise and fall of Slater Walker is that of the strategist rather than the gambler, but Slater is also tempted by the "big play." To some extent the attitude toward risk is related to the type of business involved. A Broadway impresario knows that most of his productions will fail, but that a few will be successful enough to pay for all the failures and provide something over. An oil wildcatter knows that many wells will be dry, but that some will come in to reward his efforts. An investor in the stock market knows that he is unlikely to win all the time. A real estate developer knows that there will be some failures. Each of these people expects to lose at times. For them the adage "nothing ventured, nothing gained" holds true. The nature of the retail business or the insurance business (Mark Weinberg) is not like that. There may be failures and certain things may not work out, but the idiom is that of steady growth. Something is tried out because in the light of available knowledge it is a good idea and not a gamble. There is no need to gamble in the true sense of the word. In driving a motor car there is always a certain amount of risk and uncertainty (especially as regards other drivers on the road), but the driver does not consider himself a risk-taker. He or she drives sensibly and efficiently.

Jackie Stewart, ex-champion racing driver. Does he get a buzz out of taking risks? "Absolutely not, quite the reverse. A lot of my colleagues do. I don't like taking risks. I hate fear. I hate it, really hate it. I don't like being frightened; I really get no stimulation from fear at all. Jochen Rindt, for example, loved to ski like a daredevil; loved to ride a motorcycle like a daredevil. I ride a motorcycle like an old lady. I ski like an elderly grandmother. I don't want to break my legs; I don't want to — I'm a very uncharacteristic racing driver in that respect. I've no flair for devilish pranks. Jochen Rindt just got a buzz from it, and Piers Courage was the same, exactly the same. A lot of them like going in power boats at ridiculous speeds, all those sort of things — or fly an aircraft too low or through mountains. I always saw the risks; I always saw the hazards coming up, the unseen hazards.

"When I had eliminated the unnecessary hazards, I calculated the remaining risks. I got very involved with racetrack safety, and racing safety. I spent a great deal of unpopular times with the media trying to thrash out safety to make the racetracks and racing safer. I ended up by taking a doctor everywhere with me. A doctor who had a degree in surgery, in eight different avenues of surgery, but whose main talent was that of being an anesthetist. He was a most valuable man to have around if you had a serious accident. Not a bones man, not a neurosurgeon, not an orthopedic surgeon, but an anesthetist — someone who could sustain life, keep my heart ticking and brain turning over. So I had him travel with me to races, at enormous expense, just as an insurance policy. So, I'm not a risk-taker."

This is a most interesting disclosure by Jackie Stewart, but one which seems in keeping with his thoughtful style. The flamboyant general who prides himself on taking risks may be a heroic figure but wastes a lot of lives and opportunities. Risk reduction is not the same as risk aversion. Risk aversion often means doing nothing at all, since this seems to be the best risk avoiding tactic. Deciding to take the risk of action and then setting out to reduce that risk as much as possible seems to be a sensible enough policy. It depends on the area of activity. Jackie Stewart could see himself in the "Broadway risk" type of activity — "take a huge risk and win some or lose some" — or he could see himself in the "steady business" situation. Unfortunately, being dead does not allow you to go on playing the game, so it is clearly not a "Broadway risk" scenario but a steady business — as he implies.

RISK REDUCTION

1. Work to Make a Decision Work

There is some risk in most decisions — there are factors outside one's control. But sometimes risk lies in direct proportion to how hard you are prepared to make a decision work. Lord Pennock: "I think working hard to make a decision work is possibly even more important than making the decision in the first place. One of the dangers is people making a decision then thinking, 'Oh, that's it,' when the thing has only just started.

"We here at BICC decided we were taking a risk to go into fiber optics (which are going to be the great thing for cable television). Two years ago we made that decision. It really began in the early '70's where, on the one hand, Corning, who were initially a glass making company in America, had done a lot of research into optical fiber. We as cable manufacturers recognized that particularly in telecommunication — in telephone cables — there would have to be some changes in the medium as life got more and more complex (particularly in an island like ours where so many people live and we have such sophisticated systems). So way back in '72 Corning and BICC got together. Corning said, "Well, you're the biggest cable makers in Britain; cable making is your line,' and we said, 'You're the guys who are ahead in new materials for telecommunication cables,' so we got together.

"But the big decision we had to make was in 1980, when I had just arrived. We were now coming to the stage where we had got some very practical developments in fiber optics and we said, 'Well, we must be the first people to build a plant; we've got to get cracking ahead of everyone else.' But the important thing is this: the danger (I remember it well) is that after we had made a decision at board level, everybody said, 'Well, that's it.' And I said, 'That isn't it; don't slap yourselves on the back; it's just bloody well starting. Now you've got to make it work.' The putting into practice of the decision is almost as important as making the right decision in the first place."

There are four ways of minimizing risk. First, there is assessment of the situation and a choice of taking that risk or not. Second, there is the balancing of one risk against another: as in currency hedging or countercyclic business. Third, there are actions to reduce the risk in the situation like taking a parachute when flying. Fourth, there are the actions that can be taken to modify the decision or to make it work — after the decision has been taken. There is always the risk that relates to the outside world and the risk that relates to the effectiveness of the risk-taker (there is the risk that we may not be effective enough to make this work).

2. *Learn to Wriggle*

Changes in the outside world (changes in the law, interest rates, political climate, war) may not be possible to forecast — no matter how wise people may be in hindsight. If a sufficient number of experts all predict something different, then, in hindsight, one of them is likely to be right. If we only remember the times a person is right and forget the times he is wrong, then it becomes possible to build up a considerable reputation as a forecaster. So things can change in an unexpected manner and upset the best plans of an entrepreneur. The measure of that person's worth then becomes the way he or she extricates himself or herself from the crisis.

Real estate tycoon Harry Helmsley describes one such situation: "I took a deal which required a tremendous amount of money from banks. I put it (the money) up, and just at that moment there was a drastic change in the economy. The interest rates went skyrocketing. I had to raise the interest and I had to raise the return to the investors. When I saw what was happening, I made my decision fast. I brought the investors in (negotiated with them), and I didn't make what I expected to make. I came out with my head above water and clean. It's not all success — there are plenty of risks — and you don't always come out ahead. But you must handle it. You wriggle. You get off the hook the best you can!"

Investment of money, time, or effort is almost always a risk: something has to be put in before something can come out. The mechanism for getting something out may be misconceived (a bad idea or bad market sense) or the circumstances may so change that even a well-conceived idea may fail. There are types of investment (tax-free municipal bonds in the U.S.A.) where the risks are lower, but the rewards are usually lower as well. Perhaps it might be better to look at successful people not in terms of risk-consciousness but in terms of reward-consciousness. If you feel that your ideas are going to succeed anyway, then the motivation to use risk as a path to reward is that much less.

THE RISK OF INNOVATION

Just as investment is by definition a risk, so also is innovation. There is risk as to whether the thing will work. There is risk as to whether it will have significant value. There is risk as to whether the market will accept it. There is risk as to whether the production process will be feasible. There is risk as to whether it can be sold at an acceptable price. There is risk that a competitor may catch up quickly or leapfrog what has been done. With all these risks, it is a wonder that innovation happens at all.

Some inventors take decisions which to many outsiders appear to involve lunatic risk. Herman Kahn declared: "Risk-taking is the essence of innovation." When Clive Sinclair brought out the pocket calculator, people warned him that he would lose money, that people simply would not be interested in carrying around calculators in their pockets, briefcases, etc. Sir Terence Conran (see Decision-Making, page 201), Diane von Furstenberg, and some other business people we interviewed abhor the idea of market-testing on the principle that the public do not know what they want.

"Well, in my case, it is because I'm dealing with the women's market, so my female intuition provides my consumer intuition. That's why I feel that I don't need market research and if I listen to what I think, knowing that I want the best for myself, then I think it's great. So, because I deal with women and I am a woman, and what I do is for women, to simplify their life and make it aesthetic is instinctual": Diane von Furstenberg.

Are such people gifted in being able to monitor a market need in some sort of intuitive fashion? Some people believe so. Sting: "In performance, when the audience is at one with you, what you are doing is tapping collective unconscious. Rock-and-roll music is a very simple tonal code. I have it within me to create that code. To see 20,000 people react in exactly the same way to this musical code is quite astounding. I think it is a psychic ability. You can relate it to businessmen too — the ability to foresee a market demand. There's a certain amount of psychic confidence there."

Do You Have to Take Risks to Succeed?

COURAGE TO BE AT RISK

The capacity for courage (as opposed to its near-neighbor, foolhardiness) is generally thought of as the ability to face up to enormous odds, especially on the battlefield.

The late Herman Kahn headed a team of people at the Hudson Institute who constantly put their necks on the line in a quite different field. Their business is analysis of available information and prognosis for the future, sometimes the future of the world. He has noticed that in his field there's a relationship between courage and integrity. "Over here you can afford to be very honest if you want to be. You don't have to cater to other people's big biases or ideologies or so on (but remarkably very few people take advantage of it)." Kahn uses the word "integrity" without emphasizing its moral overtones; he uses it in the sense that there are times when, to achieve, a man or woman must, in Werner Erhard's phrase, "live at risk." Erhard continues: "Whenever I've done something valuable it's always been a function operating out beyond, taking a stand out beyond that which I could justify, explain, or for which I had a strategy or prescription."

Courage, bravery, risk taking are all ingredients of success inasmuch as the successful person wants to make something happen (often something new).

VENTURE/ADVENTURE

Millionaire Malcolm Forbes, besides publishing *Forbes* magazine, is a ballooning and motorcycle enthusiast. These enthusiasms might well appear to us to be risky, but his liking for them is not a liking for risk but for adventure. Is it an important ingredient of the entrepreneurial spirit?

"Risk-taking is an integral and intrinsic part of success or living a full life. You can spend your life with regrets, saying, 'Gee, if I had done this instead of that . . .' It's a waste of time. You didn't. But I don't enjoy gambling. It just doesn't do anything for me. I enjoy adventures; but because I like being alive so much, I tend to remove risks from it. In other words, ballooning isn't risky if you do it with knowledge and care. Motorcycling isn't risky if you do it with intelligence and care. In short, I get no kicks out of risk per se. But while I'm alive I enjoy living. So, I'm not looking for the thrill of beating odds. I get kicks out of being alive, but I'm not looking for gambles. There were risks every day in the hot-air trip across the country, but I attempted to minimize them. You never eliminate them. If you want to accomplish anything, you can't eliminate all risk."

The "sense of adventure" seems to fit many successful entrepreneurs. It fits with the motivation of wanting to "make things happen." As Malcolm Forbes points out, it is not the same as the joy of gambling. The risk element may be present but is not central. There is the urge to try something out, to do something new. It is the opposite of boredom and stagnation. There is a difference between the person who sets out to be successful and to earn money so that he can then buy adventure, and the person who sets out to venture and adventure and acquires money as a by-product. This sense of adventure may be why some successful people change their marriage partners so often.

Any challenge is an adventure provided one has the confidence to feel that the challenge can be met.

Chris Bonington agrees: "I wouldn't say mountaineering is so much a gamble as a calculated risk. It's not the roulette kind of gamble. The excitement of climbing is going into a danger situation and then using your skill to obviate danger." During the Everest expedition, before Bonington took the decision to go through the Everest icefall, Monzino wanted to bring a couple of helicopters in to lift them through. Where is the point at which obviating risk disposes of the excitement and adventure of the operation? "That's going into the ethical stance within climbing. Climbing has a series of unwritten rules. In effect, the rules are introduced by the climbers themselves to maintain this level of uncertainty. For instance, there was a period where climbers started going for big rock walls using expansion bolts to aid their climb. Now, they very quickly found out that you can climb any wall — provided you've got the strength and patience — therefore, in a way, you've removed the uncertainty and you've destroyed the point of it."

T A C T I C S

1. Any successful person has chosen action as against inaction. In any initiative or opportunity pursuit there is an element of risk.

2. There are gamblers who enjoy the gamble and there are "Broadway risk" players who know that they will win some and lose some. The important point is to stay in the game.

3. There are others who try to minimize risk as much as possible because they do not need it since the steady growth of their business will ensure success.

4. Assessing uncertainties and potential dangers comes under the heading of reasonable expectations. There is a spectrum of risk, and you decide the point at which you become uncomfortable.

5. Things outside your control can go wrong. Success may then involve extricating yourself from the situation in the best way possible.

6. Risk and reward may be compared. The downside can be compared to the upside. Such comparisons aid decision taking.

7. Both investment and innovation involve risk. Both may be essential. So the emphasis is on risk reduction and reward enhancement.

8. A sense of adventure may impel successful people to take risks — the risks are then reduced as much as possible.

9. It seems that successful people like doing things that involve risk but do not like the risk itself — so they seek to reduce this.

PART THREE

MAKE IT A SUCCESS

10

Strategy

THE PLAYERS:

United States: **Malcolm Forbes · Herman Kahn · Morgan Maree**

United Kingdom and International: **Heather Jenner · Robert Maxwell · Miyomoto Musashi · Sting · Mark Weinberg · Charles Williams**

Occasionally an idea just seems to take off on its own.

"For about a year," recalls Heather Jenner, creator of the first marriage bureau, "we fiddled about thinking how we should do it. At the start, we opposed the idea of advertising: 'SCINTILLATING FEMALE WANTS TO MEET ELDERLY GENTLEMAN.'

"First, we went to a solicitor, but he was frightfully stuffy about it. Mary [her partner] got very bored with the interview, and when he asked what capital we had, she said, 'I don't know, how's your beat, Heather?' ["Beat" was a common expression for a prostitute's area of work when streetwalking prostitutes were not illegal.] We both got the most frightful giggles and left. However, I then remembered a young solicitor who had been a good friend before I left for Sri Lanka — Michael Eddows. He saw the point of what we were trying to do and said that if we did it properly it was a very good idea. He took us for counsel's opinion and showed us how to draw up our clients' form legally.

"Well, we practiced interviewing on all our reluctant friends; we read everything we possibly could, and started working to raise some capital (I was a model for a bit and Mary was a companion to some unfortunate woman — I say 'unfortunate' because I don't think Mary was ever there!). When we thought we had enough information to get started, we decided to look for an office. The one we found is next door to the one we now have, in Bond Street. We paid 55 shillings a week, which included a telephone and furniture and rates. It was a bit dusty and dingy, so we painted it yellow whilst our friends would come to see us thinking that we would be 'had up' for white-slave trafficking or something.

"However, one of them had a bit more intelligence and asked how people were going to know about us. We said that we would advertise, and he said, 'That's not good enough; you must ring up the newspapers.' This was between the Munich crisis and the war, so it was a time when papers were still going full blast and were actively looking for news that wasn't war news. So we solemnly rang up all the features editors in alphabetical order by newspaper. Eventually Godfrey Wynne came round — he was writing for the *Sunday Express* — and did a whole page on us that Sunday. That gave us leverage.

"We opened on April seventeenth, 1939, and we couldn't get the door open for letters. The post was much quicker in those days. While we were opening the letters, there was a knock on the door, and Mary went to open it. With a look of absolute horror she said, 'There's a MAN at the door who wants to be INTERVIEWED!'

"So we tossed up who should see him, and I lost, so I saw him. All the time we had thought that our clients would be in our age group, but here was a man in his late thirties in the Indian army. And he saw me through the interview. I hadn't got anyone for him, but he produced the £5 registration fee, and I took his address and information, thinking to myself that I'd send the money back at the end of the week. But this went on all day! All sorts of people we never thought would come to us, did. We rushed off to Harrods to buy a typewriter, and Mary went to the employment office to get a secretary. By the end of the week we had sorted things out and did have introductions for this man. One or two we couldn't help, so we did send them their money back — we were just so naïve! We had a bag of £5 notes, a paper bag. I remember saying that we ought to do something about that — put it in a bank or something. Mary said, "Yes, go and find a bank." I went downstairs, and the first bank I saw was across the road — the Royal Bank of Scotland — it's now on the same side of the road. I walked across and said, 'Look, we've got all this money — we may have to return a lot of it — we don't quite know what to do with it.' The man behind the counter looked at me as though I were completely dotty and said, 'You'd better see the manager.' So I went in, and there was this cherub of a man called Mr. Reynolds, and he looked at me and smiled, 'That's all right, my dear, you must have two accounts. You must have an account where you put the money you think you may have to pay back and the other for this and that.' Absolutely sweet of him! Years later, when I was married to Stephen Potter, we went to the same bank only to find that that man was Stephen's uncle! Not only his uncle but his bank manager too. (I think he was bored if there wasn't something funny happening. After a month he said, 'You must have a company.' We became two companies, in fact: we had a holding company and a company, and went on from there. We learnt the hard way."

Heather Jenner had a unique idea but no plan of how to set about achieving it. The fact that she had no premeditated strategy didn't matter a jot because it was a very good idea promoted with energy in her own natural style; the venture was in a field in which there was absolutely no competition and she had the good fortune of falling into the helping hands of trustworthy and imaginative people. How much her own "helplessness" harbored a shrewd sense of business acumen, we may never know!

DESIGN A STRATEGY

Strategy means putting things in place carefully, and with a great deal of thought. It is the opposite of just waiting for things to happen or taking a flyer. There is a strong sense of strategy in many successful people (even though we may sometimes be tempted to wonder whether this is not occasionally good luck rationalized in hindsight). Robert Maxwell, who built up his fortune from nothing to control of the largest printing operation in Europe, is known as a strategist.

Robert Maxwell: "Don't get the idea I wake up in the morning and say, 'Let's make an offer for Waddington's (or anything else).' Occasionally you do have accidents where it comes 'out of the left field' — like Oxford United [Maxwell had recently been invited to become chairman of the football club]. But, by and large, anything we do as far as business is concerned is timed and planned."

Sting: "There's a certain amount of inspiration and enjoying what you do — that's the prime mover — but then there is what you might call strategy. You look at the market and see what sells, and you see what image is required. To a certain extent you taper your creativity to that particular model. . . .

"At the time, punk rock had caused total confusion within the industry. The executives didn't have a clue what was happening, and they were terrified for their jobs. They were too old; they didn't understand what was going on; they felt isolated by the phenomenon. And they were really trying anything.

"We came in on the back end of the tidal wave of revolution (the opportunists that we are!) . . . we flew a flag of convenience, which was, 'We are marketable, yet we are part of this new revolution; take us on —

we'll succeed and you will succeed accordingly.' And that is exactly what happened: we became the biggest selling act in the world inside three years.

"I wouldn't say that we kowtowed exactly. Today, of course, we have almost total artistic freedom to do what we like. Look at the irony of my singing a 1930s song — 'Spread a Little Happiness.' It goes completely against the grain, but it became Number 1! It's fun to be able to do that, but if I'd done it at first I wouldn't have stood a chance."

GENERAL STRATEGY

An artist sets out the general composition, or placing, of his figures on the canvas. Then the detailed painting can start.

In both war and business this general placing is called strategy. There are two types of strategy: one, which we'll call general-purpose strategy, is a set of principles and guidelines that may apply to any situation. In recruiting, for example, an interviewer may have the general strategy of picking people who come in second: in each achievement they are almost as good as those who come first, but in temperament they are better because they are not prima donnas.

As a stock market investor, you may decide upon a general strategy always to do the opposite of what is recommended: when you lose out, you do not lose much, but when you win, you win big.

Morgan Maree perceives two types of general strategy: "You can structure yourself against failure by erecting all the barriers that would limit your losses, or you can structure yourself to maximize success." In the experienced and successful, strategy has long since become an integral part of their style — so much so that they may not be aware of it as anything other than commonsense. Lord Forte: "I simply followed certain practices and certain tenets and certain commonsensical things. I think I could call it 'management by commonsense.' And the thing grew." What is commonsense to Lord Forte very probably includes some sound business principles (such as "pick very capable people, pay them well, and let them get on with it").

DETAILED STRATEGY

The second type of strategy is designed for a specific purpose. At Waterloo, Wellington had a specific strategy for that battle and for that battlefield, in addition to the general strategy principles that he used in all his campaigns.

The first time around, Sir Clive Sinclair tried to do too much of his own manufacturing. The second time he had a different and more successful detailed strategy: "Have a small design team; subcontract their designs for manufacture; approach the market by mail order (so generating a good cash flow, better margins, and at the same time through the advertisements alerting the public to the product); finally, use retail chains (having negotiated a profitable deal because the market potential has already been demonstrated)." There was a strategy about pricing as well: "Price so low that the computer can enter the home market as an impulse purchase (parents for themselves and their children)."

An alternative strategy might be as follows: "Let someone else open up the market; let trends develop, and once we see clearly what is happening, move into that area with superior management, standards, and reputation." It's a "me-too" strategy, a sort of strategy which can be creatively unexciting but nevertheless can work. It works best when it is undertaken with panache by a company with a reputation for quality. IBM allowed others to develop the personal computer. They then moved very rapidly indeed, entered the field with a solid (but not specially advanced) machine, and took a very significant market share. Very probably it was not a thought-out strategy, but it could have been.

DRAWING UP A STRATEGY

Seventeenth-century Samurai warrior Miyamoto Musashi: "As a carpenter requires a building plan, so a warrior requires a plan of campaign. So great is the commander's understanding of the requirement to meet his goal that his plan is as though it were a straight road mapped out on the ground." Musashi goes on to exhort his students to take into account the intentions of any opposition, to understand what special qualities will be required to carry out your own strategies, to match strategies to resources, to employ men with apposite abilities, be fully aware of their strengths and limitations, and motivate them to achieve your ends.

Reading the opposition's intentions can be crucial to the success of a strategy, and in the case of the famous London waxworks, Madame Tussaud's, failure to read and respond to a sudden change in the plans of the opposition was to prove fatal both to their own strategy and even to their survival as an independent company. In 1978, S. Pearson and Son, the firm which owned *The Financial Times*, the Château Latour vineyard, American oil wells, and Royal Doulton china, was looking around for someone to buy Chessington Zoo in Surrey. It had been acquired several years earlier as part of another deal, but Pearson's management had neither the time nor the experience to run the zoo properly; furthermore, it had a funfair and circus attached, making it complex to maintain and handle well. The independent public company, Madame Tussaud's, which, besides the waxworks, owned the Wookey Hole Caves in the West Country and one or two other tourist attractions, came forward. But the more the two sides talked, the more Pearson began to realize that Tussaud's would make a fine centerpiece of a leisure division within their own group, Chessington included. This was not what the Tussaud directors had in mind at all, and the eventual takeover bid was strongly contested. But Pearson won, all the same.

Malcolm Forbes describes what happened to his magazine *Nation's Heritage* when he failed to match his strategy to his resources: "It was a fiscal flop; after one year we discontinued it. I think the timing was right, but what we lacked was enough money to have staying power. . . . I didn't allow for the selling process — the cost of mailings. Lots of people come up with ideas for magazines all of the time, but they never crank in the cost of getting subscribers, which is usually three or four times the cost of all the editorial content and all the print. . . . I simply didn't leave enough money over to sell it, nor was the company big enough then (1948–'49) to sustain it."

Strategies should always take into account the possibility of unforeseen problems. Product development may take longer than planned; there can be hitches.

HOW RIGID SHOULD A STRATEGY BE?

In a changing environment one of the most difficult things in business is to know when to stick to your strategy and when to change it. Strategic rigidity can be as disastrous as lack of strategy.

Herman Kahn: "We often have strategies around this place, but we tend not to use them. There are simply too many contingencies. So it is very hard to plan because you don't know which contingency is going to occur, which things will tend to become dominant and override the long-term strategy."

This is a complaint which is increasingly heard in American businesses: there are so many uncertainities and so many new developments that any long-term strategy is bound to be wrong. First, there is a sense in which strategy must remain flexible if aims are not to be achieved overnight. Second, we need to distinguish clearly between a plan and a strategy.

STRATEGY SHOULD ADAPT TO THE TIMES

A strategy should be broad and contain contingency positions; in times of uncertainty, it should be capable of taking this climate into account.

Robert Maxwell describes how he has adapted strategy to fit current circumstances in order to achieve his long-term aim to become influential in Fleet Street: "I used to want a national newspaper as a part of my efforts to wake up Britain, to make people realize we've been going backward so long. But, as I get older (and don't forget I was sixty a few weeks ago), it occurs to me that perhaps the best service I can really render, both to national newspapers and the country as a whole (as well as to our employees and shareholders), is to offer to 'contract print' national newspapers . . . to separate the publishers of national newspapers from printing.

"So, for instance, the *Financial Times* would not have the kind of trouble it is going through [a management-union dispute over new technology had brought publication to a halt]. That could not happen because I would be the printer and would deal with the problems instead of getting it all mixed up in that way.

"From the trade union point of view, they can see that if they carry on with the present method, there'll be fewer and fewer national newspapers. They'll all die. [From a would-be publisher's point of view] the price of entry into the field if you want to start a national newspaper is about £20 million. But if I had a contract printing plant for a national newspaper you were planning to set up, then your cost of entry would be relatively cheap.

HOW DOES A STRATEGY DIFFER FROM A PLAN?

For many corporations, a plan is little more than an extended budget, a strategy little more than an extended plan. But in reality, as we shall see in the following examples, they are quite different concepts and should be treated in different ways.

For merchant banker Charles Williams, strategy means designing a giant interlocking jigsaw puzzle. "We have got a business philosophy in this organization which requires putting into place certain services which we can offer which form, in my view, a coherent manageable whole. One of them is ship broking, another is insurance broking, another is banking; there are about three others. They interrelate in two senses: they relate between themselves — the bank will provide the insurance broker with corporate finance services for the insurance broker's customer and project insurance for the ship, and so on. They relate to each other, but they also interrelate to a given class of customer; one of our large shareholders is a big trading group, so part of our business concept is to relate very strongly to the trading group and its customers.

"Looking around and without mentioning any names, I cannot see anybody in this patch who has got as clearly defined a strategy as ours. You can see them adding on bits . . . people say, well, Hambro Life took over the merchant bank, Dunbar, for £10 million; that's an important part of Hambro's strategy. Ask Mark Weinberg whether there is a coherent structure; maybe there is. Maybe he cannot see what's in my strategy and what we are doing. That is always possible. But I cannot see any strategy in any similar organization to ours which is like the one

I have described. My ideas all stem from my education and my formative years. I am psychologically unhappy with unstructured situations."

Here we can see the interrelationship between personality and corporate strategy. This is quite separate from the charisma, or leadership quality of personality. Just as a person chooses the decoration and furnishing of the place in which he or she lives, so a person may structure a situation to suit his or her own personality.

HOW STRATEGY INFLUENCES PLANS

Mark Weinberg: "What we do once a year is to set aside a day for a long-term objectives meeting. We'll have five or six topics, most of which are the same every year. Every couple of years we may extend this to a whole weekend. But mostly it's a long day — twelve, fifteen hours, something like that. Each of us will present a paper which we'll have spent a day or two working on. As a result of such a meeting we will evolve a sort of broad direction. But it is broad, and the object of the game is to have a mental flexibility which enables one to take advantage of opportunities as they present themselves. Let me give you one example which has resulted in our acquisition of Dunbar [the merchant bank]."

To begin with, Dunbar wanted some of Weinberg's top clients. Weinberg couldn't see much percentage in that; only in the context of Hambro Life's overall strategy did a quite different plan begin to emerge:

"Many years ago, I felt that the life insurance industry — like other financial services industries (stockbroking, banking, etc.) had to diversify. The barriers between these subindustries would break down, and they'd be recognized as one financial services industry. That was a broad conceptual feeling, if you like. We decided to keep an eye on this, and continually provide slightly wider services in our own field so as to make sure that we didn't get out of line with developments in the market.

"Nothing very much happened until after one or two trips to America (where the problems of the financial service industry are more developed than in the U.K.). I became convinced that soon we would start facing similar problems in this country if we didn't diversify and break down the barriers between the various subindustries. At the time I had also been writing a series of papers on the commissions war in the U.K. and what threats it posed for our life insurance industry. There again I realized that the problems involved my thinking a little more broadly than just about commissions.

"So I started thinking, and making a number of presentations to people. One of the points I made was: 'Don't you realize that the banks are going to come into our industry? We are a high-cost industry and they are a low-cost.' So this was developing in my mind around the time that I met David Backhouse, who runs Dunbar.

"Then it became apparent that in America people were responding in a similar way, although there the progressive changes were being applied by the stockbrokers — the life insurance industry was on the receiving end. One particular company, Merrill Lynch (the difference between us is that they have 9,000 salesmen, we have 3,000; they have a stockbroking base, we have a life insurance base), began to diversify. But if they could diversify into life insurance from a stockbroking base, so we could diversify from our base.

"I wouldn't like to say when it happened, very likely my marketing director, Mike Wilson, said, 'Well, doesn't Dunbar fit into that? Can't *we* do that?' However it happened, my whole attitude towards Dunbar changed within a week. It was very quick; we became excited very quickly. Within a week, and almost without reference to the rest of the executive committee, Mike Wilson and I had dinner with David Backhouse and said, 'Look, we would like to work with you, but the only way we could work with you, being absolutely realistic, is for us to acquire you.' And I started having a grand design in my mind with the sales force acting as the focal point for a wide range of financial services, and Dunbar providing the link. David Backhouse immediately got caught up with the same enthusiasm."

HOW STRATEGY CAN CREATE THE CULTURE OF AN ORGANIZATION

J. Sainsbury and Marks & Spencer, two of the world's most successful retail operations, share a similar strategy: they keep costs down; they sell goods which are always in demand; they are alert enough to move with the times; and, a much-underestimated success factor, they are pleasant to do business with. It is interesting that both M&S and Woolworth began by selling purely on low retail price. On the first M&S stall, everything cost a penny; Woolworth used to boast that everything they sold was ten cents or under. But it is Woolworth that has had to be taken over in Britain, whilst M&S flourishes.

As standards of living have risen, M&S have been shrewd enough to inject that extra touch of quality to keep the public coming back — even if, as one of their buyers confided, it is just a change in the pocket decoration on a dress. M&S did make the mistake of going too far ahead of their customers in the late 1970s when they introduced coats at over £100. The move coincided with the rise of both inflation and unemployment, and it was quickly dropped. But the secret of M&S's success is its relationship with its suppliers, which enables the shops to react quickly to shifts in public mood or taste.

Manufacturers are eager to supply M&S. The name alone can get them extra business elsewhere, and as M&S has over 250 branches, it can offer the makers long production runs. In return, M&S demand, and get, absolute control. They give their type specifications on all goods, from a pair of shoes to a tub of yoghurt. What's more, they send their own staff to the factories to check that their orders have been carried out. And it goes without saying that M&S drive a very hard bargain on price, particularly if they want to keep within a psychologically important price barrier in the shop, like £4.99. Occasionally a supplier is dropped — and that can be catastrophic for them. Some sell more than half their output to M&S. But, conscious of the need to avoid bad publicity, M&S usually eases the luckless firm out over a period. However, Cliffords Dairies, a yoghurt firm, has said that it keeps its M&S business down to prevent themselves becoming too dependent and enabling them to retain some freedom to bargain. Perhaps the wisest approach, though, is the northern clothes firm which sends its staff into M&S stores every Saturday to see which lines are moving. Then they have a good idea what change of orders they're going to receive on Monday morning.

The strategy at M&S might seem to be deceptively simple: maintain high standards of quality and give the customer good service. Many successful people claim that they have no deliberate strategy but that they do to the best of their ability whatever they are doing. In the case of M&S, beneath the broad term "high quality" or "customer service," there are a multitude of substrategies. There are rules and guidelines as regards buying and as regards staff relations. Some of these may have been laid down from the beginning. Some may have been developed over the years. Taken together, they provide the "culture" of the organization. Another organization with a very strong culture is IBM. Culture is more subtle, more complex, and more comprehensive than strategy. Culture is idiom, expectation, and morale. It is also image and above all self-image, both of the organization and the people working for it. Culture guides decisions in as definite a manner as strategy guides decisions. For a long time IBM refused to give discounts on its machines because it was IBM and they believed the customer could "take it or leave it." Today there is more flexibility, and with bulk orders there may be discounts. Again it is part of the culture of IBM to be realistic and flexible and to change when the market changes.

T A C T I C S

1. Do you need a strategy? If you are being successful without one, then perhaps you do not. Otherwise, you certainly do.

2. A strategy provides you with a reason for taking an initiative, for getting moving, for taking action.

3. A strategy provides you with a long-term view and hence the ability to take risks or do things which do not make sense in the short term.

4. A strategy provides you with guidelines for making decisions: does this fit my strategy?

5. There can be a specific strategy, a game plan of the steps you are going to take in order to succeed. This is like the strategy in a particular game of chess.

6. There can also be a general strategy which consists of guidelines and principles, and this general strategy can be applied to all situations.

7. Individual style, personality, and judgment can all act as strategies, but do not rely on them unless they are being successful at the moment.

8. A strategy is not a detailed plan (which you may need as well) but a broad overview.

9. From time to time spell out your strategy in a conscious and deliberate manner. Be conscious of the changes and alterations you may want to make.

10. Strategy is not only the manipulation of resources but also the development of those resources.

11

Team Strategy

T H E   P L A Y E R S :

United States: **Alex Kroll** · **Norman Lear** · **Jerald Newman**

United Kingdom and International: **Christian Bonington** · **Mike Brearley** · **Robert Holmes à Court** · **Verity Lambert** · **Sir Peter Parker** · **Jackie Stewart** · **Sting** · **Mark Weinberg** · **Charles Williams**

DEVELOPMENT OF RESOURCES

We think of generals moving their divisions about and directing strikes here and there. There is strategy in retreat, and there is strategy in advance. There is also the strategy of investing in one's own resources.

King Gustavus Adolphus II of Sweden (1594–1632) was the commander who most clearly directed the transition from medieval to modern war. He ascended his throne in 1611. Sweden had been at war during most of his life, and though young Gustavus had much military administrative experience, Sweden was poor, with a relatively small population, and could not field large armies. During the first ten years of his reign, Gustavus instituted a number of changes intended to make best use of his limited resources. He was first to group the many independent companies that comprised his force into battalions, and the battalions into brigades — an organization that survives to this day. This created a hierarchy of command, reduced the number of subordinate officers a commander had to control, and increased the command flexibility of the force.

He then altered the standard tactical deployment of the day, a formation called the "Spanish Box," which provided a great mass of force but did not make best use of the weapons the troops carried, because only a limited number came into action at point of contact with the enemy. Gustavus required his forces to deploy in line. That done, he adopted a system whereby his musketeers fired and then countermarched to the rear to reload.

He modified the cavalry too. Instead of attacking in mass, it was required to charge in line. First rank fired its pistols at contact; succeeding lines relied on the saber, using the pistol only for emergencies. Again, the maximum use was made of the existing manpower.

Gustavus did not overlook the weapons his army used. The musket was lightened from 25 to 11 pounds, making the musketeer more mobile and, incidentally, opening the ranks to less sturdy individuals. The pike was reinforced with a longer iron shank, which was intended to defeat the defenders' swords. The artillery was rationalized, leaving just three calibers in the field. This greatly simplified logistics. The lightest gun, firing a 3-pound shot, was deployed to the line and cavalry regiments, significantly increasing the flexibility of the artillery arm and adding to the shock action of the field units.

For the first time, an army commander produced the combined attributes of his individual force components to achieve his tactical objectives.

For the entrepreneur businessman, it is important to invest equally in his resources. For him, resources are people and money; his weapons — ideas. "These are the essential ingredients the entrepreneur puts together, and the people I just pick as good resources," says Robert Holmes à Court.

PEOPLE CARE

The important difference between sophisticated criminals and business executives is that the criminal does not want to depend either on investors or on market forces. The criminal wants all the pieces under his control. Otherwise there are plans, strategies, and investments in both situations. Although the criminal does not want to depend on investors, consumers, or even a labor force in the broad sense, he (or she) usually still has to depend on people. In most sophisticated crimes there is usually a team of people and then "people choice" and "people care" are even more important than in the average enterprise. "People care" is of *huge* importance in achieving success.

"There is no one, in my opinion, who is successful today that has done the whole thing on their own," claims racing driver Jackie Stewart. "There's no one who doesn't have a backup operation. If they don't have good delegation with a good machine behind them — a people machine — they will fail; make no mistake. The market will find them out; they will go into a slump and have no reserves, and will need other peoples' energies to bring them back. It may be an economic crisis which they won't be able to handle, because they're out on a limb and can't do everything themselves. They can't answer the phone and go to the toilet and sign a check, do a letter, and answer the door at the same time. So delegation has to take place. Really successful people, in my opinion, have always seen who are most valuable to them and who they must trust. They must make sure that other people recognize the degree of confidence that has been put upon them."

HOW TO CHOOSE THE BEST PEOPLE

On the whole successful people seem to be able to pick good people to work with. This almost always seems to be a matter of inborn judgment.

Jerald Newman: "I think that's, if I may say so, one of my most important attributes as an executive, and I sometime find that my executives will ask me to interview somebody or to spend a few minutes with them. And I'll say, 'Gee, I think you ought to hire that person,' or 'I don't think that person's for us,' and they'll say, 'Why?' And I'll say, 'Well, I really don't feel they're for us.' It's instinct. And I would say in well over nine out of ten cases, ultimately, a year from now, those people aren't with us, or two years from now, they do turn into problems."

There are few people who do not pride themselves on their ability to pick people. After all, everyone picks his or her friends.

How is that instinctive feeling likely to go wrong? We may employ a plausible charmer who turns out to be useless. (The question then becomes, how much damage has he done before his removal?) The bigger danger may be to reject highly efficient people you simply don't like at first sight. Then again, even if a person is highly effective, perhaps it is counterproductive to work alongside someone we do not like.

HIRE SOMEONE LOYAL TO THE INTENTION

Some successful people isolate particular qualities which they look for in people they choose. For Verity Lambert "enthusiasm" seems to be important.

Verity Lambert: "Choosing producers and people to work around you is a combination of two things. Obviously their experience does come into it a lot (though I do like to give people opportunities to move up). It's also very much a question of who I think I will like to work with. That doesn't mean people who will agree with me. I look for enthusiasm. I think enthusiasm encompasses dedication, because people who are very, very enthusiastic about ideas are dedicated to getting it done and making it work. One follows the other: enthusiasm, dedication, loyalty."

AVOID "YES-MEN"

Politicians are supposed to pick "yes-men" in order to reassure them, constantly, that the jointly held views are right. In business that is not always the case.

Sir Peter Parker: "You cannot deal with complicated situations [if you employ people who agree with you the whole time]. Blake would say, 'Opposition is true friendship.' And you, as management, have to reject the feeling that management must reject someone who's not been cloned to your style or tradition. You may have to have someone just because he is different. That is difficult for managements and business schools to comprehend."

Here is a very important point. What *is* the value of argument, disagreement, opposition, and the whole adversarial system so beloved of Western culture? In most of my books I have attacked it as a very inefficient system designed to keep things stable rather than to effect the changes that fluid circumstances require. There is little creative content to it, since both sides become ever more rigid in their clash.

So how does this view square with that put forward by Sir Peter Parker?

Perhaps it is just the sort of disagreement that he wishes to encounter?

I see it differently. There is something I might call "creative disagreement." For example, there may be alternative explanations of the results of a scientific experiment. From these may come alternative hypotheses and progress in science. To my mind there is a huge difference between "alternative" and "opposition." "Alternative" implies different perceptions, different ways of looking at things, different strategies, different emphases, which can be put forward and discussed. They are the very essence of creative thinking (see page 116ff.).

With opposition, the emphasis is not on exploration and alternatives, but on proving a point of view wrong. I am all for people spelling out and justifying their points of view, but this is not the same as argument. In argument (as in politics), the emphasis is directly on proving yourself right and the opposing party wrong.

FINDING THE RIGHT MAN FOR THE JOB

To reach the top position, an executive may have to be without or have kept hidden exactly those qualities he will need when he gets there. As an ascending manager, the executive must be a good problem-solver; otherwise the enterprise will not survive and he will not get noticed. Once at the top, problem-solving can be delegated, and what is then needed is strategic and conceptual thinking, which is quite different.

The designer of a race car is not necessarily a good Grand Prix driver. The designer of a business is not necessarily the best person to run it.

What all this suggests is that there is rarely such a thing as a multi-purpose "good" person who can be slotted in anywhere. There are different talents, and the particular situation may require a certain type of talent. The difficulty arises when a person who has the talents needed for one area advances into an area where those talents are not appropriate (I am not writing here about incompetence and the Peter Principle). . . . The salesman is not necessarily a good sales manager. The middle manager is not necessarily a good chief executive. . . . Which leads to the difficult point: do you recruit future senior managers or people to do the job you are seeking to have done? If you recruit only for future high fliers you may find that they stay with you a while and then move on to fly higher elsewhere.

Entrepreneur Mark Weinberg, explains the need for different types to fill different positions: "A chap came to me who'd invented this microwriter. He wanted to promote it too. He's a genius in many ways, but he's a terrible organizer and doesn't follow through. He thinks he's a good salesman because he can excite people about the initial concept, but he cannot follow through. The microwriter happens to be something that you do get very excited about when you first have it explained to you, but then you think, 'Now what the hell would I actually use it for, etc. etc?' He's an impulse type. My advice to him — and I suppose it is a generalized advice — is to analyze what you're good at and what you're not good at, and make sure that you've got a partner who can do the other things. Don't try to do the things yourself that you cannot do.

"I started Abbey Life [insurance company] entirely on my own, but then it was tiny during the first couple of years. I couldn't have got Hambro Life off the ground — fast, anyway — without a good sales manager. I'm good at thinking up concepts and I can talk to my sales manager and act as a biting board for him, but I'm not a very good man-manager, not actually a very good progressive salesman either. I can't go out and find people in the street. So I need a sales manager. I'm not a good administrative, details manager because that needs application the whole time. One chap, who was at university with me, is very good at that, and he's still head of the whole administrative side here. So the success of Hambro Life was very much having a complementary team: me doing the things I do well, myself, and not trying to do the things that I don't do well. I think I'm unusually good at putting together and packaging an idea, which may include the booklet and the visualization.

I wouldn't attempt to delegate that. When I have, it hasn't succeeded.

"So I said to the microwriter inventor, 'Really, when you analyze it, you're a bloody good inventor, but for goodness' sake stay away — you're not as good at marketing as you think. You just think that because you're excited about it, and communicate that excitement, that it will last. It won't last.' So you have to cut down on his role and make sure he's got partners that can form a team. If anyone had given him a million pounds it would all have gone within six months and he would have said he was a failure."

HORSES FOR COURSES

It is fashionable (and there is some sense to it) to believe that creative people are "right-brained" and methodical linear people are "left-brained." This can be taken to the extreme of a sort of intellectual racism: "I cannot have him for this job because I need a right-brained person and he is left-brained."

Alex Kroll, chief executive, Young and Rubicam: "I think I'm reasonably good at finding the right slots for people. If you think it would make a good analogy, I can see how people fit into relations, almost spatially with each other. Maybe it sounds crazy, but it's being able to conceptualize how various geometric shapes balance each other out. I can do that. I'm not sure it's the hardest decision for me to make, but it's the most important."

CONSTRUCT A BALANCED TEAM

Making up a team for anything is a careful design process. You do not just throw in all the talent available. In a cricket team there is a need for balance, and this point is made by Mike Brearley: "In selecting a team you nearly always start by having at least six places clear and fixed. Then, balance becomes important. You don't want two on the tail of people who can't bat and you've got to have at least four front-line bowlers, preferably five. There's got to be a range. You can't have all medium pacers. At the Test Match at Lords (1982), they had four medium-pace bowlers. Absolute nonsense! There was no variety and the one bowler they could use to bowl fast was Botham, but they used him for twenty overs at a time! He never stopped bowling, so he was reduced to being just like all the others.

"Ideally your batsmen are going to be different in character too. You want some people who are steady and are going to steady the boat, as it were, who are going to battle it through when it's difficult, going to see the new ball off, not going to get flustered if you're in a mess. . . . They'll battle their way out of it — they're survivors. And you also want people who are capable of taking the other side apart. Because otherwise things are going to be all at one pace. Gooch and Boycott were a good relationship."

Here we see people choosing almost as a design exercise. Just as a painter would carefully select and distribute his colors in order to achieve an effect, so Alex Kroll and Mike Brearley pick their teams. The advantage of cricket as an idiom is that the situation and the needs are so clearly defined. This is much more so than in business, where a general purpose "all-rounder" is believed to be capable of filling any role.

Charles Williams, besides being managing director of Ansbacher, the merchant bank, was captain of cricket at Oxford University and played for Essex County between 1953 and 1959. "I think there is a useful comparison [between cricket and business] in that if you're captain of a cricket team over a long period of time you would plan, as I've planned the Oxford side, to fill certain positions with certain types of player and certain types of personality. A team is made up of a mosaic, and in planning a company — as I've planned this company — the same considerations apply. How do I judge people? First of all you have to identify in your mind the profile of the sort of person you want for a particular situation. You have to recognize that you want somebody in a particular situation — that's terribly important. A lot of people go through life simply not recognizing that there *is* a gap that needs to be filled, and that is the first important thing. If you need a 'number three' batsman, because your 'number three' batsman isn't good enough at the moment, or you need to change the management of your ship-broking operation because somehow it's not working out, you must identify where the gap is. Having identified the gap, what — in the ideal world — would be your profile of the person to fill it?"

Similarities can be drawn, too, between composing a team for a mountaineering expedition. Chris Bonington explains: "The first thing in picking a team is to decide what it is you're trying to do. You then decide how you're going to do it. And from these two things you decide both how many people you need, what kind of people, and what skills you require. Having decided all those things, you then sit down and try to fit the right person into the job. This might sound terribly obvious, but it's amazing how many expeditions (and I suspect how many other functions) don't allow that very simple kind of line.

"Then the difficult thing is in deciding how people are going to work together. Of course it's made a lot easier if you've all actually climbed together before. But inevitably — on the larger expeditions, hopefully — you widen it slightly. For instance, we decided we would have one young climber for the Everest expedition and we had a short list of about six people. We, the inner core if you like — Doug Scott, Dougal Haston, and myself — tossed around all kinds of names before finally Peter

Boardman came up to see me. I had never met him before. We had a weekend's climb and he was a really nice guy, and so we plonked on him, and it worked out really well."

In personality assessment there is no substitute for working with someone in the equivalent of the "weekend climb." It might take much longer to assess the business ability of someone (it may be necessary to see how he responds to real pressures and problems), but personality can be assessed quite quickly. Robert Holmes à Court believes in the importance of trying people out:

"I cannot forecast how they'll come out, but I'm very capable of telling after the event whether they are any good or not. Once I had a short list of three financial people, and I employed all three and just waited to see which two faltered; the third one is actually here now. I give people the opportunities to succeed and do something well; that's the sense I use them in. I place the person in a position which is challenging and exciting, and I get a lot of enjoyment in watching them succeed, and it's my responsibility to replace him very quickly if he's not the right horse for that course. You cannot judge people well in advance. You cannot judge how they're going to perform. There are too many invisible factors, so I put them in and try them. I give a person complete freedom to develop his own style — he is absolutely free to do that and work in his own way."

PLANT A CATALYST

Sometimes it is not simply a question of recognizing the weaknesses in a team, or the skill gaps, it is also recognizing the need for catalysts in a team: it's being sensitive to the way individuals react to one another, how they complement one another.

Norman Lear, the TV writer, puts his success down to the people he worked with. "Simmons was very important to me, and Bud Yorkin was important. I view show business as a collaboration. I'm not about to sell myself short, but I am a collaborative individual, and I need collaboration, though I do do a lot of things alone. But one of my strengths is working with people and helping them achieve their best. I do that by giving my best, I guess, and caring about theirs."

The manager of Sting's group, Police, is Miles Copeland, who has approached the overseas markets, particularly, in a very considered way, with careful planning. "He is really the other side of the coin to me. In many ways I'm left to be creative," said Sting. "Miles is terribly militaristic and right-wing and very direct. In a sense, having those two sides of the coin working together (sometimes against each other, but usually to the same end) is really the key to our success. Miles has this world overview."

Does he take the role of a general? "More of a colonel! Although I don't like to think of myself as a puppet. I'm not. There is no feudal system here."

There is the backup type of partnership which is to be found among many successful people. There is also the "energizer" type of person who inspires people and gives them confidence to get going. This area of interaction of successful people with key people is important. It rarely seems to be a matter of creating the potential for success; it is more a matter of providing the right microenvironment in which the talents of a successful person can flourish.

"Without Hammett," said Lillian Hellman, "I felt I might not have written."

12

Team Motivation

T H E   P L A Y E R S :

United States: **Nolan Bushnell · Roy Cohn · Werner Erhard · Rafer Johnson · Herman Kahn · Billie Jean King · Alex Kroll · David Mahoney · Jerald Newman**

United Kingdom and International: **Professor John Adair · Mike Brearley · Sir Terence Conran · Mickey Duff · Hans Eysenck · Alan Fine · Lord Forte · Robert Holmes à Court · Robert Maxwell · Sir Peter Parker · Lord Pennock · Ron Pickering · John Ritblat · Lord Robens · Margaret Thatcher · Mark Weinberg · Charles Williams · Bob Willis**

USE PEOPLE WISELY

Some people say what they mean without any euphemisms. That might be expected from Roy Cohn, the famous tough lawyer, who tells how people get used: "Let's face it, life is a mutual thing. Being 'used' may be a little bit of a tough word, but it's probably an accurate word, politically."

Sir Terence Conran: "It is very important that we in Habitat give everybody the opportunity to be shareholders in the business. I think this is very effective and useful. It is something we began seven or eight years ago. But I think the last thing you should ever make people think is that they're being used. Never exploit people. What you do is see that their talents and qualities are exploited to the best. People whose talents are not exploited become disenchanted and disruptive."

Here we have another of these problems which crop up so often with language. The word "exploited" is used with opposite meanings. The words "exploited," "manipulated," and "used" all have dreadfully negative meanings. They suggest that people are being used as puppets, slaves, automata, and all for the benefit of a greedy capitalist boss. Yet, as Sir Terence points out, there is the opposite meaning: placing someone in the best surroundings for that person, allowing that person to use his or her talents; appreciating and rewarding those talents.

CREATE A SENSE OF INVOLVEMENT

There are successful people who work very much on their own or with a small staff. There are others whose medium of action is a large organization. For them it is vital that the employees are involved and know what is going on.

"The important thing is that managements must involve employees, lead employees, and make sure that they comprehend the real economic facts of the business. At least twice in my life I have been faced with enormous problems of near bankruptcy," recalls Lord Pennock. "On each occasion I have found that I worked very hard not for a day, not for a week, not for a month, but for two, three, four years making sure that the shop floor understood the problems and helped to solve them. Let me give you an example:

"In 1965–6 I became chairman of ICI's Agricultural Division. In the three years previous to that, the business had moved from having five 30,000-ton ammonia plants, which were closed down, to having two 200,000-ton plants and building three 300,000-ton plants — all in four years. When I arrived, the 300,000-ton plants had just been built and none were working! Now, the problems of that were absolutely immense. The business had been capitalized by £400 million, yet it was only earning £4 million profit — it was a disaster! I had eighteen months to two years of doing a lot of painful things: getting rid of top people who obviously couldn't cope, bringing in people who could, but recognizing that they wouldn't do it in five minutes, and getting the shop stewards on my side. I had to say to them, 'Look, if you don't recognize the difficulties we're in and give all the help you can, this place, which is the biggest chemical factory in Europe, will close.' And I remember taking 35 shop stewards up to the top of the tower on the office block at the divisional HQ at Billingham, and saying: 'Here it is — seven miles round and two miles across; it's the biggest chemical factory in Europe and I'm telling you that just like Rolls Royce (which had recently closed), in two years' time it will be shut if you and I, together, don't do something about it.'

"My wife will tell you privately that it put ten years on me physically, that time. But the point is that I recognized that I had to get everybody with me on the plant — particularly the militant shop stewards. I also had to get management with me. I had to get management to feel 'Jesus, this guy's got the toughest bloody job and we've got to do all we can to see him through (which incidentally will see us through as well).' So I had to generate that without creating panic. I had to unleash their efforts, if you like."

Mike Brearley: "When I came back to captain England against Australia when Ian Botham was kicked out, they hadn't won a Test Match for 13 Tests, Botham hadn't scored a 50 for 12 Tests or taken 5 wickets in an innings for 13 Tests. First of all, I wanted to find out what the attitude was in the team. I asked Graham Gooch because he was a sensible bloke; I knew John Enbury and Mike Gatting, so I began to get an image of what was going on in the side. One of the things that Graham Gooch said was that we were losing matches because of poor catching. He said that the whole attitude to practicing catching, getting fielders in the right position, and generating a feeling of confidence had gone. So I just said that what I always did as captain was have a lot of catching practice before each day's play — especially sharp close stuff, slip fielding. It became a key part of the day. We'd fix a time for it — 35 or 40 minutes before the start — and at that time it would take precedence over everything else. . . . Gradually it worked, partly we started to win; each bit feeds off the other bit. You can't actually say, 'This was better, so that got better,' because once it begins to happen everyone gets excited and starts to do it naturally."

Good motivation is an infectious thing. It may start at the top but soon travels right through a company. "People who have been here at the Institute," says Herman Kahn, "have done better work than they've done in their entire lives. In many cases I don't know why they do better work; there's something in the atmosphere that does it."

DISPLAY A SENSE OF INVOLVEMENT

One way of getting involved is to show that you have "hands on" experience. Another is deliberately to cross barriers and boundaries that normally separate bosses from workers. Kahn talks about the value of "hands-on" experience for its own sake: "Pick up a shovel; work a computer. You need hands-on experience. If you don't have hands-on experience, be conscious that you don't have it. You need confidence to get anything done, but you don't want blind confidence, foolish confidence. You have to understand that if you lack hands-on experience, you lack something important. It shouldn't paralyze you, but be aware of it."

Lord Robens, ex-chairman of the Coal Board, made a point of going down the pits and he continued to go down the pits, even though after the first few visits he knew what was happening. Was this to sell himself? To try and get himself known to everybody? "No, it wasn't. The main job inside the Coal Board was the human engineering. It was to enable the men who worked down the pits to see this chap who was the chairman of the board and recognize that he was an ordinary human being and didn't have horns and a tail and was ready to listen to problems. I didn't just go down the pit — I'd go down in the morning, but when I came up about noon or one o'clock, then we'd have a buffet lunch at which representatives from various parts of the pit (such as the trade union or the lodge committee) came along too. That enabled me to move around and chat to everybody. This was contrived so I could maximize the number of chaps I met. I met some fine people. I met painters. I met men who wrote poetry. Men who wrote books. It was a rich experience. And I just wasn't going down pits to inspect new machinery and new devices. It was very much to meet the chaps, both on the job and off the job; to give a much better understanding of their hopes, their ambitions, and their aspirations. And their fears. Yes, and their fears. And I think we did our pit closures well, because we understood their apprehension and fears. And we took all the steps it was possible to take to remove those fears and apprehensions.'

In an interview with the *London Evening Standard*, Professor John Adair noted a distinct lack of talent in this area within British management: "Our great weaknesses are too many class barriers, too many chairmen sitting behind desks. Joe Gormley [ex-leader miners' union] was right when he told a TUC conference in the '60's, 'What we want now is leaders, not bosses.' "

It's nothing new — inspiration by example: the same that Napoleon used. His personal bravery, characterized by his presence in the leading files of a bayonet attack which captured an important bridge, won him the nickname "the little corporal." His greatest adversary, Arthur Wellesley, the First Duke of Wellington, had personal qualities which meant that his very presence gave inspiration and heart to his troops. His men trusted him to see that casualties were as light as possible; he trusted them to fight. He took pride in them — and they knew it.

YOU DON'T HAVE TO BE LIKED

Charm is a useful tool for getting things done. Sometimes it is sufficient by itself. It can, however, be a liability in two ways: when the charm is turned off, there is a noticeable difference; also, it may preclude the ruthlessness needed for a particular decision. A leader's need to be loved may place him in a similarly vulnerable position. His actions may be governed by his wish to preserve this image. Yet a beloved leader can achieve wonders, especially in difficult times. We can solve this dilemma with a form of words: a leader should not "need" to be loved but should behave in such a manner that he (or she) is loved. The second case does not have the dependence of the first case. We can also solve the dilemma by bringing in the word "respect."

David Mahoney: "I'm not so insecure to think that that's important. I want the respect. I'd like them to like me. I do the very best I can. But I can't forget what my role is. My role is to run this company as well as I can financially, substantively, pick the right people, get the goals correct, see that they're implemented." And Harold Evans: "If you can forget about wanting to be popular or ruling people, then really that is a better way."

GIVE THEM GOALS

In the first place, people must have a clear idea of what is expected of them. Where do they fit into the overall strategy? One very good reason why they should know this is that later, the achievement of clearly defined goals will be a prime motivator. Success is self-perpetutating.

Mike Brearley: "Before the afternoon's play begins I decide in a clear way how we are going to play, so that the boys know exactly what we're going to do. For example I might say, 'I want you to bowl for 4 overs flat out, and if you haven't got X out by then I shan't keep you bowling — give it 4 overs.' So, the fellow knows what he has to do and that I don't want him to hold anything back.

"You must give the team a feeling that you're thinking about the game. It's no good walking onto the field saying, 'Who the hell's going to bowl?' or 'Oh, he's batting, is he?' I have already entered into the afternoon's play. I have an idea for the policy or strategy of it and try to give bowlers and fielders the feeling that we have got other tricks up our sleeve, that what we are doing now is not our last resort."

Coach Rafer Johnson agrees but argues for an inspired and almost sensitive matching of goals to resources: "You get the best out of people by establishing what the program is, letting your people know what you would like the results to be. But not so specifically, or you will make them a little uptight; you must have a little flexibility in what those results can be; allow people to bring their own personal touch to what they're doing; allow them to expand on their strengths, rather than spending a whole lot of time yelling at them about how you expect them to perform or about what you think those final results should be. I think this is true in both sport and business. The key is to understand that just because you are coach or you are boss, it doesn't mean you know everything there is to know. You may know the most, but you do not know what's going on inside every individual. What you really want is to get every person producing to their maximum. The most effective way is not only to let them know what the goal is or the goals are, but to let them know that they can bring themselves to that point without being ridiculed.

"Find a spot for each person in terms of what their production level is, and make them the best at what they are."

HOW ATTAINABLE DO THEY HAVE TO BE?

This is a difficult matter because this is where the value of dreams and objectives gets mixed up. It seems that successful people do have both. At different times they may, however, emphasize distant targets or attainable targets. You do have to have something within range to shoot at.

Sir Peter Parker: "I always say to people who come up with big plans, 'What's the attainable target?' If you're having a big appeal for charity, say, don't make it overwhelmingly big! Let people feel you're winning and that you're building. I think that Utopian visions unnerve people. I am not a Utopian; I am a pluralist. And I want to see attainable objectives appear from people."

While Alex Kroll would not sanction unrealistic targets, built in to his philosophy of success is the notion of stretching oneself: "Mine are all uncomfortable goals." As we have seen (page 31) the concept is taken from his own experience. Perhaps the most practical advice, however, is a kind of middle way between Kroll's "uncomfortable goals" and Parker's "attainable targets." Inherent in the management philosophy of Lord Weinstock, managing director of GEC (Britain's largest industrial group), is a sense of self-reliance. Weinstock is a second-generation immigrant whose parents died when he was still a child: the self-reliance this taught him was reinforced by two years' wartime evacuation. In the 1950s Weinstock rode the TV boom in company with his father-in-law, an early television manufacturer, whose daughter he had met when he was still helping his brother, a hairdresser. In 1960 the company was taken over by General Electric Company — but with Weinstock in charge, as GE's management was growing old. His watchword continued to be self-reliance; he questioned everything and made sure that every operation paid by setting his managers targets (if they failed, they were warned a couple of times, and then "Out!"). The skill lay in his personal credo: pitch the targets high enough to extract the maximum, but not so high as to be out of reach.

Part of both Kroll's and Weinstock's approach to target-setting is an unwillingness to articulate an upper limit: trainers of athletes feel the same. "Because a man cannot run 100 yards in zero seconds, logically there is a limit," admits Ron Pickering. "But I have been involved in sport for 30 years and never failed to be amazed at how frequently the records are broken and by what margins. These limits are not there at the moment, and certainly they're not in the minds of kids. Don't tell Daley Thompson that his world record is unbreakable; he knows that he can break it tomorrow. The day any athlete feels he has arrived, he has arrived."

HOW TO COMMUNICATE GOALS

The function of communication in spelling out goals is clearly not the same as what we might call "oiling the wheels of everyday life." A visitor from outer space with no knowledge of human relationships, but a sophisticated familiarity with computers, might assume that all communication was primarily concerned with the transfer of factual information. To him, the question "How are you today?" would be a request for details of the other person's state of health, rather than a commonplace ritual greeting, a drop of social oil. Failing to recognize the difference between the two can sometimes lead to a breakdown in communication altogether. As Oscar Wilde said, "A bore is someone who when asked how he is, tells you."

KEEP IT CLEAR

At the lowest level, the function of communication in spelling out goals is to transfer factual information. This is not as straightforward as it sounds. For example, it has been clearly shown that the average student's concentration lapses after 20 minutes and that around 90 percent of material spoken in a lecture is forgotten. Yet many universities still rely heavily on the one-hour lecture as a central part of the teaching course. Again, there is a high likelihood that what is said will be misinterpreted:

"Everyday Americanese can be misinterpreted depending on where the other person is coming from," agrees David Mahoney. "We use the English language as sloppy as hell in the world! American is the only language which has one word for 'love' — you love your children; you love the Yankees; you love apple pie; you love your wife and your girlfriend. Everything you love! There are about 30 words in the Greek. There are about 25 in the Latin. There is eternal love, this love, that love, etc. So, we throw things out and wonder why people have trouble in understanding and communicating.

"We all have trouble communicating. You know what my intensity comes through to many people as? It comes through as angry! I'm intense as I'm talking to you about what I'm thinking. But to some people it's 'Christ, he's angry again . . . he's mad!'"

As a lawyer, Roy Cohn depends on people being able to interpret him correctly: "I try to make it simple. I try consistently to do two things. I do try to be grammatical, but I also try to use simple language. Pithy and effective. I use key phrases, and I don't talk down to juries."

OBTAIN A RESPONSE

"Sometimes humor is the tool that crosses all barriers of communication. We're in the business of selling ideas," says Herman Kahn. "I particularly use humor a lot in our briefings and I use it in a way which helps carry conviction."

"Humor? It's great," agrees David Mahoney. "Most people don't appreciate it, or are afraid of it. But I use it a lot, though sometimes I have found that what I think is amusing offends somebody."

"LISTEN TO THE OTHER PERSON LISTENING"

To reduce the possibility of misinterpretation in communication, Werner Erhard prescribes a measure of empathy with an interlocutor: "I don't listen to myself when I talk; I listen to the other person's listening. When I'm speaking, I am not trying to say it accurately; I am trying to have it heard accurately."

GIVE IT PERSONAL RELEVANCE

If you think back over the newspaper that you read a few hours ago, a few points will be remembered, while most is forgotten. If you take that farther and ask yourself why certain things have stuck in your mind, it will probably be because many of the things remembered have some special significance for you. One characteristic of the successful teacher is that he is able to make his students see the value of what is being taught in terms of their own lives.

Jerald Newman: "I think what goes into good communication is not only what you're presenting but the entire background of the individual who is listening: their religious background, their educational background, their experiential background, their parentage, everything."

Billie Jean King about the tennis coach she had when she was sixteen years old: "The main thing Alice Marble did was help me to understand how to win. And it was important to me that she wasn't just a champion talking to me — she was a woman who was a champion. For the first time in my life I sensed a sort of legacy that I was part of."

Communication involves both context and content. The content is the script, and we tend to feel that it is the most important part. In the sense of communicating goals, context covers the way the content is put (words, phrasing, sequence, aids) and where the receiver is at (mood, history, concepts, peer pressure, etc.). Later, in "Tactical Play," we will see how such things as image and appearance might prove similarly useful to the negotiator.

GIVE THEM YOUR TRUST

The late Sir Maxwell Joseph was one of property man John Ritblat's most important mentors: "I saw from him that if you wanted to do what I'll term 'great things,' then the only way is to put your trust in good people and let them get on with it. Now when I say, 'Put your trust in good people,' that doesn't mean that you neglect them or fail to look over their shoulder. But you so arrange matters that you're constantly accessible so that they can chew it over with you. This means that you become a sounding board for them just as they are for you. And you make sure that in your crew of talent you have people who are very orderly and have the attribute to keep great control, particularly financial control, on your various activities."

"If you've got the right people around you," says Margaret Thatcher, "and they can come in to see you and talk to you, tell you what you've asked them to find out, you can often knock off what might be three hours' paperwork in thirty minutes."

Sometimes it is difficult to get people to accept confidence in their abilities — this may need to be forced upon them: "I almost absolutely delegate," say Mark Weinberg. "The control of the sales force I delegate so absolutely that the marketing director has to make the initiative to get me to comment on what he is doing. He came up through the ranks, actually, although I recognized his strengths more than the person he reported to. When he eventually succeeded the person who'd done it before, he'd been used to reporting quite closely to that chap. So he'd come each week to me, expecting me to give him directions and answers. Although he's a very strong-minded person, he's been so conditioned to expect someone to tell him what to do or OK what he wants to do that you would almost have to *sell* delegation to him. So I would say, 'OK, that's fine, and look, Mike, I can trust your judgment; you're the person that's got to do it.' And then we would have difficulty making a weekly meeting, perhaps, and I would say, 'Well, I don't mind very much, Mike; I'm basically relying on you to make the judgment.' So we stopped meeeting."

Nolan Bushnell agrees: "If you try to delegate responsibility without authority, you end up with a 'yes-man'; then it's cheaper to buy a mirror. A lot of people get carried away with a sense of self-importance and find it very ego-stroking to have others ask, 'Hey, boss, should I do this, this, and this?' I really prefer to force people to make their own decisions. Often they're closer to the problem than I am and if I can't trust their judgment, then they ought not to work here."

But delegation must not mean an absence of communication. Lord Forte: "Without delegation we couldn't have reached where we are in a very difficult trade [catering/hotelkeeping], because the trade is so detailed. I delegate on a very long string — as long as possible. I keep hold of that string, however, and occasionally want to know what is happening." Charles Williams: "If you've got the right people, you are confident that you can delegate. But I always like to keep my toe somewhere near the water. I regard communication as being very important. . . . I always keep the door open and regard it as symbolically very important that people can just walk into the office."

The nature of delegation clearly depends in the first place on the nature of the business. Where there are a number of small decisions that have to be taken, but the broad direction is unchanged, then it should be easy to delegate. Where the decisions are big and creative, then delegation is more difficult. A key question is whether the entrepreneur has confidence that the other person will carry out instructions or make important decisions in his own right. "If I don't trust their judgement," Bushnell correctly points out, "then they ought not to work here." But does the general want company commanders that follow the master plan or ones that take the initiative within the overall direction? There are circumstances where individual initiative could be disastrous; there are circumstances where the inability of company commanders to take the initiative has been equally disastrous. In the end, feedback and communication is a vital part of delegation.

HOW TO PRODUCE CHANGE IN PERSONNEL

Rewards are a powerful way of producing change, though subject to certain limitations. We tend to think of rewards in terms of cash or presents; the model here is getting one's way through bribery. Unfortunately, the more rewards are used, the weaker the effect. To achieve the same result, the price has to be increased. Another problem is that the recipient can become satiated. Money can become as meaningless to the rich man as sweets can become nauseating to the child with a full stomach. It has been shown that such rewards can be effective, if given intermittently, so these problems can be partly overcome. However, a much more important discovery in the psychology of learning is that whereas rats and pigeons like to be rewarded with food, humans may be just as pleased to receive approval and appreciation rather than material rewards. Although an advertisement might say, "When did you last buy her flowers?" the marriage counselor may ask, "When did you last tell her how much you appreciate her energy and sense of humor?"

"I have executives on low salaries who deal with millions of pounds," says Robert Holmes à Court. "If they suddenly owned those millions, would it matter very much? I'm sure that people feel they want money; the factor that's really important is that people want what they feel they are entitled to. If a person is on a salary and he feels he's entitled to another £1,000 a year, he can get quite hung up if he doesn't get what he thinks he's worth, whether he needs it or not. It's a measurement of his work."

Robert Maxwell: "My worst fault, I'd say, is in not handing out the honey spoon more often. I still tend to be the barrel of vinegar of complaint rather than thanking people often enough for the excellent contribution they've made to the company."

DIFFERENT APPROACHES FOR DIFFERENT PEOPLE?

Bob Willis, current England cricket captain: "Mike Brearley is quietly ruthless, and he knows the difference between a stick and a carrot." The stick he has applied in the past so successfully on Ian Botham, England's fiery fast bowler — it consists of hard looks, baiting. "If Mike told *me* I was bowling like an old woman," says Willis, "I'd believe him and fold up." The carrot — encouraging positive remarks about what in a person's performance is going right — the calm and friendly approach — is reserved for Willis.

"I'm a bit of a tub thumper," admits Ron Pickering. "I'm recognized in that light — going around and banging tables and saying, 'This is what we in Britain can do, and this is what you kids can do.' So people expect that from me, and I can personalize that.

"But that is not to say that you can use the one rule to cover all. You tend to get branded as a verbal motivator and from then on people think you shout at everybody in the same way and that you don't take individual personalities into consideration. That would be grossly wrong. My personality, as a coach, is very useful for 75 percent of the journey. At that point I will have either alienated some athletes forever or involved those who want to follow my path and become disciples. Then I will have to start learning about them in a highly personal way.

"It's a very difficult thing to explain. You can talk to an athlete in mechanical terms, or in physiological terms, and you'll talk to each athlete differently. All you're trying to do is to create a personal language between the two of you. It really doesn't matter what the scrutineer thinks about that language. It doesn't really matter if it stands up to scientific scrutiny or not. It's like a coach standing on the side of a track when a guy has run three-quarters of his race and he's way out front and he's given 98 percent of his effort, and there's the coach on the track screaming at him, 'Relax.' Of all the absurd ironies, you might say. But he has a language that that guy might understand, while you stand back and observe the coach doing that and think the man's a fool. But if the coach is trying to say to the kid, 'Conserve your energy, put all your efforts into your legs and get rid of the tension, head and shoulders up' — that one word 'relax' might mean that to the kid. Whereas anyone watching might think, 'What's the fool talking about?' It's a personal language an intensely personal thing."

Pickering goes on to explain how he motivated Lynn Davies to win an Olympic gold medal at the long jump: "Lynn was very shy — it was really part of his social development. As a seventeen-year-old, fairly diffident youth, he showed a tremendous amount of talent in rugby, in soccer, and in athletics. And I stood over him and said things like 'Do you want to be the greatest athlete that Wales has ever seen? If you do, you're going to have to take a unique course of action. You're going to have to train harder than anybody's perceived before. You're going to have to do things that nobody has considered before. You're going to have to go places. I'm telling you now that I think you have the talent to be the best athlete that Wales ever saw.' I said, 'I'm going to go home, I'm going to write you a letter, and I'm going to tell you what you ought to start doing to follow this way of life, and you let me know whether you want to do it.' He wrote back, and it was one of those 'Dear Sir, thank you very much for your interest and I'd be very happy to be the first man on your squad when you come to Wales.' It was a very nice and very modest acceptance of a job.

"So our relationship just grew. And it was a very intense one, but it wasn't without its problems. I realized that if I couldn't earn his respect in other aspects of life, then I'd be no good to him as a coach. I'm not saying that he needed my approval; I'm saying our relationship was so strong that he would automatically discuss things with me. The thing that I knew in my heart of hearts was that the way to get the best out of Lynn Davies, in a motivational sense, was for me to almost alienate the audience. I would put all the sympathy on his side, but I would be the bully and castigate him in front of everybody. I would cast every aspersion in his direction; I would berate him. I would make all sorts of horrendous remarks. He would lay on a demonstration in front of 200 people and he'd jump 25 feet, which they'd never seen in their lives; they'd all break out into rapturous applause. But I would say, 'Do you honestly think 200 people have traveled thousands of miles to see crap like that? Do you really seriously believe that is something you ought to feel inordinately proud of? I've seen you do that in training in the rain. It's sunshine now and the wind's behind you; do you not think these people deserve something slightly better than that?' So immediately the sympathy would go on his side, and I would be the enemy of the piece. He always reacted. In a lecture, he'd be the butt of all my jokes, but he thrived — he could come back. There were always escape routes, and he thrived when he came to demonstrate. He would respond."

Mary Rand was the first British woman athlete to win an Olympic gold medal. Again it was the long jump, again it was in 1964 in Tokyo. "She was a great competitor — besides long jumping, hurdling, sprinting, and competing in the pentathlon was her forte." Pickering didn't personally coach Mary Rand — she was coached by John Mazure — "but I helped her with her weight lifting and her strength training. She was so vocal and verbal; she'd tell you to get stuffed. Quite different from Lynn Davies in her reactions. If I said, "OK, so you're a pretty bird and you think you look fantastic and everybody admires you, do you think we could see you jumping?' She'd say, 'Balls.' "

Mike Brearley, noted for his perception of what makes people tick, explains how different relationships between leader and team player arise. "It isn't often that I sit down and decide *that* is how I will approach somebody. It's a much more instinctive thing. In fact, we all alter our behavior with different people. Different people draw out different things in us. Some people draw out the cantankerous, some people draw out the tender. It's not that you're a chameleon. You've got your own identity clearly there. There are *ranges* in personalities. There are different *tunes* you can play on your own instrument (rather than being played upon, as Hamlet put it).

"Obviously you hope there's enough of your identity as a person and as a captain that isn't just borrowed from other people, that isn't influenced too regularly by other people's styles." But occasionally he admits to adopting a specific tactic: "I developed a policy to deal with Geoff Boycott. At times he could be very cooperative; at other times — if he wasn't feeling right — he'd 'take his bat home,' as it were. Also, the great danger with him is that he talked down to people. He'd tell you something fairly sensible as if you'd never thought of it before and make you feel like a fifteen-year-old schoolboy. He thought he should be captain. So I decided after feeling really furious with him that although I was 'grateful' to him for being so helpful, that I wouldn't rely on him too much. I would pick my moment to ask him what he thinks — and be rather brief about it. And at the same time I would tell him when he's playing well, or encourage him with his batting in a way one might not expect he needs. That was a little bit of a policy. Sometimes you work out why things are going wrong and you try and adopt a policy to deal with them, to help you through it. Somehow or other you have to get people to want to play well when you're captain. You can be more or less authoritarian, more or less jokey, more or less pally. Captains have got to be able to stand back and not just be one of the boys; that's for sure."

USING THE STICK

The basic problem with punishment is that it leads to resentment and antagonism. This is particularly noticeable in close relationships: for example, in an unsuccessful marriage where communication has become almost exclusively punitive — even to the point where attempts at reconciliation lead to abrasive rows. Nevertheless, there are some occasions when admonishment, criticism, and reprimand are *skills* which the man-manager will need to perfect.

THE VALUE OF CONFRONTATION

"There will be times," agrees Alan Fine of the Inner Game Organisation, "when I will scream and shout at somebody if that's what they need. It is not often there's a need for that. Ninety percent of people are overaroused, overanxious — at least that's how it seems to me — and what they need is relaxing. But occasionally it is the only way you can communicate. If their mind is in a tizz, you scream and it gets through."

The purpose of confrontation is to challenge the attitudes, beliefs, or behavior of another person in such a way that he will at least consider change. It is one of the hardest interpersonal skills to master effectively. The problem with many confrontations, is, as we have said, that they are experienced by some people as punishing or attacking. This leads to alienation. Attitudes harden, and change becomes less likely — the reverse of what is intended.

But, in order for rewards to be credible they must be interspersed with criticism when this is needed. Some people are so skilled at human relations that they can even make the criticism sound like a reward: "I am disappointed in this — it is not up to your usual standards." Rewards can be given in the form of specific praise or through the transmission of an "image." The reward is to know that the rewarded person has that image or picture of you.

There are people who resent criticism because it is offered harshly and apparently without respect.

Be clear as to what is being criticized. Is it a particular action? Is it general performance? Is it an attitude?

Giving the person an insight into his (or her) own mind is a good way of doing it. "Imagine you were sitting in this chair and looking at your performance, what might you say?" "If you were to describe your sales performance over the last month, how would you describe it?" Another neat way is to use the PMI (Plus, Minus, Interesting) technique from the thinking lessons I developed.

Another approach is to take the criticism for granted and immediately to look for explanations: "These sales figures are well below what we expected, let's try and see what went wrong and the reasons for this." Having sorted out some possible reasons (and been careful about excuses), the next stage is to move on to what can be done in the future. Alternative strategies can be discussed. Underlying the whole discussion is the realization that what is being done is not good enough.

GETTING RID OF PEOPLE

Just as individuals can react in different ways to confrontation techniques, so some managers find it more difficult than others to get rid of employees even when it is absolutely necessary.

Robert Holmes à Court: "There have been executives that have been no good, that fail, so you quit them."

Do you find that an easy process?

"Very easy."

Because it is business, after all?

"Because it's the goal of success, and an incompetent executive stands in the way, so you drop him out. If you select a cricket team, your goal is to win the game, so you say to the fellow who hasn't been scoring very well, 'I'm going to drop you from the team.' If he says, 'Well, I've known you for a long time. I enjoy playing the game,' it's not our objective really. You do it for the club, and you bring in the other one who you don't know but who's scoring well. I treat my executives and racehorses like that. The ones that win go in. Executives I have to change, change their duties, drop them — constant monitoring and changing."

Professor Eysenck: "When people are ideologically motivated to deny the truth for a political rather than a scientific argument, I don't mind hurting them if needs be."

John Ritblat: "I think firing people is an obligation of management. I don't think you have any choice. I mean, I don't like it at all, but my experience is that when you bring unpleasant things to an end, it's better for everybody. I'm a great believer in being cruel to be kind. There's nothing worse, for instance, than employing people in the wrong slot. You know there can be no future for them and that it's only going to go downhill. It would affect a great number of people. In public companies you have no choice. In a company like ours with employees and shareholders and loan stockholders and suppliers from other industries, where you may be affecting 20,000 other people, you cannot allow sentiment to influence you over a handful of people."

Lord Forte: "It would affect me, in nearly every case — good, bad, or indifferent though the person may be. But not in *all* cases. In some cases I'm very delighted to see the back of people. But I don't like doing it myself. I'm a bit hypocritical in that way. I don't like saying to a man, 'You've got to go'; I always like someone else to do that. And I have the privilege of not having to do that, so I use that privilege."

That's the privilege you've worked for?

"I had to do it once."

Sir Peter Parker: "I have tried to nurse some people along too long after I've realized I was being overoptimistic."

Because you won't admit to yourself that you were wrong?

"That's right! It's nothing to do with whether I'm being ruthless or not ruthless. It's really that I'm trying to kid myself, not facing up to my wrong decision. I don't find it a trouble to deal with human situations in the sense that we've got to part company or have a row or something. But I find that very often I've made a choice and not been quick enough to say: 'I've made a wrong choice.' "

Nolan Bushnell: "I think it's better to be a really good firer than necessarily a good hirer. I mean, that sounds really rough and tough, but the fact is there are a lot of people who take wonderful interviews, can put together impeccable résumés, and charm you out of your socks, then two months into the job you say, 'Hey, this guy's not right!' "

Robert Maxwell: "I'm enormously aware of the problem because I come from a very poor family. My father was an unemployed farm worker, and I remember, as a young man, asking my mother why my father wasn't working. And she told me that Conservative politicians had so arranged matters that there were millions of people unemployed all over the world.

"So I feel deeply the responsibility I have when terminating anyone's job.

"But as a manager, who is responsible, say, for some 12,000 people, it is imperative that I save the maximum number of jobs I can. And if this means having to ask people to give up their jobs — in fact, compelling them to give up their jobs in agreement with their trade unions — I must do it. On the same principle, if you suffer an illness in which, if you don't cut off a finger it means the whole body will die, you must do it, no matter how hurtful, how upsetting, it is to you as well as to the person concerned."

Herman Kahn: "It's almost like getting rid of a mother or a wife because someone prettier came around. In other words, you are loyal to each other, but the loyalty is not absolute. It's hard."

David Mahoney: "When you let somebody go, it affects their family; more important, it affects their psyche. I'm aware of it. It's the high risk. It's the high-wire act. It's the high-wire act for them in the sense they're paid a lot, they're up on that wire, and they fall. Nobody likes to see the crash."

Mickey Duff: "The most unpleasant task anyone in boxing has is to tell a boxer to retire. Most times it doesn't happen, as you can gradually ease a boxer out and let him keep his macho — let him believe it was his own decision. But I had a very bad experience not long ago. John Conteh came to me and wanted to continue boxing. I didn't see any reason why he shouldn't. I knew he was going to continue because he needed the money. But I said, 'You know, you're going to have a problem with your license. You've just written a story to say that you get dizzy spells. It would be very difficult for you to go to the Board of Control and tell them, "I did that for money and I was telling lies" — they won't accept that. They'll say they've got it in writing, you'll have to do something about it.'

"So I sent him to a top neurologist. And the report came back, and I had to send it straightaway to the British Boxing Board of Control. Then I had the unpleasant duty of telling him that he'd never get a license again.

"I had to think as I was telling him, 'I was present at all the adulation and back-slapping when he won the World Title, and I'd got him that title here.' Conteh and I had had a great love-hate relationship for many years. He left me on four or five occasions, but he always came back. The funny thing is that we never stopped talking. There are fighters I've fallen out with, managers I've fallen out with. But I don't fall out with fighters usually."

Mark Weinberg: "I'm not a person who enjoys shouting and dismissing people. Some people love it; it gives them adrenaline. I'm not like that at all. Luckily for me, there's only been three or four times when I've really had to get the person who reports directly to me and either criticize them or dismiss them. I do it in a quietly rational way. I almost sell it to them by saying 'Look, here are your strong points and here are your weak points, and this is why we have to do this or that or the other.' I tell them the position. I think that's probably right."

There are people who are dangers and disasters and if they are not removed from their positions, then much damage will be done. There are others who are adequate but are occupying a position that should be occupied by someone who can do a lot better (it may even be that the same person has done better in the past and has got tired or bored). Then there are others who are passengers.

These passengers are not getting in anyone's way. They are simply an expense which the company carries as an overhead. Getting rid of such people is emotionally more difficult, because there is often nowhere for them to go. The high-flier can go and high-fly somewhere else. It is also much easier to point out where a person has gone wrong than to say: "You are good but not good enough." In practice, what often happens is that the person is shifted to some other position and then resigns. The difficult point is to decide whether a corporation exists to make profits, satisfy its investors, and to survive in a competitive world, or whether it exists to provide work for its employees. It is clear that the second aim is the more important, but the second aim can only be followed if the organization can exist, and that may depend on following the first aim. An organization like IBM comes close to satisfying the second aim because they have done so well with the first.

TACTICS

1. In taking someone on, decide quite clearly whether you want a general-purpose "all rounder" or someone for a specific job. If the latter, decide what profile you want. Getting the right people into the right places is a design exercise.

2. If there is a chance to try someone out, that is the best test of all. A short tryout may help with personality, but a real tryout must be long enough to allow the experience of proper pressures.

3. If your style is to be an impresario or circus master of talent, then make this an objective and choose the best people around. If you want to exploit your own ideas, then choose a support team.

4. Remember that many successful people have depended on a partnership in which the second party has supplied qualities needed for the success of the first party.

5. In almost all cases a success person needs the support of a good team.

6. Delegation is essential, but decide whether you trust someone to carry out your wishes or to have valuable wishes of his of her own.

7. Delegation does not mean lack of communication.

8. The motivation of others can require a clear definition of roles and goals.

9. The motivation of others means leading them, involving them, and giving them a sense of achievement. All this requires communication.

10. The reward of recognition or appreciation is as powerful as more material rewards.

11. Be definite about criticism but criticize the performance not the performer.

12. Lead the person to realize his (or her) own failure.

13. Decide whether a person can do the job for which he or she is employed. Keep that decision separate from the action that may then follow.

14. Communication depends on both content and context. Personal image is a powerful way of creating a permanent context.

15. Everyone wants to be an individual and at the same time to belong.

16. In the long run, human values may be good business values. It may seem otherwise at a particular moment in time.

13

Tactical Play

THE PLAYERS

United States: **Angelo Dundee · Harry Helmsley · Henry Kissinger · Alex Kroll · Morgan Maree · Mark McCormack · Jerald Newman**

United Kingdom and International: **Sir Ove Arup · Jarvis Astaire · Mike Brearley · Sir Terence Conran · Mickey Duff · Lord Forte · John Fowles · Margery Hurst · Lionel Murray · Lord Pennock · Baroness Seear · Jackie Stewart · Virginia Wade**

Just how transferable are sets of operating rules from one situation to another?

"I happen to think that management and the principles of management and planning and tactics is the same no matter what business you're in": Jerald Newman, President Bowery Savings Bank.

"I place a very black mark against the ubiquitous commentator-pundit who sees all in terms of short-term tactics and calculation, or the strategy of the football match. This reduces politics to public entertainment or the bread-and-circus view of what the people need": John Fowles, author.

Poker is not bridge. Bridge is not chess. Chess is not Monopoly. It has often been said that one of the difficulties of the cold war confrontation is that the Russians play chess and the Americans tend to play poker and bridge. Each type of situation requires a certain type of play. Bridge requires a careful calculation of possibilities and an understanding of the psychology of the opponent. Poker is bluff and counterbluff and brinkmanship. Chess involves a steady development of strategy on a long-term basis. With bridge and poker, you lose one hand but win the next. With chess, a game lasts much longer.

Tactics are the servant of strategy. The overall goal and the guidelines are set by strategy. Behavior on the way to that goal is determined by strategy. Tactics span a wide range: from the straightforward and necessary to the devious and cunning. It is said that when the great Turkish reformer, Kemal Atatürk, wanted women to stop wearing the veil, he issued a decree that all prostitutes must wear veils. The story is probably untrue, but it illustrates the nature and purpose of tactics. Instead of just ordering that women should no longer wear veils, he employed an indirect tactic.

GIVE A LITTLE TO GAIN A LOT

Mike Brearley, the cricketer, recalls one situation in the Test Match against Pakistan in 1982 when tactics were sadly lacking: "I was watching it on television at Lords. Pakistan had this marvelous leg spinner called Qadir — he's a terrific attacking bowler. He's also a bit of a gambler. He's going to get hit every now and then because he does so much with his wrist to get his spin (to get his variety) that he can't possibly be quite as accurate as some other bowlers. Mike Gatting was playing Qadir quite easily — not scoring many runs off him but obviously in control against him. At the other end was a young batsman, Gregg or Pringle, who hadn't got a clue how to play this bowler. Yet Mike Gatting was getting the bowler all of the time. The Pakistan captain, Imran Khan, took ages to realize this and give Gatting a single — it didn't matter a run here or there — the important thing was to get the young batsman down the leg spinner's end. It was so obvious to me."

JOURNEYING SOUTH TO MAKE HEADWAY NORTH

The idea of giving away something in order to achieve something much more important is one of the basic rules of tactics. A good tactician knows that he may have to retreat at times. This leads on to the major question which has plagued moralists over the ages and still does today: does the end justify the means? If a move is going to help toward the overall goal, does the value of that goal justify the tactic? In general terms the answer must be "yes," but in moral terms it is usually held to be "no." Do some of the tactics sometimes attributed to the CIA become valid because the overall aim of the defense of freedom is so worthwhile? It is obvious that in heading north you may sometimes need to journey south for a while in order to get around an obstacle. An entrepreneur who is very short of money might have to spend money on an expensive car and house in order to convince others that his credit is good and that he can be given a loan. Much of tactics are concerned with appearance and reality, as in bridge or poker.

In business too, says Alex Kroll of Young and Rubicam. "You have to be willing to use unusual tactics and be daring, to win. You have to understand that you can get clobbered by doing so, but I think there's a certain exultation when you go after something in an unusual way. I would say that it can be fun. I don't think you should do it because it's fun, but do it in a very reasoned way and calculate the odds — yet there's always a subjective part that's more instinctual than it is rational."

THE TACTICS OF COMMUNICATION

Some people are extremely good at communicating. Others are not. Some people do not need to be good at it in their position in a company, but others would certainly like to be better. Communication is, indeed, a skill. The ingredients for success in this field can be taught.

Communication of confidence may be vitally important to the negotiator, for example. The possession of such confidence is one thing, the display of it another. The display of it can rightly be called a tactic and may very well make the "opponent" feel one-down before the game even starts.

It can be a very great help to know how to put across a feeling of confidence even if one doesn't feel it. The actor as murderer need not kill, nor the actor as lover actually fall in love; his goal is to make the audience believe.

Margery Hurst went to the Royal Academy of Dramatic Art in London before creating her internationally successful employment bureau, and sees it as excellent training for her work. "I firmly believe the acting in me has made me what I am. I am completely honest with myself and know what I aim to be, but the acting technique enabled me to put it across to other people. I made it more interesting by delivering it and expressing myself to best advantage."

Baroness Seear remembers going to hear some of the great speakers at the Cambridge Union. "There was one who said to me: 'Throw away your notes when you speak. They're no good to you; you'll never speak unless you can speak without notes.' And I thought about that and made myself do it, and I must say it is advice for which I have been extremely grateful. You get a totally false, exaggerated amount of credit for being able to speak without notes; it's a trick I have passed on to my students. A sheet of paper cuts you off from your audience. How can you speak and get what you want to say over to people if you're hiding behind sheets of paper? But it was terrifying at first. I remember forgetting completely what I was going to say next, and saying the same thing about four times over like a gramophone record that had got stuck . . . until I managed to pick up and go on again."

These are minor, but nonetheless effective exploitations of the context of communication. For the then union leader Lionel Murray, image was deemed a powerful element in the same context: "Soon after I became general secretary, someone said to me: 'Len, make yourself look different. Those suits you wear; those ties you wear!' I was appalled by the idea that I should wear purple ties or wear a beard. You know — wear a cloth cap or something like that! OK, so it's showbiz and we're all in the act together. I know that, and you've got to make an impact as best you can."

Does it matter, appearance? Or is it simply something for the press to use in support of an image created by all sorts of different factors? On Remembrance Day (November 9, 1981) the then Labour leader, Michael Foot, was conspicuous on the steps of the Cenotaph. Described as looking like "a bored tourist at a bus stop," he was wearing a green donkey jacket, full flapping trousers, and casual shoes. The contrast was with smart civilians and old soldiers replete with rows of gleaming medals. During the traditional two minutes' silence in honor of those killed in the war, he was seen to swing his head from side to side and when called upon to lay his wreath of poppies at the memorial, he did so "with all the reverent dignity of a tramp bending down to inspect a cigarette end" (*Daily Telegraph* editorial). In hindsight, how much did his image contribute to that humiliating defeat in the General Election of June, 1983?

HOW FAR SHOULD YOU GO?

Does the end justify the means? Is the goal of success so important that all is fair in love, war and achievement?

Mike Brearley: "You don't win at absolutely any cost: it is a game. I usually feel clear in my mind about where the line should or shouldn't be drawn — though not always."

" 'When a guy comes into the business he looks to make as many contacts as he can . . . to grab as many boxers as he can . . . to make as much money as he can. But after you've been around for twenty years . . . you're around for just one reason, to get even with people.' I've tried to use Eddie Walker [retired manager] as a guide whenever I'm really mad at someone": Mickey Duff.

Even some philosophers have not accepted that there are such things as moral rules. There is a story about Karl Popper, who had been invited by the Moral Sciences Club at Cambridge University to give a paper. Ludwig Wittgenstein, one of the most influential figures in philosophy in the first part of this century, was clearly irritated by Popper's performance (which had developed to include a discussion on the validity of moral rules. Wittgenstein, who had been sitting by a fire, fidgeting with a poker, suddenly leapt to his feet and demanded: "Give me an example of a moral rule!" Popper, unperturbed, replied: "Not to threaten visiting lecturers with pokers." Whereupon Wittgenstein dropped the poker and stormed from the room!

"One very important thing to remember in business . . . you mustn't squeeze the orange too hard. Some people squeeze the orange until the pips pop out . . . but if people don't make money with you, they won't come back a second or third time": Jarvis Astaire.

There are laws and there are moral laws. There are idioms in any field. There are the ways in which things are done and unwritten rules that are followed. There are gentlemanly things and ungentlemanly things. This is an immensely complex area. On the one hand there is the power of innovation and escaping from old ways of doing things; on the other hand there are idioms that have evolved because they are necessary for the smooth running of a business. There are rules which have evolved for the behavior of a small "in-group" and rules that apply to all business. The City of London is notorious for its dislike of outsiders who challenge the rules.

There are cheats who take advantage of the system, and others who do not actually cheat but take advantage of the system. France can afford not to belong to NATO because everyone else belongs to NATO and in defending themselves would also be protecting France. Italy does not allow patents on pharmaceuticals, which is a splendid system so long as other countries allow patents and so fund the research from which Italy then benefits. When does ingenuity become cunning and cunning deceit? There is a legal distinction between tax evasion and tax avoidance. In practice, people seem to make a distinction between telling an outright lie and omitting to tell an important part of the truth.

Creativity almost always involves breaking some rules and overturning expectations of the way things should be done. On the other hand, someone who knows the rules and can work cleverly within them is far more likely to get something done than the pioneer who tries to rewrite the rules.

There are people who agree to a deal in principle informally and later simply go back on what has been said: because they have changed their minds or because circumstances have changed. There is no law which says that a person may not change his or her mind. In practice it also works in another way: "That is not what I said and not what I agreed to." Each side can claim a faulty interpretation or extrapolation. In contrast to this is the handshake deal and "my word is my bond" type of ethic. Without it, life becomes impossible as it can be in American business. Everything has to be written down and everything has to be passed through lawyers. I remember being told by one major European company that one of their divisions in Europe shared a lawyer with another division. In the U.S. an equivalent division had fifty full-time lawyers. Every detail has to be spelled out because what is not specifically excluded from the contract is assumed to be included. There are apocryphal stories of how someone sued the maker of a microwave oven for not stating that such ovens were not suitable for drying out poodles dampened by the rain. Legal departments may be a bigger source of profit or loss than main operating divisions. Lawyers have to live and often have to create their own work. Now the pendulum is beginning to swing back, and there are times when bringing a frivolous suit rebounds against the claimants, who have to pay costs. There is also a move toward arbitration and minitrials in which executives settle disputes within a day instead of having them settled in court by lawyers over many months.

It is easy to see why unwritten rules and codes of practice are so treasured and protected. The ultimate sanction is that if you break the rules you lose credibility and get excluded from the club. The recent troubles regarding Lloyds Insurance market in the U.K. arose because some people within the organization were alleged to have bent some rules. Conversely, people outside were alleged to have defrauded Lloyds by taking advantage of the Lloyds reputation that required payment of all claims. Sometimes it is a matter of perception. Lloyds underwriters are not allowed to insure financial risks. Are computer-leasing contracts financial risks? They may be seen as such, or they may not. Many difficulties arise when rules have simply not kept up with modern developments: for example, the copyright law does not cover computer software adequately.

It is alleged that Jim Slater was initially successful because he bucked some of the unwritten rules in the City of London, but when the crash came there was a reluctance to help him.

It is important to distinguish between "This is the way things are done because of tradition and history" and "This is the way things need to be done because of the operating value of certain rules." A person who bucks the first set of rules is often as unpopular with competitors as someone who bucks the second set — but there is a clear difference. The insurance industry has usually been run through moderate competence and the momentum of a solid business base and a club-type atmosphere. From time to time an innovator (like Mark Weinberg) comes along and introduces a new or improved way of selling. That individual can be extremely successful. One of the very largest foundations in the U.S.A. (the MacArthur Foundation in Chicago) was set up by an individual with an innovation in the insurance field.

The first set of rules is moral or ethical. What you do may be legal but it may not be moral. Before the rise of consumerism, the law used to advise the buyer to beware (*caveat emptor*). The consumer should check out their purchase. A seller could therefore make a legal sale which would not be acceptable on moral grounds. Where consumers are concerned, the law is indeed catching up with moral considerations.

When we look at gain what are our criteria for judgment? Should a factory contribute to acid rain in the U.S.A., and so damage Canada or, in the case of the U.K., damage Sweden? Should there be a global ecological view of benefit? If you sell technology to Taiwan and, as a result, the products produced undercut those made in the U.K. and so throw people out of work, is that allowable? The usual answer is that if you do not supply the technology, someone else will: the result will be the same except that you and your workers will go out of business in addition. Is protectionism allowable to protect certain workers and at the same time impose poorer-quality goods at a higher price on their fellow citizens?

As an architct and construction engineer, Sir Ove Arup can perhaps afford to have a broader view of total benefit, because with his work the total benefit is still quite local in effect.

Sir Ove Arup declares: "It is obvious that what we are not just interested in is action, which can be good or bad, but in what I may call 'beneficial' action. Beneficial to whom? That is where strife comes in. If I only want to benefit myself, I will have few allies . . . if I want to benefit my country — that's OK — but other countries might object. The fact is, we need to have aims which benefit us without harming others, and preferably which also benefit others. This means that both our aims and our means and all the consequences of our actions must be judged from this standpoint."

When asked what advice he has given to his son Rocco, who will very likely take over the business when Lord Forte of Trust House Forte retires, the man declared: "I've said to him that he must have complete integrity in everything he does. I don't mean not robbing people of money; that's basic. Integrity in his thoughts, in his complete approach to life. When he was sixteen, seventeen, eighteen, and nineteen I have said to him: 'Look, you must be able to go into any room anywhere in the world and know there'll be no one there who can point a finger at you and say, 'That man did me down.' "

It might be argued by a smaller entrepreneur that Lord Forte and his son can well afford to have such high standards because the business is now established. There are, however, two practical gains attached to this sort of integrity. The first is that decisions and strategies are made much simpler, as anything dubious is immediately eliminated. The second is that personal credibility is a valuable capital asset.

People like to know that when a deal is made, both parties will stick to it. In some areas this is the very basis of business. People take risks and make a deal at some point in time. If things go against them, they suffer. If things go the way they hope, they benefit. Some years ago there was a big upset when the Japanese offered a different concept of a deal.

At the time when sugar prices were about $400 a ton, the Japanese made a very beneficial long-term contract with Australia for sugar at $200 a ton. If world sugar prices continued at that high level, the Japanese would have benefited greatly from the deal. Quite soon afterward, however (ironically, in part due to Japanese work in developing enzymes that would convert cornstarch into sugar), the world price dropped to about $100 a ton. The Japanese immediately repudiated the contract and refused to accept sugar at the contract price of $200, which was now much higher than the world price. The Australians put the sugar into ships and sent it to Japan anyway.

From the Australian point of view, the Japanese were violating the very basis of commodity contracts (and business in general): repudiating a contract when it becomes unfavorable. The Australians asked whether the Japanese would have been as willing to alter the contract price upward if the world price of sugar had risen even higher than $400. The Japanese claimed that their culture had a different concept of a contract. For them a contract was an agreement between two parties to do business to their mutual benefit. If conditions changed, then the contract could be changed so that the mutual-benefit part persisted. Even though the suspicion lingers that the Japanese might be inclined to use whichever version of contract (fixed or flexible) that suits them at any time, there is something to be said for this concept of a contract — provided that both sides know what the ground rules are.

THE GAME'S THE THING

Some people have such an urge to be sincere that they regard the ritual game-playing of negotiation as dishonest and a waste of time. For others negotiation is a genuine exercise in value assessment and exchange. "I always remember the difference between Hong Kong and Red China," says Sir Terence Conran. "You cross that little bridge and go into an atmosphere where if anybody says something they mean it. But on the Hong Kong side of the bridge they never mean anything they say, and it's all negotiation.

"I don't mind it. I accept it as the sort of economic circumstances in which we live. You have to view it as a game and not mind losing. It's even worse in Japan, where a friend of mine negotiated for a license for his product designs. He had two people that he was negotiating with, and eventually made a decision in favor of one set of people, whereupon the other person went and committed suicide! Apparently he couldn't bear the thought that he'd lose face by losing the negotiation. He didn't even know that he was in competition with somebody else. And of course my friend felt so awful about this. He said, 'I didn't know that you were supposed to tell the other side that you were in negotiation. It would have been all right if I had.' I think it's acceptable if you spend only a small part of your life negotiating, because you can look upon it as a game of bridge, look upon it as a little bit of brinkmanship. And I've enjoyed that. Usually it's been in property. Luckily, I've never had to do any serious union negotiation, which always strikes me as brinkmanship — you have to go through, walking away from things. Negotiating to purchase Mothercare was a bit like this. Selim [Zilkha] is an extremely tough cookie and he didn't want to lose, either.

"Of course, you could stand away from him and let your merchant bankers do the negotiating and then come back to talk to you and then sit there while they do the negotiating. Basically, you instruct them what to do. You say to them, 'I think if you offered such-and-such in exchange for such-and-such, then maybe . . .' Sometimes they suggest strategies to you."

To let someone else do that is a tactic in itself. The Japanese are very good at this. There is a whole negotiating team, and the lone Western negotiator does not know who he is actually dealing with. At crucial points the Japanese disappear to confer or they claim that they can take it no farther but must report to the head office. This type of negotiation arises from the nature of their culture but is disconcerting to the West. If you speak a foreign language, should you negotiate in that language or in your own? Many fluent English speakers prefer to use an interpreter if they want to change their minds. The political leak is a much-used form of tactic. A controversial idea is leaked to the press. The government denies it but watches the reaction. The purpose is twofold: to pretest the idea (kite flying) and to draw the fire. If opposition is too great, the idea is dropped. Otherwise the idea is introduced when everyone has got bored with the matter.

KNOW YOUR OPPONENT

Total understanding of an opponent's strengths and weaknesses involves thinking yourself into his position. It does not necessarily entail sympathizing with it; on the contrary, it enables you to understand his Achilles' heel, his fears, and the strategy that he may use in response to his particular predicament.

Virginia Wade makes the point more directly: "Everybody has got a weakness. It's a matter of persistence — to really look for that chink, to really go for it. Now, if you know the word has gone around that you have a particular preference, a preferential shot, then you've just got to force yourself to do the opposite of that very early on. If you always hit forehands down the line, you've got to — right at the beginning — hit them crosswards to show them. You really should give them a feel of your whole armor even if, when it comes to the crunch, you're going to go with your preferential shot. Once you've employed the other ones at the beginning, they have to hesitate. It follows that the most difficult player to play against is the one that continually produces a wide range of play." Who would Virginia Wade regard as the best tactical player in the world today? "Probably somebody like Jimmy Mayer. He always does the right thing at the right time. He's always thinking. He absolutely thinks on his feet. He knows exactly how to confuse the opponent. And I think people don't play well against him. He has both hands on both sides, but he also has so much touch, he can do so much with the ball. He keeps you thinking all the time." And are there similarities between business and tennis in this respect? "I think it's all part of this sensitivity — understanding the opponent and knowing how best to deal with him," says Lord Pennock. "I find in the tennis world it's fascinating that Borg always beats Conners and Conners always beats Lendl and Lendl always beats McEnroe and McEnroe beats Borg. It's a battle of the different styles, the different games; they're all different, and that's how life is. You come to a situation in which you've got to size up either the opponent or the man who's coming with you. You have to recognize what he's thinking and what his reaction is going to be, and then you start to play. Is he a guy who comes up or is he a guy who stays at the back? If he's a guy who stands back all the time, is he a guy you can tempt to come up? Life's just the same."

Mark McCormack: "I try to judge. If I'm trying to negotiate with somebody, I try to judge them. I try to figure out where I want to get. What is the minimum I want to get and what is the maximum? Not necessarily in dollars, but in pieces of an arrangement. I try to judge the person and where he's coming from. I try to figure out which of the six points to get into first — maybe I try to make a concession to him before I want him to make one to me. Maybe I inject humor into it if I feel he has a sense of humor. It's just a feel for people."

Jackie Stewart: "When I was stalking another car, I would get to know the driver's weaknesses. Maybe I see him making slight errors of judgment or I see him driving very well. In order to outmaneuver him, I have to sit and watch for a little while and see how he conducts himself — not just one, two, or three laps — maybe I sit behind him for five to ten laps (that's only twenty or thirty miles). I sit behind him and see it all happening. Occasionally I give him a little pressure, to see if he's affected by pressure, and then I back off and make him feel a little more confident because he's feeling a little more secure (it might also mean that he thinks he's going a little faster when that's not at all the case). In other words, he's really not quite sure where I am and what advantage he has (if any). So he'll be in a slightly turbulent state, mentally, and most people make mistakes when they are under pressure (or when they're a little relaxed because they think they have an advantage that they didn't think they'd get).

"If I were getting into the traditional movement for passing the fellow
. . . I'd wait for a little crack in his armor and put myself into position.
Now this is where experience comes in — it's very cold and calculated — what you have to have is the ability to see everything in slow
motion, as it were. You have to eliminate the element of speed, eliminate the things that you are competing against, which are speed, the track,
and the car, and the other driver (but he's the weakest link). You eliminate speed so that you have plenty of time to place the car where you
want it to be, in a position where he cannot retaliate. People may see it
as a risky pass, but what I will have done is to put him 'behind the black
ball.' I've snookered him; there is no way that he can come in. If I'm
going into a left-hander I come up on his lefthand side, and I go just a
little bit ahead of him, just a tiny bit. It's only a foot, but he can't go
round me because there's really only one groove round the corner —
 elsewhere there's ball bearings, dirt, sand, and muck that's been swept
out there by the tires; it's all loose and a bit slippery there. So, if he can
only go into the groove, and if I overdrive slightly into that corner, he
cannot take me; he's got to drop behind me. Of course, he could try to
run into me, but I have already worked out that he's the kind of driver
that is not going to do that."

Unless you know your opponent well, don't presume how a deceptive
tactic will turn out.

"Speaking of human expectations and human nature," says A. Morgan
Maree, "there's a story about a young boy whose friends jeered and
derided him because when they offered him a nickel and a dime, he would
always take the nickel. And they would laugh at his stupidity until one
of his friends took pity on him and said to him, 'Let me tell you, the
dime — even though it's smaller — is worth twice as much as the nickel.
So when they offer you a nickel or dime, you should take the dime.' The
kid said: 'But if I ever took the dime, they'd quit offering.' "

This is a superb example of good tactics. The boy who took the nickel
knew that he was going for the long play. Taking the dime would only
have meant an immediate advantage. This would have been exactly the
opposite of good tactics. As I wrote at the beginning of this section, the
purpose of tactics is to *win the main strategy.* Once a player starts to
think of tactics as a short-term end in itself, then the strategy is lost from
sight. In negotiation you may concede something in the normal process
of bargaining where each side ends up by conceding something. You may
also make a concession precisely to lure the opponent into a position of
weakness. A general may retreat in order to lure the opponent onto a
field of battle that is not to the enemy's liking.

Be sensitive to the situation in which you're operating and to the true
circumstances of any deal.

"You have to feel where you have to give in, and if you're going to give in — give in fast! Then go on to something else. Save your energy for where you're not going to give in": Harry Helmsley.

THE MERIT OF SURPRISE

A simple tactic is to do something unexpected. This can have the merit of surprise, and it can also confuse the opponent, who tries to figure out what is happening. In my early days at Oxford, I remember a poker game played between some good card players and a poet. The poet was so unpredictable in his play that he won and went on winning. Whenever the skilled players reckoned they had got him figured out, he did something which threw them again. This was all done quite unconsciously. He just did not understand the game properly.

In his book *Years of Upheaval* (Little, Brown and Company, 1982), Henry Kissinger — a great tactician himself — recalls that on the final days of the 1976 Summit between Brezhnev and Nixon, Brezhnev retired early, the Soviet Party excusing itself on the pretext that rest was required before traveling the following morning. "At ten o'clock my phone rang," explains Kissinger. "It was the Secret Service informing me that Brezhnev was up and demanding an immediate meeting with the President, who was asleep. It was a gross breach of protocol. . . . It was also a transparent ploy to catch Nixon off-guard, and with luck to separate him from his advisors." It was the sort of maneuver that costs more in confidence than can possibly be gained in substance. Concessions achieved by subterfuge may embarrass; they are never the basis of a continuing action between sovereign nations because they will simply not be maintained.

"When I interview a guy who comes to see me about a job or about a problem or something," says Lord Pennock, "I usually tend to throw him. He'll come in and he'll know I'm going to ask certain questions in a certain sort of way and he's got himself all ready for it. So I always begin by talking about something else entirely different. It gets him off his mechanistic approach; then I get to know the real man."

Stephan Kindel (senior editor of *Forbes* magazine) finally defeated a chess-playing computer by opening with his king's rook's pawn. The machine took one look and its screen went blank. Programmed to deal with "sensible" openings, it could not cope with a silly one.

Doing something unexpected can be a ploy to disconcert an opponent. It may also be a move to shift the whole perspective of the situation. At the time of the Tehran hostage crisis, I had suggested on a television show that one way to shift perspective might have been for the U.S. government to compensate the hostages at $1,000 a day for every day of captivity. This would have made their captivity more tolerable in their eyes and in the eyes of the U.S. public. This in turn would have signaled patience to the Iranians. This in turn would have made it point-less to hang onto the hostages (the point of hanging onto them was that it upset the U.S. so much). The suggestion was actually debated in the U.S. Senate, but the point was missed; it was treated as ordinary com-pensation, and it was felt this might set an expensive precedent for fu-ture prisoners. At that time the total cost was about half the price of one helicopter.

GAMESMANSHIP

In medieval philosophy there was a type of argument which was called "ad hominem." It meant that you forgot all about the substance of the argument and attacked the person instead. So much of modern argu-ment is similarly based that we no longer need to give it a special name. There is a whole body of tactics that is concerned not with the game itself but with upsetting the psychology of the opponent. It is often called "gamesmanship" after Stephen Potter's very amusing book on the mat-ter.

Gamesmanship in chess had begun more than a century earlier. When Paul Morphy traveled from New Orleans to Europe as a young man, what he most wanted to do was play a challenge match against the much older Howard Staunton of England, the foremost analyst and authority on chess. Ernest Jones concluded that for Morphy, Staunton was the supreme fa-ther image; defeating him was the test case of Morphy's capacity to play chess, and unconsciously of much else besides.

Now, this was dangerous for Staunton, who appears to have been a typically pompous, stuffy, arrogant Victorian. Morphy was a genius, probably unbeatable. He would probably demolish Staunton, however politely, and Victorian English gentlemen did not relish being demol-ished. So Staunton engaged in gamesmanship of a high order, conceal-ing his fears by standing on his dignity.

Morphy was introduced to him and immediately asked for a game. . . . Staunton pleaded a previous engagement. For three months Morphy "in the most dignified manner" tried to arrange a match. Staunton re-sponded "by a series of evasions, postponements, broken promises and pretexts that his brain 'was overtaxed by more important pursuits.' " This last dodge deliberately conveyed the impression from the older estab-lished man to the youngster that chess was a "childish" business. Throughout, Staunton in his chess magazine maintained a steady fire of criticism against Morphy, "deprecating his play, hinting that he was a monetary adventurer, and so on."

It was a disgraceful performance, but in its limited aim successful. In the longer run, it failed: Staunton's behavior is seen as unworthy and Morphy's candle is undimmed. But in the short run it had an immediate effect on poor Morphy, who revolted against chess. One biographer wrote: "Morphy sickened of chess tactics — off the board. Is there any wonder?"

The most brilliant genius in the history of the game returned to New Orleans and more or less abandoned the game. He sank into a state of seclusion and introversion, culminating in unmistakable paranoia, and died a quarter of a century later from apoplexy.

Alas, Staunton set a precedent which has bedeviled chess ever since.

Emanuel Lasker was world champion from 1894 to 1921, largely because "he evaded many of his most dangerous rivals." The champion in those days could do more or less as he pleased, and it was only in 1921 that Lasker finally agreed to play Capablanca. This only happened because he desperately needed the $20,000 purse, having been ruined by the postwar inflation in Germany.

In 1927 Capa lost to Alexander Alekhine, a Russian aristocrat, who successfully avoided a return match. "If Capa arranged a match for the summer, Alekhine asked for the winter; if Capa agreed to the winter the Russian wanted the summer." The chess world eagerly wanted a return match, but it never happened. They did not meet until the Nottingham tournament in 1936, when Capa and Botvinnik tied for first place and Alekhine came sixth. Clearly, he had been tactically correct in refusing to play a challenge match for the world title.

Alekhine continued to thwart the chess world until his death in 1946, which left an interregnum. This was to be ended by a six-man tournament in Holland in 1947, but a Dutch newspaper came up with the charge that the Russians planned to "throw" games to each other to make sure the new champion would be a Soviet. Fischer was to make an essentially similar charge fifteen years later, in 1962, and to withdraw voluntarily from official events.

The Russians demanded that the Dutch government censor the newspaper and refused to have a world championship match unless it was played in Russia.

And so it went on. In settting up the 1972 match the cities chosen as possible venues by Spassky were unacceptable to Fischer, and vice versa. Fischer tried a totally new gambit in demanding 30 percent of the gate receipts, over and above the guaranteed prize money. Fischer made all sorts of demands about playing conditions (lighting, table, chairs, etc.), and after the sixteenth game the Russians charged the Americans with maybe using electronic devices and chemical substances to weaken Spassky's playing ability.

Even when Fischer and Spassky had left the scene, the gamesmanship went on. The next title match was between Karpov and Korchnoi in 1975, and Korchnoi objected to a figure in the audience who he said was Karpov's parapsychologist, there to disturb his, Korchnoi's, concentration. Whatever the truth of this, Korchnoi did not play his best chess. Maybe he psyched himself.

PSYCHING THE OPPONENT

"We got Randall out for two noughts in Middlesex versus Nottingham-shire," recalls Mike Brearley. "In the first innings he was caught hook-ing the second ball — a bouncer. He's a compulsive hooker, and al-though he scores runs, he'll make a mistake and get out. Actually he's a good friend of mine. I spent the night with him on the following Mon-day night. He was going to bat on the Tuesday morning. And so I was talking to him about when he'd get the bouncer this time. Did he think it would be the second ball again? Or did he think it was going to be some other ball? I was just playing with him. It was all set to make him wonder which ball it was going to be, make him think he couldn't pos-sibly know which ball it was going to be. And we did the same thing again! He was out. It was a fluke, of course, but it worked. A rather delightful fluke, but he was out second ball again. So it's bluff and coun-terbluff."

Angelo Dundee describes the famous occasion of Muhammad Ali's psyching of Sonny Liston at the weigh-in before their championship fight: "Muhammad was screaming and carrying on, and screaming he wanted to get at 'the big ugly bear,' right now! Well, it was all staged. I was holding Muhammad off with my pinky.

"Actually, we came into the convention hall for the weigh-in with a big procession, twice. The first time we came too early. The place was empty. Then we went back, waited for the crowd to arrive, and did it all over again.

"Muhammad's blood pressure shot up, and everyone thought he was either frightened to death or he was a real nut. We wanted Liston not to know what to think. Liston was a toughie, a bully, and with a guy like that you show him you're so crazy he doesn't know what you're trying to do. A half-hour later Muhammad was sitting on the stoop playing with some children."

Muhammad Ali beat Liston, who refused to come out in the eighth round because he said his shoulder hurt. . . .

A NATURAL PECKING ORDER

Most people regard gamesmanship and psyching the opponent as im-moral or, at least, as detracting from the true merits of a contest. The "win at any cost" may benefit the winner but does not benefit the spec-tators or the sport itself. The tennis player who upsets his opponent by screaming at the umpire is not doing tennis any good and may be de-tracting from his own talent. In matters of morality we seek for what is true and natural and we throw out what is false. Very often we go to the world of nature in order to discover what is "true" because behavior in the natural world has not been tainted by man. To our amazement, we find that psyching the opponent and gamesmanship is rife in the animal world. In fighting for the leadership of a herd or for the right to mate or for territory, there is a great deal of psychological gamesmanship that takes place. There is very little real fighting. There are displays and roars and posturings. It is mainly done by signals and psychology. One or other of the contestants backs down first and slinks away in defeat. This is the way the "pecking order" or dominance order is established. So Muhammad Ali's behavior was very "natural." It is easy to see why this psyching of an opponent has such a high value in nature. If there had to be a real fight each time then the hero would quite soon be exhausted and killed. So his powerful genes would be lost. The purpose of all the competition is to ensure that the best genes get to fertilize the females and so maintain the species. Psychological warfare means that the hero can maintain this dominance without killing himself. How does psychological warfare work? There are brain chemicals that set our mood, and basic among these are some that are concerned with fear and with aggression. There comes a point at which the build-up of the fear chemicals exceeds that of the aggression chemicals, and at that point the animal slinks away. In this way the dominant male tends to be aggressive and insensitive. This idea of the natural leader is well illustrated by Jackie Stewart, the famous Grand Prix ace.

"I think, as in business or in any form of success pattern, there comes a time when you begin to recognize that other people have accepted you as the natural leader, and when you achieve that dominance you can do almost anything to control pace, as long as you're not totally stupid. In my case, in motor racing, it first appeared in 1968 after Jim Clark died. He had been accepted as 'the man to beat.' That year I won the U.S. Grand Prix, and I was in the lead of the race and found that the second man was giving me a hard time and not really letting me get away. I had a cushion but not a big cushion. I increased it slightly and got myself what I considered to be an acceptable advantage. I don't know whether it was ten seconds or nine seconds; whatever it was, I was in the lead. But after I'd consolidated that advantage, I thought, 'I'm going to give myself a breather.' I thought I'd give myself two laps not driving quite as hard. I suddenly found that he was reacting to my slower pace — not by accelerating but by going slower. In fact, after giving myself two laps' breather, I then went faster, and he went faster. We then learnt that I could control the pace of what I was doing. That worked tremendously well until one or two young, uninhibited drivers arrived, and I had to exercise my authority on them before they got the idea."

ILLUSION AND BLUFF

Very often tactics (especially in negotiation) seem designed to give a false impression. There is a story in World War II of how the famous stage magician Maskelyne created a whole false port in Egypt for the Germans to bomb in the belief that they were bombing the true supply port. There are times (outside of war) when tactics and deception come close. It is true that value is often in the eye of the beholder, and in takeover battles the only true value is what someone is willing to pay. But that payment is related to some sense of underlying value.

True negotiations — and in this sense union negotiations are often more true than business ones — involve real values that are known to both sides. The management knows what a day's lost production costs. The union knows what an increase in wages means. Such values are known. Negotiations then take place with regard to the subjective values. When a hotel chain is negotiating to take over a hotel, it is working from its own subjective value as to how badly it needs that particular hotel. The actual profit-and-loss account of the hotel is a real value.

Where real values can be disclosed there is no problem in distinguishing them from subjective values. Where real values are hidden, then the distinction is lost. Poker is a game in which real and subjective values are the same. So bluffing comes into play.

The Theory of Games was created by the great American mathematician John von Neumann in the 1920s and '30's. The classic problem that started the whole subject was the poker decision of whether to bluff and, if so, how often, when playing against perfect opposition.

The surprising result that von Neumann discovered was that it is indeed correct to bluff some of the time, even if your opponent knows that bluffing is part of your repertoire. When the various strategies are examined, it turns out that bluffing with a particular frequency wins more money than either not bluffing at all or bluffing too much. In turn, the second player minimizes his loss by calling with a certain critical level of frequency. Lower or higher calling frequencies lead to greater losses.

Do the idioms of poker apply to business? The answer is that those who want to get on and run a business do not care for the tactics of negotiations. Those whose business it is to negotiate naturally regard this as an important area in its own right. Is it honest, through skillful negotiation, to sell something at more than its proper value? The negotiator would answer that proper value is only determined by what the buyer is willing to pay. He would also argue that what is being sold is "potential value" and that there is no way of assessing this except in terms of "belief," and that is something the buyer (helped by the negotiator) has to decide upon. It is immoral to sell lead as gold. But it is moral to sell gold at a high price because the buyer believes inflation may be coming.

WHAT, THEN, IS THE PROPER PLACE OF TACTICS?

Consider two announcements made to passengers waiting on an aircraft for takeoff. The first: "We regret to have to inform you that because . . .

and because . . . and because . . . there will be a delay of five minutes in our departure." And the alternative: "We are pleased to tell you that there will be no more than five minutes' delay in our departure, which is due to . . ."

In the first example, the passengers do not know what is going to follow the "We regret to have to inform you . . ." It could mean a long delay, even having to change planes, etc. In the second case the minor delay is immediately announced as such. In doing anything there is rarely a neutral position: something is done in a good way or a bad way. Tactics can be the art of doing something in the best way. But from whose point of view? Clearly from the point of view of the person operating the strategy, but this includes morals and also consideration for other parties.

The war or combat analogy can be taken too far. We can get into the habit of thinking only in terms of win-lose situations: "I can only win if the other party loses." Yet in many situations the purpose of negotiations or tactics is to ensure that all parties benefit: a win-win situation. In the example of the airline announcement the second version is better for all parties. A powerful general tactic is to align your interests with those of the other party so that both parties are working in roughly the same direction.

Nor should it be assumed that tactics only involve other parties. There may be tactics in building up a business or in doing a scientific experiment. Tactics refer to the implementation of the overall stragegy — not just to beating an opponent.

A key element in tactics (or it may be part of strategy) is to provide a "fallback" position. If things do not work out as desired where does that leave you? This may seem to be the opposite of risk-taking and commitment, but it is not. The better able you are to design your fallback position, the better able you are to take a risk. There is a saying (attributed to Martina Navratilova among others) that in a plate of ham and eggs the ham is involved but the pig is committed. I am not convinced that that shows good sense on the part of the pig.

T A C T I C S

1. The fast-buck, "what you can get away with," idiom may be very successful on a short-term basis but is very difficult to live down and is no basis for sustained success.

2. Integrity and credibility have practical value quite apart from what they do for your soul. They make decisions easier and bring deals to you.

3. Learn to distinguish between those things which are only done in a certain way because they have always been done in that way and those things which are done in a certain way because business would be impossible without unwritten rules.

4. If you can learn to work within the system, you are far more likely to get things done than if you set out to pioneer and change the rules.

5. Cheating the sysem is neither clever nor heroic.

6. It may be necessary to go south for a while in order to journey north.

7. Different games and different situations have different sets of rules and styles of play. Be clear as to what they are.

8. In a bargaining situation there are subjective values and variable values in addition to the real values.

9. Psychological tactics will be used on you even if you do not care to use them on others.

10. Play the percentages rather than the flashy strokes.

11. Tactics are never an end in themselves but only serve the long-term goal.

12. Be prepared to concede things as part of the bargaining and also to move your opponent to ground more favorable to you.

13. Some situations are win-lose but others are win-win. The other party does not have to lose for you to win.

14. An unexpected (and even irrational) move can throw the other party.

15. If you are not getting anywhere, try shifting the perspective or frame.

16. Decide whether you want to conceal what you are up to, or to make it very clear. Both types of tactics have their merits.

17. There is a good way and a bad way to do most things. Design or choose the better way.

18. Always try to take the initiative rather than just responding to the situation or the other party. Be active rather than reactive.

19. Do not get so fascinated by tactics that the overall purpose is lost from sight.

DECISION-MAKING AND THINKING

14

Decision-Making and Thinking

THINKERS AND DOERS

A man who started out as a philosopher and then spent a very successful life as a doer (the world's leading construction engineer) has this to say about doing and thinking. "The natural thinkers tend to strive for perfection, whereas the natural doers act quickly, relying on intuition, and they're the ones that often get most done": Sir Ove Arup.

This is a very complex matter. It is suggested that some people are oriented toward description, analysis, and thinking, whereas others are oriented toward action.

I strongly disagree with this distinction between thinking and doing: that thought is the enemy of action. For me, there is thinking concerned with description and there is thinking concerned with action. I have, in fact, invented a word to cover the thinking involved in getting things done: the word is "operacy." Much of the thinking that I have designed for use in education is directed toward operacy. It is true that academics are seen to think, more than to act, and hence the sort of thinking they do becomes equated with thinking in general (the striving toward perfection as an end in itself). As shown in this book, entrepreneurs do a great deal of thinking as well. It is not so visible, because such people are made visible only by their actions.

There is another suggestion behind the Ove Arup quote. This is the suggestion that all the important thinking has largely been done by the brain in a holistic and unconscious fashion, and so that action can be taken. Conscious thinking only clouds the issue in the same way as a centipede's self-consciousness would confuse the sequence of its gait. This implies a reliance on instinct and style and internalized knowledge of the field — which may indeed to valid in some cases. But it is highly dangerous in others.

There is yet a further suggestion. Take a decision. Take action. Bring thinking to bear only to modify and adjust and make your decision work. The suggestion here is that everything cannot be thought out in advance, but that there is a continuous synergy between thought and action. The suggestion is that you cannot smell a flower at a distance — you have to get up close to it. Again, this can be dangerous. The general who sets out to fight a battle by getting on with it and then adjusting may lose out to the general who has put in some strategic thinking in the first place.

"You must think before you hit the ball. That's the main thing. What are you going to do? Why are you going to be doing it? Where are you going to hit the ball, to whom are you going to hit the ball? These are really the main things": Antonio Herrara.

Scientists and engineers had proved that man-powered flight was impossible because a human being could never generate the horsepower needed to raise a plane off the ground. Paul MacCready did not know it was impossible, so he set out to do it and succeeded. This is the contrast hinted at by Sir Ove Arup, and in this respect I agree that too much thinking along old lines will not lead to innovation. I am also inclined to agree that there are "describers" and "doers." It is my experience, however, that thinking is used by both groups. I feel it is very dangerous to pretend that doers do not use and have no need for thinking.

If thinking does matter, than on what does thinking depend?

Hans Eysenck: "There is no question at all that IQ is the most valid predictor of intellectual success. We have recently conducted a study on the Isle of Wight. We chose the Isle of Wight because the Isle of Wight children all go to the same school, so there is greater uniformity. We took IQ measures at the age of five and then again at sixteen, and also looked at their achievements at school. And the predictive accuracy of the early IQ test is really remarkable. It correlates very highly with much later success and much later IQ. (The first evaluation) predicted very accurately how well they would do at school; and that, of course, determines whether you can go to university or later have success in the professions and so on."

Since IQ tests are concerned with very much the same sorts of abilities that are tested in traditional school examinations it is no surprise that there may be a correlation between performance on the tests and performance in these exams. As Eysenck points out, the way society is presently structured, success in the exams means entry to university and that in turn means entry to other jobs. It is also assumed that those who do not do well at school or who do not enter university are somehow "stupid." Yet if we look at successful people we find that some of them have done rather poorly at school (Churchill) or have not had a professional training (Clive Sinclair). It is possible that the constellation of qualities required for success are not best tested by IQ tests or school exams as we now know them. The great danger is that society may be wasting some of its best talent by setting up a system that only selects those who may not be best suited to bring about the dynamic growth of society.

Professor Eysenck is a firm believer in the genetic basis of intelligence: "We also have lots of studies of identical twins brought up in very different environments; yet the IQ remains almost identical . . .

"Jews are highly intelligent. It comes out in all the tests that have been done; especially the Ashkanazi. There is a very good reason for this in their history. Amongst Catholics, the priests are not allowed to marry, and so their genes are lost. But amongst Jews, the rabbi is enjoined to have as many children as possible. It is a part of his duty. As for his genes, he is highly educated and very intelligent. His genes are multiplied and, as it is an honor to marry a rabbi, all the rich Jews coming from families of high intelligence are vying with each other to marry a rabbi. In the end, this combination of assortative mating pushes the genes pooled in the direction of high intelligence. . . .

"If you look at intelligence, you find that though men and women have the same average, the curve of distribution of the males is wider. There are more at the top and more at the bottom. And what is relevant here, of course, is that top group. There you have many more males than females in the outstanding intelligence group. There is another factor which is equally important, and that is, genetically, women value family and home life much more highly than the male, and they value commerce and success in committees and government much less. A very good example is in the kibbutz, where they started out with the express purpose that men and women would be completely equal, with pressure for women to go into government, run the kibbutz, and be on committees. In effect, they pass rules that at least one third of the committees should be women.

"Nevertheless, women never took this up at all eagerly. And the next generation, not having been brainwashed, wouldn't accept this rule and simply overthrew it. It was the genetic factor: a very strong factor which feminists won't normally recognize, but which is there.

"The point about women is that they score fifteen points lower in IQ. And, in spite of all the help they've been given, they're doing just as they did eighty years ago. There's been no change in that."

There are people who take an opposite view and dispute both the statistical bases for these claims and also the interpretation of the data. I do not intend to pursue that particular controversy here. The key point is whether a high intelligence (as measured by traditional IQ tests) leads to success and whether a high intelligence is required for success.

INTELLIGENT PEOPLE MAY NOT BE THE BEST THINKERS

There is something I have come to call the "intelligence trap." This means that some highly intelligent people may turn out to be rather poor thinkers: they are caught in the "intelligence trap." There are many aspects of this. For example, someone whose self-image depends on being right and on being the cleverest is unwilling to admit error or take the intellectual risks necessary for creativity. Highly intelligent people are often able to construct a coherent support for a particular point of view. The more able they are to construct such a support, the less do they see any need actually to explore the subject. Hence they remain locked into a particular point of view. And so it goes on.

I like to think of intelligence as being equivalent to the horsepower of a car. The skill of thinking is then the skill of the driver. There may be a powerful car driven badly and a humble car driven well. Indeed, a powerful car may be particularly dangerous because it demands a higher degree of driving skill. I believe that thinking skill, like driving skill, can be developed through training and deliberate effort.

If we tested the raw natural mathematical abilities of a group of people, we would get a scatter of talent. But even the best of these people would probably fall far behind someone who had learned the notations, methods, and systems that have been developed for the operation of mathematics. Because we have made so very little effort to *train* thinking deliberately as a skill, we have to rely on untutored natural ability. When we start to treat thinking as a skill and to train it, we may find that skill in thinking is more important than genetic endowment in this area (within certain limits). For example, the use of the random word as a deliberate creative technique can yield a higher output of ideas than an effort without such a technique. The teaching of thinking directly as a skill in schools has already started. In Venezuela my program for the direct teaching of thinking as a skill is used with every child at the age of ten to eleven, and, by law, every child in Venezuela must devote two hours a week to thinking skills throughout education. The same methodology is used in Canada, Australia, New Zealand, U.K., Eire, and the U.S.A. The extent of the use depends on the motivation of local school boards and individual school principals. I have also set up pilot programs in Bulgaria, Malta, and Malaysia. The material has been used in Israel for training teachers. All this is but a start. In years to come we may find "thinking" taught deliberately as a skill as a routine part of education.

I would regard the notion that thinking is the same as IQ as being highly dangerous, because from it follow two suppositions: first, that people with high IQ do not need to learn thinking; second, that people with a lesser IQ cannot be taught thinking anyway. The result is that nothing is done in this direction.

Note that these considerations do not contradict Professor Eysenck's claims as to the genetic basis of intelligence. They do, however, challenge the implications of those findings. We may find that all houses in a country are white. This may be a fact. But it does not mean that all houses *have to be* white. That may only last until someone takes action to paint them different colors. Within certain limits, the training of thinking may be even more important for success than performance on the IQ test.

It is possible that some successful people have developed a powerful thinking style on their own and without specific training. The ability to focus and to assess priorities seems to be a component of this style.

Conscious or Unconscious Thought?

In discussing the role of thinking with successful people, it is interesting to see how conscious/unconscious the process is claimed to be.

(Unprompted, in the following quote, Professor Eysenck chose the same analogy as that used earlier by me, albeit with a quite different purpose.)

"I rely on my brain, essentially, to come to the right decision for me. In fact, I often feel — and it's a funny feeling — you might have a very ordinary car and put an eighteen-cylinder engine into it from an aeroplane. That's how I feel about myself; a very ordinary person at games and boxing and so on, with a happy marriage, and with an acceptable personality, who gets on reasonably well with people; but superimposed on that is a brain that is almost an alien, which dictates my books and tells me what to do in the way of research. I am almost possessed by it."

This suggests that Eysenck's brain, like an autonomous computer, does his thinking for him. Much will depend on the input to that computer: the concepts, possible relationships, experience packages, etc. An emphasis on input is shown in the following quotation by Sir Huw Wheldon:

"One of the things that I have learnt is that good television programs come out of *preoccupation*. I believe you should be constantly thinking whether to mention that tree before you mention that gate (for instance), or whether you should mention the gate first, or possibly mention neither of them, but to see them instead. Should the gate be revealed or should it be disclosed? Should it be explored or should it be found? In what way is this gate going to come to the attention of the audience? When and under what circumstances, and is it going to be called a gate, or an entrance, or a wicket?

"Preoccupation is all, I think. Eventually you make a decision — somehow or other — that the best way is actually to have this motorbike roaring along and just give the audience a flash of both tree and gate. Somehow the gate is now a thing taken in only on the edge of the mind."

Deliberation or Instinctual Thought?

Category thinking is a widely used type of thinking that relies upon past experience as its input. Harry Helmsley: "Most decisions fall into categories that we've had before (for instance, every lease that we make). There could be thirty or forty leases a day coming across my desk. I only bother with them when they fall out of the category. In other words, there is a rate per square foot and certain clauses that have to be checked off. If something doesn't fall into a slot, then I go further, but most do. Decisions are easy, until you begin buying real estate. Then, nothing falls into a slot."

Lord Pennock, who was deputy chairman of ICI before becoming chariman of BICC: "I was amazed coming into this cable business (about which I knew nothing) two and a half years ago, how the fundamental problems that I have to get involved in and solve have happened in the chemical industry. Exactly the same."

The creative ego rightly sneers at category thinking. Yet in real life, category thinking is valuable if only because it frees the mind to apply creative thinking to areas where it really matters. Many successful people have established thinking categories: types of deal, types of investment, state of the market, types of design. This thinking is directed toward seeing whether what is in front of them fits into a category. If it does not, then there are two choices: reject it or work creatively upon it.

Of course, there can be a great deal of creative skill in designing the categories. Perhaps this is where the successful person may win out over others.

Champions of the markedly conscious, "preoccupation" method of thinking (as well as those whose repertoire is confined solely to category thinking) somehow seem inadequate to the increasingly complex problems affecting top executives, politicians, and generals today. Since the advent of the industrial age, armies have become larger and their weapons more sophisticated. The battlefield is now not only much more widespread but also has become multidimensional.

It has moved from a few fields to an entire country and could involve continents. The sea lanes over which supplies must pass must be protected from attack from vessels on and under the surface, from aircraft, and from missiles launched many miles away and guided by their own integral electronic mechanisms. The battlefield itself may come under attack from long-range missiles or from air attack, and their missiles and aircraft may have to be defended. More insidious, more difficult to combat, is the attack on the will of the populace, military and civilian, through ideological weapons: subversion and propaganda.

No one commander can carry in his head the detail required to fight in this complex environment. He needs staffs of specialists to deal with the minutiae of information-gathering, operational matters, the administration of logistics and of political affairs. These staffs in their turn are complex, and the administration of them diffuse and complicated.

It is assumed that therefore war must be a matter of decision-making by committee. At first sight it seems so. Committees are indeed made up of individuals, many with knowledge of their own specialities.

A few businessmen too claim to make decisions by the so-called "think-tank" philosophy: Sir Peter Parker —"I am tremendously conscious that there's a better chance of a solution if you dare to share your problems; and if you dare to get people to listen to them. Organizations are never the shadow of one man. My instinct is to mix sweat. It complicates life, of course, and other people ask, 'Aren't you slowing it all up to the slowest in the convoy of consensus?' and so on. I find that the Conservatives — especially this present government — don't rate very highly the need for representation or the old Republican sense of "opinion." The government doesn't see the importance of consulting, like Japanese industrialists who give special time for acceptance."

Earlier in the book there have been occasions where a successful person has described discussions with colleagues. Perhaps an entrepreneur proposed an idea which was then solidified by discussion; sometimes the discussion may have been geared to shaping an idea; or they were "enthusing" or "communicating" discussions in which the entrepreneur seeks to involve his colleagues in the business to hand. But in every case responsibility remained firmly in the hands of the entrepreneur. It may be the dominance of the successful person that gives this impression. Then again, there are meetings that can be dominated by active listeners, just as there are those which are dominated by active talkers.

There are design partnerships and design teams; there are also firms of architects. Nevertheless, the basic design is done by one person; it is difficult for a creative process to occur across a number of different minds (though different minds can input ingredients and, later, modifications). So the design of a successful concept tends to occur in one person's mind. The successful person tends to be a creative designer in his or her chosen field. So there is a tendency to take the responsibility for decision-making, to work alone. Communication is still essential, however. Let's return to the military example. Why was it implied that war, despite its complexities, is not in fact a matter of decision-making by committee?

Committees are groupings of individuals, many with much knowledge of their specialties. It is the role of the group leader to frame the questions that are put to the specialists so that the answers given should be useful to the leader's analysis. One major weakness is that the experts are pushing their own points of view and may overstate their case. (It is possible that in the Falklands war President Galtiere was given bad expert advice by his naval team.) Another weakness is that, try as the group leaders might to reduce complex matters to a high order of simplicity, there is danger and delusion in this. It may not be possible to describe the behavior of a complex system to someone who does not understand the full "information universe" in which that system is operating. It is difficult to see how, in this situation, some one individual is supposed to *weigh* the information and make the right decision. Is this indeed what happens?

In the realm of business Lord Pennock leaves no doubt as to what in fact happens. (Interesting how both Sir Peter Parker and Lord Pennock call up Margaret Thatcher as their "evidence" for quite different cases.) Lord Forte, in the second quote, claims unconvincingly to be a proponent of the "think-tank" approach:

"I saw quite a lot of Margaret Thatcher as president of the CBI. The common picture of her being a domineering, insensitive person who just shuts people up isn't true. She listens a lot, concentrates hard on what you say, especially if she respects your view. You've got to listen. . . . You do have this gut feeling, but then you've got to go round testing it; you have to think of all the people it is going to affect before you come to a decision. You have your own hypothesis, if you like, and you test it; sometimes you modify it, sometimes you confirm it, but finally you have to decide and then go. The great danger today is to just go on and on and on consulting, and I don't think you can do that and lead. . . . In the final issue it's me." Lord Forte: "I like to spark my views and thoughts with other people. I like throwing something out and saying, 'I think we should do this.' Then maybe exaggerating a bit and listening to what the others have to say. Some may well say, 'Well, I'm not sure. I think maybe if we do this, I think we could do this that way.' At the end of this conversation, which may last ten minutes, an hour, or a week, I've made up my mind on the right thing to do. The Americans call it group thinking; I think I believe in that in a big way. I'm able to change my mind."

The fact that Lord Forte is able to have his mind changed does not make it any less his decision. Although it is a sort of group thinking, it sounds very much like a Forte decision, in fact. This is in contrast to the Japanese idea of group thinking, in which no one has a defined idea, but everyone puts in their piece of information and experience. Gradually an idea shapes up — almost as if it were out on the table in front of them all. They all watch the idea and tend it. Finally, there is a decision. In the Western world, the closest we get to this is probably in an advertising agency. We saw the way (page 25) Alex Kroll uses games to encourage imaginative input: "But we could do a better job of helping our people think through problems. What I wanted to do," claims Kroll, "was to develop a worldwide process system — schools, training programs — so that our people could filter through the data, the information, better."

Filtering through the data, communicating it to the "leader" successfully so that it becomes a valuable and appropriate element in his analysis of the situation . . . there really would seem to be a serious danger that matters have reached such a point of complexity (in economics, ecology, and war particularly) that it may not be within the power of the individual to make the right decisions. Perhaps we shall be in this state until our "fifth generation" computers can take over this thinking job for us. That may herald even greater dangers.

David Mahoney puts store by the executive's ability to ask the right questions and judge the import of the answers received:

"Let me put it this way: I agonize a lot, but agonizing is not procrastinating. They're two separate things. I'll try and look that thing over 95 different ways to find out which way is best and I'll agonize over it, and I'll look at all 360 degrees the best I can, so it's not hip-shooting.

"The problem is getting all the facts together and eliminating. The toughest part of a decision is getting what you should make the decision on, and that doesn't come out of computers; that comes out of human beings — each with his own vested interest — getting people to level with you. What you're dealing with is people's innate security. Let's say (a hypothetical situation) you tell me that's the only machine made like that, I've got to say, 'Does he know what the hell he's talking about? *Is* that the only one? . . .' Maybe I go on a five-day trip to five companies in five different cities. My role is to find out if what they're saying is accurate, if that's the way we want to go. The whole quest for information is the role of the good executive. Some people you can discount because they're extremely conservative; some people you know you're just gambling with; others are wild-eyed dreamers! In your own mind you go through them, and you compute it. We're talking about agonizing. The reverse is procrastinating and doing nothing."

Here we see two important aspects of thinking. One is extracting and

209

assessing information. The other is constructing a sort of perceptual map. This map shows the information and the biases and the areas of uncertainty. The more complete the map, the easier it becomes to find your way to where you want to go. This is exactly the approach that we take in the teaching of thinking in schools. If the map is good enough, then the actual "thinking" part becomes very easy because the map shows you the route. The problem is that it is a "perceptual" map and not just an information map. People always make the mistake of believing that you can put all the information onto the map (or into the computer), and the right answer will pop out. But information is only one part of it. The more important part is perception: the way the information is looked at. That is why David Mahoney puts so much emphasis on looking at it "in 95 different ways." There never is a correct perception: only alternative perceptions. They all go down onto the map. The task of the thinker is to make that map rather than to fiddle with syllogisms. Syllogisms are fine when perceptions are fixed and for playing around with language, but thinking in real situations is more complex.

Jim Rogers would have to glean the true picture of a company (a potential investment) from what he read and what he heard outside and from the company executives themselves. "I would go to see X, Y, Z and discuss with them their business. OK, you would be bound to tell me the best things about your business, especially if I were an outside investor. And that's fine and dandy. That's not really misleading me. Most of the time they actually believe and honestly accept what they tell me. But what you then have to bring to bear is a lot of judgment, a lot of knowledge. A lot of perception and a lot of other outside knowledge. I talked to dozens of guys who told me, 'Listen, that is a terrible business to invest in. You really shouldn't.' But what I would want were the facts. Answer this question, this question, and this question, factually. So I would discover things the company didn't know about itself, or I could interpret things it didn't know."

INTUITION—MAGIC OF THE MUSE?

Intuition may represent processes that were once conscious and have since been internalized. Some of those interviewed based intuitive judgment on experience.

For those decisions about real estate which do not fit into the "slots" of category thinking, billionaire Harry Helmsley declares, "You have to have a feel. Well, I guess I should have a feel for it by now, I've been doing it for fifty years. But I've always had a pretty good feel for it from the very beginning."

Jackie Stewart: "What I developed was a very complete consumption of visual fact which gets analyzed very clearly. I became able to dispose very fast of the unimportant elements of a situation, and take exactly what I required as input so as to be able to see all the relative advantages open to me on the track. Now, if there is a slow-moving vehicle in front, a less experienced driver might say, 'Ah, a slow-moving vehicle.' Whereas mine might say, 'Why is there a slow-moving vehicle? Is it a blown engine? (When an engine blows you usually have oil all over the track.) Where is the oil? Where was the car when it happened? etc.,' and use that. . . . My vision has become extremely analytical. It's one of the advantages I had over other people — that I was able to assemble what I saw, clearly analyze it, bank it, and deal with it. You're talking of microseconds of decision, and it's quite different to an inexperienced driver saying, 'Hey, there's an accident!' When you do that, you generally freeze. Good racers don't freeze. They always act positively, in an immediate sense. . . . People think of you having to have fast reactions. It's nothing to do with reactions or being able to take a pound note when it slips between your finger and thumb — I'm not very good at that — my motor reactions, if they were analyzed, might not be very fast. They're not slow, but they're not superfast."

When a person has been doing a certain type of thinking for a long time, the processes can become internalized just as software can be programmed into a computer chip. The thinking may then not be as conscious as it was. What has really happened is that the thinker has moved into a higher-order thinking habit. A complex thinking habit can thus be "switched on" just as a subroutine can be switched on in a computer.

It is a mistake to suppose that this thinking is hunch or intuition simply because it is no longer conscious at every step. One of the purposes of training thinking is precisely to have the habit and technique internalized so that they can be used in this manner. The point is illustrated by Jim Rogers:

"I'd take everything in, in two or three hours, and throw it, as it were, into a computer, and I'd come to the computer and say, 'Do x' — that was what I was doing. I was throwing everything I could into my mind to the exclusion of everything else in my life, and a decision would come out. It would grow; it was organic. A decision would sort of grow out of it, and I would say, 'This is what we must do next.' Today, there is a great deal less input, but I would still trust my decisions. It's instinct based on twelve to fourteen years' 'education.' It's as though I had gone to medical school for eight years and was making decisions based on my education. My decisions would be better based than when I first went to medical school because I know a lot more. It's an instinct which has been honed by twelve years, twenty hours a day. I don't believe in hunches. Hunches always lead to bankruptcy. Instincts always brook disasters."

At other times intuition is treated almost as an aesthetic value: this looks right.

Sir Terence Conran: "People don't recognize what they want until it is put in front of them. This is why market research is so much bunkum. I'm extraordinarily good at being able to put my finger on the pulse of the public. I don't know how it actually happens, but it probably happens because I travel very widely, read a great deal, look at a certain amount of television . . . it's a whole mass of different media things. I look, listen and hear."

In Sir Terence Conran's sense, intuition is a sort of complex judgment that brings together subtle trends, changes, insights, opinions, experiences, and comments to produce a design that is new — but not too new. It is a design that will be acceptable to all the elements of his trade: the consumer, the commentator, and the retailer. You do not recognize a friend through detailed analysis of the length of his nose and the spacing of his eyes. There is a complex, composite judgment. We know enough about how the brain works to understand this type of judgment. It is quite different from our linear type of logic; it is the logic of patterns. With designers, there are three possible ways in which an intuition can crystallize into a design (or design trend). The first is on an ego level, where the design is a visible extension of that designer's self-image — and most useful in terms of critical acclaim. The second level is where the optimizing influence is the design itself. The result may be a striking design but without the stamp of a particular designer. The third level is where the "acceptance of the user" exerts influence and the end design is eminently salable.

Mickey Duff recalling one of the biggest successes he had in the early days — British heavyweight champion, Billy Walker: "He was strictly a gut feeling. You've got to develop something that you think the public will follow. I never thought that Walker was a great fighter, but he had an indefinable quality — a star quality. He had macho; he had box-office appeal. We sold out Wembley Arena for eleven consecutive shows with Billy Walker. I always remember getting on an underground train at Baker Street to travel to Wembley where Walker was matched against Karl Mildenberg. I was reading a newspaper. There was a boxing crowd in the same compartment talking about the fight. Not one of them gave Walker a ghost of a chance. One said, 'So, what are we all doing here?'

"Then another said, 'I don't know about you, but I go to watch him because, win or lose, you know you'll get a bloody good fight for your money!' He had a magic. That's what Billy Walker had."

Verity Lambert: "I have to get some kind of buzz from the script or the idea. I have to feel. . . . Before I even look at it in any kind of detail, I have to respond in some kind of way, emotionally, instinctively, if you like, to what is being put forward. That is the initial thing. . . . I don't think flair comes out of knowledge. I don't know what it comes out of. I think it is indefinable."

Norman Lear: "Writers and artists have their own slide rule in the belly."

Harold Evans: "I think the strongest thing I've been to journalism, one might say, is my capacity to bleed easily. I'm sympathetic to hurt and I have a sense of what is just or unjust . . . for what is wrong. And I can feel angry! A bleeding heart I try to ally to technical strength. My most difficult decision was probably publishing the Crossman Diaries and defying the government on it. It was important because if I'd got it wrong and the paper had been damaged, or I'd been prosecuted, I think I might have lost the support I'd had from Thompson and Hamilton. I get convictions about a few things, and these are very quick. I was absolutely convinced I had to publish the Crossman Diaries come what may. That was a gut feeling, if you like; straight, instinctive, supported by a rationale afterwards.

"On other things, a decision on whether to promote A or B, I would worry for a very long time. . . . At the *Sunday Times*, I eventually learned to say, 'I think we ought to give the main spread to Brezhnev; that's my present feeling.' But it might change, and it would change. I was prepared to change my mind as the week went on . . . but I wasn't approachable at all on decisions such as Crossman, thalidomide, or Philby."

Alex Kroll: "To me, in the end, the fundamental decisions that a leader makes are decisions of character. We presume that he or she has all those other characteristics which are required. But the last decisions are the ones that are the loneliest. The ones that only the leader can make. The ones that there's no book on, no precedent. In the end it's the reading of his or her character that is fundamental. I'm convinced that that is true."

Style, aesthetics, and character may all refer to the same thing in this context. We saw previously how a complex thinking process may be internalized so that it appears to operate as an instinct but is really a process. This may happen when decisions are referred to style or character. Sometimes it is the emotional content of a decision that requires the character — for example, the willingness to take risks or to innovate. Aesthetics is what works for a designer, an artist, or an architect. For example, Sir Ove Arup has to work, as a structural engineer, in fields that demand precise thinking. His team was responsible for erecting the very difficult roof of the Sydney Opera House, when others seemed incapable of accomplishing the task. yet he realizes the limits of logic and the value of the "aesthetic" input.

Sir Ove Arup: "Logical thinking alone will not be enough. The relevant data can never be assembled 'in toto'; they stretch out indefinitely in all directions. We can only estimate the short-term results of our actions. And, more important still, to decide what invariably involves value judgments, ethical and aesthetic considerations, and an understanding of human aspirations and behaviors — all of which cannot logically be deduced. We need intuition and what the Germans call *Einfuhlung,* or what we — at the risk of sounding bombastic — may call love."

Different people have different thinking styles. Different situations demand different thinking styles. Different areas of activity demand different thinking styles. What is important is that we recognize these different styles and do not make the mistake of saying that there are some things we think about and some things we do not. The mind is a thinking machine whether we are consciously in control or not. The only alternative to thinking is blind action or chance.

Roy Cohn, the New York lawyer, operates on instinctual judgments under the guidance of one or two key people he respects. "You see, I'm not a thinker, because I find life propels me from course to course. If somebody says, 'Why did you go with Senator McCarthy and become chief counsel for the Committee and you were a Jewish Democrat from New York?' the answer is, I believe that I had as strong feelings about communism as I did about Nazism. These are not the kind of things that I sit down and hold conferences about or try to make decisions on. Life's so quick for me that I operate almost instinctually, and I don't think out where I am going to go. I am just propelled. The opportunity presents itself, and I don't call a meeting with thirty advisors. I make up my mind and I do it. Now, I have checks on my decision-making. One of my law partners, Tom Bolan, who's very, very bright and has wonderful judgment — that's his strong suit — if I have a question I will go to him and say, 'Here's A, B, C, and D; what do you recommend?' Yes, it's certainly recognized publicly that we're a very good combination —for over twenty-five years!"

This is a very clear example of two things. There is the strength of a partnership in which the partner supplies complementary qualities (something that has been mentioned at many points in this book). There is also the separation of one sort of judgment from another. Clearly Cohn exercises his own judgment, but he recognizes that there is a value in another sort (more broadly tuned) of judgment. I often think that in the advertising world the stength is not so much in the generation of concepts but in the judgment of how they will work. I have often found the generative side to be somewhat weak (in relation to the demand put upon it). Perhaps advertising should separate into two specialties: generators and judges. Of course, there has to be an interaction, since judgment can also shape ideas and change them into better ideas.

"In banking," says Charles Williams, chief executive and managing director of Ansbacher, the merchant bank, "90 percent of your decisions are of the type that 'I must talk to so-and-so; I must get so-and-so on my side, get his views, and so on,' and generally try and distill the views around you — put your views, but be flexible. Ninety percent of banking decisions are like that, because banking is a very risky business, and nobody in his sane and sensible mind will take banking decisions instinctually."

What is important is that we recognize these different styles of saying that there are some things we think about and some things we do not. The mind is a thinking machine whether we are consciously in control or not. The only alternative to thinking is blind action or chance.

Mark McCormack looks at his thinking styles: "Sometimes (in making a decision) I have a gut feeling. Sometimes I think it out very carefully. The method relates to different decisions. I have to be in Paris for a very important meeting at eight in the morning; there is a flight that lands at seven and leaves at six; do I go on the six A.M. flight and risk the fact there might be bad weather, or do I leave the night before, and if I leave the night before, do I miss something else I might have done the night before? I weigh that.

"There are certain things at the core of our business where you are forced into a decision. If you are going to be in tennis management, then you've got to have a reasonable percentage of the top tennis players — ten years from now as well as today. As far as new businesses are concerned, when a thing like the Papal visit comes along, that's a one-off thing and it's something you ask yourself, 'Can I do a good job so that I am perceived to be doing so by my client: in this case the Vatican?' 'Can I, having done the job, make reasonable profit?' The people working on the project won't work unless they're making a reasonable profit. If it's only a one-off, 'Is it worth the diversion of the manpower for the profit you make?' Because, otherwise, that manpower could have been developing something that could have more longevity. In the Papal situation, we decided we did want that diversion. but trying to decide who's going to be a good tennis player — a lot of that is intuitive."

And the best example of a gut feeling where Mark McCormack was right? "Borg. I was up in Sweden talking to a lot of people up there. I was there with Arnold Palmer. Borg was fifteen years old at the time. So he's twenty-eight now (1982), so that's thirteen years ago. So that's 1971, and I was talking to some of the people up there, and the Swedish people said, 'There's a really young boy here.' We weren't that much into tennis at that time. We were into it, but we weren't all that highly structured in tennis, and I wasn't looking for anybody at the time . . . but they said, 'There's a young boy that looks very good in tennis,' and I knew that when Gary Player became good in golf it did amazing things for sport in South Africa. So I know that if a young Swedish boy became good in tennis, there'd be an uplift in sport in Sweden and produce a lot of opportunities. Because I knew that all sports, and tennis in particular, were getting more and more international, and I knew that we were an international company and therefore we could service an international player better than anybody that wasn't an international company. It was pretty easy, because Borg had only one alternative offer, and the offer wasn't even that serious. You can't recognize talent [at that stage]; you just guess. The kid wins the junior when she's eleven; you probably figure she might have a chance of winning the sixteens; if she wins those, who knows? She might do well at Wimbledon."

T A C T I C S

1. There are many different types of thinking: logic, perception (and lateral thinking), and intutition (including aesthetic, complex judgment, and internalized processes).

2. There is thinking concerned with description and thinking concerned with action (with getting things done).

3. Intuition can lead to great successes and it can lead to disasters.

4. Intuition may represent processes that were once conscious and have now been internalized.

5. When used for judgment, intuition may be based on experience and aesthetics (for that field) and may provide a complex judgment of many factors, not all of which can be spelled out.

6. Category thinking can be very valuable. Create your categories and then see if apparent opportunities fit them.

7. There is value in feeding material into the mind and then "sleeping on it" or otherwise letting things sort themselves out.

8. One powerful approach to thinking is to create a map out of information and perceptions and then to find your way about that map.

9. It can be useful to work with others, but if you are going to be responsible for the idea, then you have to "design" it.

10. Thinking is an operating skill that can be learned; it is not just a matter of intelligence.

11. Different situations require different thinking styles just as in a car you shift gears according to the situation.

12. Remember that the purpose of thinking is to so arrange the world, in our minds, that our actions and decisions become obvious.

13. Trust your intuition as you might a friend: on the basis of past experience and a consciousness of human nature.

14. Thinking is an aid to action, not an excuse for inaction.

Epilogue

This is an inspiring book.

I am not, of course, referring to my contribution but to the words and thoughts of those successful people who have contributed so much more to the book. Whenever I reread the book I find it inspiring. So I hope readers may do likewise.

At the end of the book the reader should say: "Why not me?"

I have written twenty-two other books in which I put forward my thoughts, provocations, insights, and suggestions for the betterment of human thinking. In some places I make clear my view that human thinking — outside the purely technical area — is all unbelievably backward and primitive. Those who are interested in these views should read my other books. My role in this book is totally different.

In this book I have set out simply to frame the words and thoughts of a variety of successful people. These words are the book. My comments are just the frame. The words are not there to support my views. On the contrary, my views are there only to frame the comments that have been provided by the contributors. As I read these words they seem to me to ring true. In his or her words the successful person comes alive. There is a lot of wisdom, a lot of honesty, and a lot of insight in the comments. I encourage the reader to pause at the quoted comments and to read them slowly with full attention. For my part I have been impressed by the focus of these comments. At the start of the project I half suspected that many successful people would have very little to say. Their success might have just been part of their life-style and they might have been incapable of verbalizing their thoughts about it. This has not been the case. I find the comments real and valuable.

My role has been that of impresario: to provide a platform for the observations of those whose success is so visible. I could use another analogy. That of the bird-watcher. At first the novice watcher just sees some birds hopping about. Nothing of much interest. Then the more experienced commentator starts to point some things out: "Observe how the bird hops away from the nest. Observe how it is the male that sits on the eggs. Observe that dull-looking bird — it has probably just flown a thousand miles," etc. In this way the novice bird-watcher finds his or her attention directed to points of interest. In this book I have sought to draw the reader's attention to various aspects of success: risk taking, background influence, dealing with people, negotiation, expectations, etc.

I would suggest that the keen student of success read the book over and over again in order to learn the many lessons that are on offer. There may be observations that become apparent from the quotations and to which I have not drawn attention. The experienced bird-watcher is soon making observations which go beyond those of the tutor.

WIDE RANGE

The book covers a wide range of successful people. From one of the greatest motor racing champions of all time (Jackie Stewart) to one of the toughest lawyers (Roy Cohn). From a fashion tycoon (Diane von Furstenberg) to the top television producer (Norman Lear). From an inventive entrepreneur (Sir Clive Sinclair) to a king of real estate (Harry Helmsley). From a pop star (Sting) to the world's greatest hotelier (Lord Forte). From a millionaire publisher (Malcolm Forbes) to the inventor of man-powered flight (Paul MacCready). From the head of the world's largest advertising agency (Alex Kroll) to a publishing giant (Robert Maxwell). From a renowned deal maker (Robert Holmes à Court) to a boxing promoter (Mickey Duff). From bankers to chief executives, etc., etc.

THE LESSONS

What can we learn from the comments and thoughts of these people? There is a great deal to be learned. It is obvious that there are very many styles of success. The style depends both on the personality of the person and also, to some extent, on the field of success. There is the drive of Alex Kroll; the patient stalking of Robert Holmes à Court; the energy of David Mahoney; the "can do" attitude of Paul MacCready; the efficiency of Mark McCormack; the toughness of Roy Cohn.

It may come as a surprise to many readers that the Grand Prix champion Jackie Stewart hated taking risks. Others took calculated risks. Some even liked to gamble. All of them were willing to dare. As Malcolm Forbes puts it: "You can never eliminate risks. If you want to accomplish anything you can't eliminate all risks."

In spite of the huge differences in styles and approaches, there do seem to be some strong underlying agreements.

Energy, persistence, determination and singlemindedness seem important in all cases.

There is action. Successful people do not stand still and expect things to happen to them. They take a step and then the next step.

There seems to be a sense of integrity. Integrity towards oneself and also towards others.

There is always the "expectation of success" and the ability to think big.

There is the ability to define goals and targets and also to have dreams.

There is a certain daring.

There is creativity and the ability to see things differently and to think new thoughts.

There is both a seizing of opportunities and also a creation of opportunities.

There is eagerness and enthusiasm and the willingness to make things happen. The rewards of success are summarized by Diane von Furstenberg: "It's the warmth that you get in the fruit of your work or in the fruit of your efforts. It fills you up with a warmth and you wink at yourself, you smile at yourself. You don't need to share it with anybody, and it's not 'ha ha'; it's just warmth."

NEW HORIZONS

Have successful people all reached their ultimate goals? Does the future hold a number of challenges which will be met one after another? In many cases success has become a life-style, and the successful person only has to be alive and eager for the success to continue. For the mountaineer there is always a higher peak to be conquered. As many readers of this book will know, I have pioneered the teaching of thinking as a skill in schools, and I now run what is the largest program in the world for the direct teaching of thinking as part of the curriculum. This is now happening in many countries. In Venezuela, by law, every child does two hours a week on thinking skills. The program is in use in Canada, the United Kingdom, Eire, Australia, New Zealand, Bulgaria, Malaysia, Malta, etc. In the United States there is an important pilot project in Santa Barbara which may provide a community model. Since this trend is now established, what is the next horizon?

I feel that the conflicts, crises, problems, and changes in the world need a good deal of thinking attention. This needs to be done outside the sectional interests of nations, creeds, and ideologies. It can never be done by bodies like the United Nations which have to represent the bloc views of national representatives. So I am setting up a supranational independent thinking organization (SITO) to provide thinking that is permanently neutral and independent: to provide concept maps much as a geographer provides physical maps. What concepts do we have? What concepts do we need? What new concepts can we design? I know it to be a difficult task which lies halfway between a target and a dream. The first steps have already been taken.

NOTE: There will be readers of this book who are achievers, who are success-oriented, and who pride themselves on their effectiveness. I see "effectiveness" as that marriage of thought and action which makes things happen. I am setting up "E-Clubs" as a structure for such people to develop, use, share, and focus their effectiveness. This book will be required reading for all members.

Index

Self-analysis, 78–79, 82
Self-confidence, 33–35
Self-examination, 79–80, 82
Self-knowledge, 38, 77–82
  interpreting strengths and weaknesses, 81–82
  recognizing limitations, 80–81
Self-organization, 62–63
Selznick, David, O., 17
Shrimpton, Jean, 10, 130
Sinclair, Sir Clive, 4, 78, 95, 218
  background of, 19, 203
  on creative opportunity, 105–106
  creativity of, 121, 126
  on ideas, 16
  on making things happen, 54
  risk taking by, 134
  on strategy, 144–145
Single-mindedness, 3–5
Slater, Jim:
  as risk taker, 130, 131
  and rules of tactical play, 184
  Zulu principle of, 109, 110
Slater Walker: An Investigation of a Financial Phenomenon (Raw), 110
Soros, George, 19
Spanier, David, 34
Spassky, Boris, 192
Spock, Dr. Benjamin, 58
Stamina, 35–36
Status, 53
Staunton, Howard, 191–192
Stewart, Jackie, 36, 218
  background of, 19
  on decision making, 210–211
  on limitations, 81
  on luck, 71
  as natural leader, 194
  on opponents, 188–189
  on people selection, 154
  on rewards of success, 46, 51
  on risk taking, 131–132
  targets of, 83
Stimulants. *See* Negative stimulants; Positive stimulants
Sting, 218
  background of, 19–20
  on creativity, 121, 123
  on failure, 43
  on image, 62
  on intuition, 134
  motivation of, 47
  natural talents of, 60
  on self-awareness, 81
  on strategy, 143–144
  on teams, 159–160
Stracey, John, 72
Strategy, 141–151
  culture of an organization and, 149–150
  defined, 144

designing, 143–144
detailed, 144–145
drawing up, 145–146
flexibility of, 146–147
general, 144
vs. plan, 147–149
See also Team strategy
Strengths:
  awareness of, 79–80
  interpretation of, 81–82
Styles, 23–45
  characteristics of, 31–45
  copying, 62–64
  entrepreneurial, 27–30
  failure, 40–41
  macro-, 24
  management, 26
  micro-, 24
  natural vs. artificial, 66–68
Success:
  chosen field and, 6–7
  confidence and, 33–35
  copying and, 62–64
  cultural attitudes toward, 61–62
  defined, 1
  determination and, 3–5, 31
  efficiency and, 36–37
  ego and, 32–33
  energy and, 32
  expectations and, 60–62, 74
  failure and, 40–45
  hard work and, 5–6, 35–36
  heredity and, 59–60
  image and, 62, 65
  luck and, 2–3, 69–74
  negative stimulants of, 47–50
  positive attitude and, 8, 33
  positive stimulants of, 50–55
  role-living and, 65–66
  role-playing and, 62, 64–65
  ruthlessness and, 3–4, 5, 37–40
  stamina and, 35–36
  talent and, 5–6
  timing and, 72–73
  upbringing and, 57–59
Sumner, Gordon. *See* Sting
Sunday Times, 12, 24, 37, 213

Tactical play, 179–197
  communication and, 181–182
  fallback position in, 196
  gamesmanship, 191–192
  illusion and bluff, 194–195
  opponents in, 187–190, 193
  pecking order in, 193–194
  rules in, 182–186
  strategy and, 180
  surprise and, 190–191
Talent, 5–6

INDEX